Nutrition in the '90s means more than preparing a well-balanced meal. It means choosing the freshest, most wholesome foods. It means knowing how to avoid harmful preservatives, additives, and pesticides. It means being aware of labeling practices that may be misleading. And it means discovering the truth about fat, salt, and sugar in your baby's diet.

The Complete New Guide to Preparing Baby Foods is the most comprehensive, easy-to-follow guide you will find on child nutrition. For years a bestselling classic, it is now completely revised and updated for the '90s.

THE COMPLETE NEW GUIDE TO PREPARING BABY FOODS

The Complete New Guide to
PREPARING BABY FOODS

Sue Castle

Foreword by Jeffrey L. Brown, M.D., F.A.A.P.

BANTAM BOOKS
NEW YORK • TORONTO • LONDON • SYDNEY • AUCKLAND

This edition contains the complete text
of the original hardcover edition.
NOT ONE WORD HAS BEEN OMITTED.

THE COMPLETE NEW GUIDE TO
PREPARING BABY FOODS

A Bantam Nonfiction Book / published by arrangement with
Doubleday

PRINTING HISTORY
Doubleday edition published June 1981
Bantam edition / March 1983
Bantam revised edition / June 1992

ISBN 0-553-29183-1
Published simultaneously in the United States and Canada

Bantam Books are published by Bantam Books, a division of Bantam
Doubleday Dell Publishing Group, Inc. Its trademark, consisting of the
words "Bantam Books" and the portrayal of a rooster, is Registered in U.S.
Patent and Trademark Office and in other countries. Marca Registrada.
Bantam Books, 1540 Broadway, New York, New York 10036.

PRINTED IN THE UNITED STATES OF AMERICA
OPM   0 9 8 7 6 5 4

Contents

Contents

Foreword

There are few parenting responsibilities more important than knowing that your baby is well fed and well nourished. It is not a surprise that parenting magazines often feature nutritional issues on their covers and that parents spend more time discussing nutrition and feeding techniques than any other baby-related topic. During recent years the manufacturers of commercial baby foods and infant formulas have become more responsive to the requests of physicians and consumers to make their foods safe to eat, have good nutritional content, and be flavorful. But, thank goodness, there are still a large number of parents who believe that the only foods good enough for their babies to eat are the ones they prepared themselves. This thinking is not old-fashioned: Preparing your baby's food is a way of showing your love as well as tending to your baby's nutritional well-being.

But where does a parent start? How can you be sure that the diet you are planning for your baby is well balanced and appropriate for your child? What can you do to make tasty dishes without destroying the valuable vitamins, minerals, and good-for-growth resources? Sue Castle has revised her popular *The Complete New Guide to Preparing Baby Food* to answer these questions and others commonly asked by responsible parents. In addition, she has given special attention to considerations of time—making this book especially valuable for use by parents working outside the home as well as those who have the luxury of full-time parenting.

As a pediatrician with twenty years of practical experience, I would like to offer some additional tips to new parents as they offer these homemade foods to their small children.

There is no absolutely correct time to introduce solid food into your baby's diet. And contrary to popular belief, starting solid foods early does not help a baby to sleep through the night sooner. The author has offered an excellent guide for the introduction of specific solid foods, but don't be afraid to experiment within the boundaries of your own good common sense. You may also wish to discuss feeding issues with your child's doctor at the time of the first few "well baby" visits.

Although it is a good practice to offer a small infant more than one food at a given meal, it is not necessary to do so. Small babies are often more accepting of a bland food like cereal when it is mixed with a sweeter food such as fruit, but this may not always be the best policy. Teaching infants to accept foods that are not sweet may be important to good nutrition later on.

Parents often mislabel their child as a picky eater when he or she doesn't like specific foods. Try experimenting with the same food in different textures and avoid adding unnecessary seasoning. Babies frequently enjoy foods that are toward the bland side, and remember that food does not have to taste good to you in order for your child to like it. Also, adding a seasoning like salt may not be healthy for the baby.

Try offering your baby foods that you don't like. It is frequently stated that "babies are picky eaters because they don't get to pick the food." There are many infants who will refuse the traditional baby vegetables of carrots, peas, and string beans, but will readily accept the less-traditional Brussels Sprouts, cauliflower, spinach, and squash. If a parent doesn't like these foods he or she may not even bring them into the house.

Experiment with different feeding patterns: Until the first year of age most babies will eat three equal-size meals a day. But, after twelve months, children will often eat one large meal mixed with many smaller ones. The time of the large meal may vary from day to day and the small meals should not be thought of as snacks. Instead, children should be offered the same food that was rejected at mealtime but in smaller quantities all day long. Pieces of fruit, vegetable, and meat can be offered from plastic containers or plastic sandwich bags while avoiding junk foods with less nutritional value. When babies eat this way, they are responding to the message that their bodies are giving them. Remember, your baby may not be hungry when you are.

Think of feeding your child as a fun time. If you do, your baby will too.

Jeffrey L. Brown, M.D., F.A.A.P.
Attending Pediatrician, United Hospital Medical Center,
Port Chester, New York; Clinical Assistant Professor of
      Pediatrics in Pediatrics and Psychiatry,
The New York Hospital—Cornell Medical Center

The Complete New Guide to Preparing Baby Foods

1
Nutrition

There is a growing awareness that Americans, with a high standard of living and a large selection of food, are in many ways overfed but undernourished. This condition is not simply a result of low family income or the amount spent on food.

We can only assume that the problem is one of not understanding the basics of nutrition. This subject is usually taught early in high school, when we are least interested or least likely to use this information. By the time we are buying and preparing food for our own families, we have forgotten the essentials and do not have time to catch up, especially with an infant in the house.

There are also very few sources of specific information on a baby's nutritional needs. Because your baby is eating a limited diet and is growing at a rapid rate, his needs are not the same as those of an adult. Good nutrition is even more important in a baby's first year, as research has shown that the earlier a nutritional deficiency occurs, the more serious and permanent the effect. Also, many deficiencies in infancy do not show up until later years, as in the case of rickets. So a good understanding of infant nutrition is essential and worth going into in some detail.

The advisable daily intake of various nutrients is based on recommendations from the American Academy of Pediatrics' *Pediatric Nutrition Handbook;* also the Food and Nutrition Board, National Academy of Sciences—National Research Council. I have included these amounts so that you can have some basis for interpreting the "Nutritive Values of Foods" tables and the amounts of nutrients that are often listed on product labels. You might also occasionally look at an average daily menu to see if you are supplying your baby with the advisable daily intakes. However, unless you happen to have a lot of spare time and enjoy arithmetic, you do not have to use these specific amounts in planning your baby's daily meals.

The easiest way to ensure your baby's good nutrition is to understand the general principles of good nutrition and to serve a balanced selection of the foods that supply the essential nutrients. These nutrients are calories, protein, carbohydrates, fat, vitamins, and minerals.

CALORIES

Calorie is probably the most familiar word in nutrition. Many people have the idea that calories are something bad in food that cause you to gain weight. In fact, a calorie is really only a measure of how much energy a particular food supplies. If you consume more calories than your body needs, the excess will be stored as fat.

There is also the misconception that foods high in protein, such as meat, are low-calorie foods; whereas high-carbohydrate foods, such as pasta and rice, are high-calorie foods. In fact:

1 gram of protein supplies 4 calories.

1 gram of carbohydrates supplies 4 calories.

How many calories does a healthy full-term baby need on the average every day to maintain good growth and energy?

Birth to six months (up to 13 pounds): 52 calories per pound

six to twelve months (up to 20 pounds): 48 calories per pound

one to three years (up to 29 pounds): 1,300 calories, total

The following table will save you time calculating:

Daily Calorie Requirements for Growing Infants

POUNDS	DAILY CALORIES	POUNDS	DAILY CALORIES
6	312	14	672
7	364	15	720
8	416	16	768
9	468	17	816
10	520	18	864
11	572	19	912
12	624	20	960
13	676	21–28	1,300

Of course, individual growth and activity levels vary and could increase or decrease the calories required for optimal weight gain. So be sure to discuss your infant's needs with your doctor.

In the first four to six months, your baby will be getting all his calories from breast milk (about 21 calories per ounce) or commercial formula (20 calories per ounce). As solid foods are introduced, about 35 to 50 percent of the daily calories should come from a variety of these foods.

PROTEIN

Protein is the main material for growth and development of many parts of the body—muscles, glands, blood, heart, nerves, brain, and skin. It also forms an important part of the enzymes that aid in the digestion and absorption of food. Protein is especially important in the rapid body building that your baby will do in his first years. A lack of protein in infancy can cause serious problems such as mental retardation and physical impairment, during childhood and in adult life. Resistance to infection can also be lowered.

Fortunately, in our society, a protein deficiency is rare. Of more concern is consuming too much, which can strain an infant's digestive system. There is considerable medical criticism of the low-carbohydrate, high-protein diets, and they are definitely not advised for infants and children.

Because protein cannot be stored in the body, your baby should eat protein foods throughout the day, including some complete protein foods. They should account for about 15 percent of the total daily calories.

The following table gives the recommended daily amounts by weight and age:

Protein Needs by Weight and Age

BIRTH TO 6 MONTHS		6 TO 12 MONTHS		1 TO 3 YEARS	
Weight (lb)	Protein (gm)	Weight (lb)	Protein (gm)	Weight (lb)	Protein (gm)
6	6	14	12.6	21	18.4
7	7	15	13.5	22	18.4
8	8	16	14.4	23	18.4
9	9	17	15.3	24	20.0
10	10	18	16.2	25	20.0
11	11	19	17.1	26	20.0
12	12	20	18.0	27	21.6
13	13			28	21.6
				29	23.0

Note: Formulas (containing 15 gm protein per quart) supply 0.5 gm per ounce. Breast milk supplies about 0.3 gm per ounce. Cow's milk (skim or whole) supplies 1 gm per ounce. Even though formulas and breast milk contain less protein per ounce than cow's milk, it is in a form that is more efficiently assimilated.

Human milk contains only one-third the amount of protein as in cow's milk, but if nursing is the main source of food, a baby will still receive adequate amounts of protein. It is important, if your baby breast-feeds and also eats a good amount of solid food, that you select those foods which contain high amounts of complete protein.

COMPLETE PROTEIN. Some foods contain all the elements, called amino acids, that are contained in protein and are required by the body. The following foods are excellent sources of complete protein:

Milk	Fish	Yogurt
Meat	Eggs	Nonfat dry milk
Poultry	Cheese	Soybeans

INCOMPLETE PROTEIN. Other foods supply only some of the protein elements that are essential for nutrition and are considered incomplete protein foods. These foods are still an important source of protein, and because they are usually inexpensive, they are good to serve as a supplement:

Whole grain cereals, bread

Dried peas, beans, lentils

Nuts, peanut butter

Enriched pastas

Brown and converted rice

Wheat germ

CARBOHYDRATES

Carbohydrates, in the form of sugar and starch, should provide about 55 percent of the total calories that an active baby needs for heat and energy. They are the main source of immediate energy and the only energy source for the central nervous system. If the daily carbohydrate intake is too low, valuable protein will be converted for energy instead of for growth and other necessary functions. If an excess of carbohydrates is eaten, they will be stored in the body as fat. A moderate amount of carbohydrates is necessary each day for an active, healthy baby.

In the first months, the milk sugar, lactose, will supply carbohydrates. As solids are added to the diet, carbohydrates will come from other sources.

STARCH SOURCES. There are many complex starches among foods that you will serve your baby:

Bananas	Dried beans, peas	Potatoes

Cereals	Noodles	Rice
Corn	Peas	Winter squash

SUGAR SOURCES. There are also many natural sources of sugar in fruits and vegetables:

Apples	Carrots	Orange juice
Bananas	Grape juice	Peas
Beets	Grapes	Sweet potatoes

EMPTY NUTRITION SOURCES. If your baby is eating a balanced daily diet that includes cereals, fruits, and vegetables, he will be receiving an adequate amount of carbohydrates. In view of the abundance of natural sugars and starches, the addition of refined sugar and starches, such as cornstarch, modified food starch, and tapioca starch, to any food is unnecessary (see "Sweeteners," in Chapter 6).

An overabundance of these "empty nutrition" carbohydrates can affect your baby in several ways. They can give him a false sense of being full, thus decreasing his appetite for other necessary foods. Because these sugars and starches are nutritionally empty, your baby may become deficient in many vitamins and minerals while giving the appearance of being "fat" and "healthy." The extra fat will be produced because the baby is consuming more carbohydrates than he requires. Research now indicates that being fat during infancy may lead to a tendency to become overweight as an adult. If your baby becomes accustomed to sweet food, he may also grow up with a craving for sweets that can result in nutritional deficiencies and tooth decay.

FATS

Fat, usually thought of as a nasty word, is also a necessary element in nutrition. The calories in fat provide a concentrated source of energy and prevent the loss of protein being burned as energy. Fat helps in the absorption of the fat-soluble vitamins, A, D, E, and K, into the body. Stored fat protects the body from excessive loss of heat and supports and protects the vital organs.

The various forms of fat and their effect on cardiovascular disease have become a familiar part of our language. Here's a brief review.

Cholesterol is naturally present in the body and is essential for proper development of the nervous system. It is also present in all foods of animal origin, such as meats and whole milk dairy products, and is especially high in butter, organ meats, and egg yolks. It may form deposits in the arteries and in large amounts can cause heart disease and stroke.

Saturated Fats tend to raise the level of cholesterol in the blood. They are also found in high amounts in animal origin foods:

Egg yolks

Organ meats

Red meats

Whole milk dairy products—cream, milk, cheese, butter, ice cream

Coconut and palm oils, as well as chocolate, are vegetable foods that contain saturated fats.

Polyunsaturated Fats have been shown to actually reduce the levels of cholesterol in the body. They are found mainly in vegetable sources:

Corn oil	Sesame oil
Cottonseed oil°	Soybean oil
Safflower oil	Sunflower oil

Fish also contains mostly polyunsaturated fat.

Monounsaturated Fats neither raise nor lower the level of cholesterol. They are high in olive oil, peanut oil, and avocados.

°Cottonseed oil should be avoided because cotton is not considered a food crop and may be treated with many pesticides.

Now that you understand the different types of fat and the way each one contributes to the possible development of cardiovascular disease, it *may* seem the best way to protect your child is to eliminate saturated fats and cholesterol from your baby's diet, but *this is not true*.

Cholesterol is present in breast milk and is essential for an infant's growth and development. There is the possibility that cholesterol in the diet during infancy helps the body develop mechanisms to handle cholesterol efficiently later in life. Many of the high-cholesterol foods such as eggs and liver are also good sources of vitamins and minerals.

The American Academy of Pediatrics, concerned about the trend toward eliminating fats, has given the following recommendations:

- Dietary fat and cholesterol should not be limited during the first year. When a baby switches to cow's milk, it should be whole milk, not skim or fat reduced.
- After one year of age, a varied diet from each of the major food groups provides the best insurance of nutritional adequacy.
- About 35 percent of the daily calories in the diet should come from fat.
- Children over two years old who are at risk due to a family history of cardiovascular disease should be regularly screened for serum cholesterol levels.

In short, even if *you* are cutting down on fats, do not modify your baby's diet without specific instructions from his doctor.

Finally, a word of warning about mineral oil. It is totally lacking in nutrients and is nondigestible. Because it absorbs the fat-soluble vitamins in the body, it can cause deficiences. *Never give mineral oil to your baby*.

VITAMINS

Vitamins are small substances found in food and are necessary for growth and all the bodily functions. All the vitamins needed for good health can be found in food, or are synthesized in the body.

WATER-SOLUBLE. These vitamins cannot be stored in the body and foods containing these vitamins should be eaten every day. They are very perishable and can be lost in water, heat, and exposure to air. They are vitamin C and vitamin-B complex (thiamine, or B_1; riboflavin, or B_2; niacin; pyridoxine, or B_6; pantothenic acid; folic acid; B_{12}; choline; and biotin).

FAT-SOLUBLE. These vitamins can be stored in the body. The amounts that occur naturally in food consumed in moderation cannot cause a harmful surplus in the body. However, supplemental forms of the vitamins can be taken in harmful amounts and should only be given under a doctor's supervision. They can be destroyed by high heat, drying, exposure to air, and rancidity. These vitamins are A, D, E, and K.

Vitamin A Vitamin A is essential for growth, good vision, and healthy skin and for keeping the lining of the mouth, nose, throat, and digestive tract healthy and resistant to infection. Babies are unable to store this vitamin before birth, so it is necessary in their diet. The following animal foods supply large amounts of vitamin A:

Butter	Fish liver oil
Cheese	Kidneys
Egg yolk	Liver
Fish	Whole milk, breast milk

Plant foods contain large amounts of carotene, which is converted by the body into vitamin A. The highest sources are dark green and leafy vegetables, and the deep yellow fruits and vegetables:

Apricots	Green beans
Asparagus	Leafy greens
Broccoli	Mangoes
Cantaloupe	Sweet potatoes
Carrots	Tomatoes
Chard	Winter squash

The vitamin, while found in many foods, can be destroyed by exposure to air (wilting), high heat, and rancidity. Skim milk and skim milk products are very low in the vitamin because it is removed with the fat, and so they are often fortified with vitamin A.

Because the vitamin can be stored in the body, a continual overdose can be harmful to your baby. The amount of the vitamin that naturally occurs in food cannot result in overdose (when the food is consumed in normal amounts); however, the amounts in supplements can reach high levels. Also, many foods have been fortified with vitamin A, especially nonfat dry milk, skim and whole milk, margarine, and cereals.

The suggested daily intake of vitamin A for a normal infant is 375 micrograms of retinol equivalents. A daily dosage of 6,000 micrograms (or more) of retinol equivalents for as long as a month can result in toxicity with symptoms of loss of appetite, skin rashes, listlessness, and injury to the nervous system.

Vitamin-B Complex There are at least fifteen different B vitamins, which occur in many of the same foods. The best-known ones are thiamine (B_1), riboflavin (B_2), niacin, B_6, and B_{12}. These B vitamins are essential to the growing infant in many ways. They enable body cells to obtain energy from carbohydrates; they promote growth, good appetite, digestion, and healthy skin; and they keep the nervous system in balance. A deficiency in these vitamins can result in loss of appetite, irritability, fatigue, eye and skin problems, and poor growth. The B vitamins are found in high amounts in a variety of foods:

Bananas	Green leafy vegetables
Breast milk	Liver and organ meats
Brewer's yeast	Milk (whole, skim)
Brown rice	Peanut butter
Cheese	Pork
Dried peas, beans, lentils	Poultry
Egg yolk	Soybeans
Enriched cereals	Sweet potatoes
Fish	Wheat germ

All the B vitamins are water soluble, so they are easily lost in cooking water. They cannot be stored in the body and should be eaten daily. The vitamins are quite stable to heat, with the exception of B_6. Riboflavin is particularly sensitive to light, and foods that are served as main sources, such as milk, should not be stored in clear containers or left out in the light. The B vitamins are also lost when soda is used in the cooking water.

A deficiency in some of the B vitamins may be more prevalent today because of the practice of refining flours, cereals, and rice, which results in a large loss of all the B vitamins. The Food and Drug Administration has approved levels of enrichment for refined flours and cereals; however, only thiamine, riboflavin, and niacin are added. Even a large intake of enriched foods can leave a baby deficient in the other B vitamins. One answer is to serve whole grain cereals, unbleached or whole grain flour, converted or brown rice, and other foods that are high in the B vitamins. Wheat germ and brewer's yeast can also be used as added fortifiers in your baby's food.

In general, if your baby drinks an adequate amount of breast milk, commercial formula, or cow's milk, he will be receiving a good amount of the B vitamins, with the exception of niacin, which can be supplied by meats, poultry, and enriched cereals. The commercial formulas should be fortified with B_6 and will state so on the label. Advisable daily intakes of some of the B vitamins are:

	BIRTH TO 6 MONTHS	6 TO 12 MONTHS	1 TO 3 YEARS
Thiamine	0.3 mg	0.5 mg	0.7 mg
Riboflavin	0.4 mg	0.6 mg	0.8 mg
Niacin	6.0 mg	8.0 mg	9.0 mg

An excess of niacin can cause abnormal liver function and a rise in blood sugar.

Vitamin C Vitamin C, or ascorbic acid, is needed by all body cells. It is crucial to growth, strong bones, and teeth. Current research indicates that it plays an important role in the body's resistance to infection, which is especially important for infants. Vitamin C cannot be stored in the body and must be supplied daily. A deficiency can result in scurvy, gum problems, and frequent infections. There are many high sources of this vitamin among foods:

Breast milk	Kiwi
Broccoli	Lemon juice
Cantaloupe	Orange juice
Guava	Oranges
Grapefruit	Papaya
Grapefruit juice	Parsley
Green pepper	Strawberries

There are also many fair sources of vitamin C:

Asparagus	Spinach
Collard greens	Tomato juice
Kale	Tomatoes
Kohlrabi	Watercress
Potatoes	

In spite of the abundance of vitamin C in foods, the vitamin is highly unstable and can be lost in cooking or soaking water or by exposure to heat, light, and air.

While the vitamin is usually adequately supplied through breast milk and commercial formulas, cow's milk is a poor source.

The recommended daily allowance of vitamin C is 35 milligrams for the first year and 45 milligrams from age one to three.

Vitamin D Vitamin D is one of the most important vitamins for babies. The first formation of bone is cartilage, and this vitamin is necessary for the absorption of calcium and phosphorus, which cause the cartilage to harden into bone. When a baby is deficient in vitamin D, he may have rickets, which is characterized by soft, curved bones, bowed legs, or knock-knees.

The vitamin can be produced in the body by the action of the sun on the skin, but this is not a reliable source. The main food sources are:

Cod liver oil
Halibut liver oil

It is also present in fair amounts in liver, salmon, tuna fish, and egg yolk. The vitamin is added to most formulas and many kinds of milk—whole, skim, evaporated, and non-fat dry milk powder.

Breast-fed babies require vitamin D supplements because it is not adequately supplied by human milk. You should give it during or just after a feeding to make sure it is well absorbed. The advisable daily intake for birth to six months is 7.5 micrograms (300 International Units); for six months to one year, it is 10 micrograms (400 International Units).

Since the vitamin is stored in the body, an overdose of as little as 45 micrograms (1,800 International Units) daily for a month can result in toxicity with symptoms of poor growth, weight loss, vomiting, and excessive calcium in the kidneys and blood. Bone deformities and multiple fractures are also common. In fact, many of the symptoms from an excess of vitamin D are similar to those caused by a deficiency. So never give more than the prescribed amount.

Vitamin E Vitamin E is essential for your baby's development. It plays an important part in cell structure and contributes to growth, good muscles, nerves, and skin. The vitamin can be extracted and is available as alpha-tocopherol. It is also found in some foods:

Breast milk
Nuts
Peanut, soy, and safflower oil
Wheat germ, wheat germ oil
Whole grain cereals

The vitamin can be destroyed by high heat and exposure to air. The practice of refining flours and cereals has removed much natural vitamin E from our diets, and the enrichment of flour and cereal does not include vitamin E.

Because heating and chemical extraction of oils can destroy the vitamin, nutritionists recommend using unrefined oils.

Breast milk contains more vitamin E than cow's milk. All commercial formulas are fortified with vitamin E. The advisable daily intake of vitamin E (alpha-tocopherol) is

BIRTH TO 6 MONTHS	6 MONTHS TO 1 YEAR	1 TO 3 YEARS
3 mg	4 mg	5 mg

While there are no known risks of megadoses, there is no reason to give them.

Vitamin K Vitamin K is a fat-soluble vitamin that is essential in blood clotting and liver function. It is found in several foods:

Breast milk   Spinach
Cabbage   Tomatoes
Cauliflower   Turnip greens
Cow's milk

Yogurt is also a source since the yogurt bacteria will produce vitamin K in the body. The vitamin is adequately supplied for normal babies in breast milk, cow's milk, and formulas. A single injection of vitamin K is usually given at birth. Again, this vitamin can be stored in the body and overdoses will result in jaundice (with yellowing of the skin).

MINERALS

Minerals are present in the body fluids as soluble salts and affect many bodily functions. Calcium and phosphorus are the basic elements of bones and teeth. Iron and copper are elements in the red blood cells. Iodine is essential for proper functioning of the thyroid gland. Sodium, potassium, and magnesium are other important minerals.

Most minerals are adequately supplied by a balanced selection of food. However, minerals are water soluble and can easily be lost if you soak food or cook with a large amount of water. Refining of flours, cereals, and rice also destroys minerals, so the whole grain cereals and brown rice are better sources. Breast milk and cow's milk can supply your baby with adequate amounts of most minerals, with the exception of iron.

Iron Iron is a mineral that is essential to your baby's health. It combines with protein in the body to form hemoglobin, the substance that carries oxygen from the lungs to all the parts of the body. The body cells must be supplied with oxygen to sustain life. Iron also forms part of several enzymes that break food down so that it can be digested in the body. These foods are high in iron:

Dried fruits   Kidneys
Dried peas, beans, lentils   Liver
Egg yolk   Meat
Enriched bread and cereals   Molasses
Green leafy vegetables

Unless a mother is iron deficient during pregnancy, the baby will be born with enough stored iron for at least the first four to six months. Both human and cow's milk are low in iron, but many commercial formulas are iron fortified. Your baby's doctor may prescribe an iron supplement. Never give more than the recommended amount. Excess iron may cause damage to the liver, pancreas, and heart. It can also increase the likelihood of bacterial and fungal infections.

When your baby is eating solid food, you can add iron-fortified cereals, egg yolks, and the above foods to his daily diet as a source of iron. The dry infant cereals are fortified to meet a baby's daily need for iron. Molasses can be added to food or a bottle, but because it is a laxative, it must be used in very small amounts.

Although a baby's daily requirements for iron can vary with individual needs, an average daily intake of 10 milligrams is advised for the first six months, then 15 milligrams to age three. Babies who are most likely to develop iron deficiency are those with low birth weight, those of multiple births (twins, etc.), and those who are born to mothers who have had several closely spaced pregnancies, or possibly who are low in iron during pregnancy.

Calcium Calcium is the most important mineral in the building of strong bones and teeth. Infants have a particularly high need for calcium in the conversion of cartilage to bone and for their rapid growth. It also plays a larger part in the prevention and relief of nervous tension and irritability. A calcium deficiency can result in rickets.

The highest source of calcium is milk, both whole and skim, breast and cow's milk. Other foods contain calcium in good amounts:

Broccoli	Ice cream
Cheese	Kale
Collard greens	Nonfat dry milk powder
Green beans	

Although spinach, chard, and beet greens also contain calcium, it is not in a form that is usable by the body and should not be considered a source of calcium. Fat is also important in the absorption of calcium by the body.

By the time your baby is a few months old, he should be drinking 24 to 32 ounces (3 to 4 cups) of milk a day and continue to do so through childhood. This will adequately supply his need for calcium. The following foods contain the same amount of calcium as 1 cup of milk and can be used as supplements, but should not be considered substitutes:

1 ounce semifirm cheese—Swiss, Cheddar, Muenster, etc.
3 tablespoons nonfat dry milk powder
1 cup custard

The advisable daily intake of calcium is 360 milligrams up to six months; 540 milligrams to one year; and 800 milligrams to three years.

Bone meal, a food supplement that may be sold as a source of supplemental calcium (there are better sources), may also be consumed at toxic levels. Bone meal contains a high level of phosphorus that, if the diet is already high in phosphorus, can actually decrease the amount of calcium in the body and create a deficiency. Do not give to children unless advised by a doctor.

Sodium Your baby will receive an adequate amount of sodium, or salt, from milk, meat, and vegetables. It is unnecessary to salt your baby's food to your own taste, because babies do not show any preference for salted foods—this is an acquired habit. Research has indicated that a high intake of sodium by infant animals results in high blood pressure and hypertension in adult life. So the safest course is to avoid adding salt to your baby's food, and avoid those prepared foods that are highly salted. Be aware that sodium compounds are also used as preservatives in many foods.

The advisable daily intake of sodium is 115 to 350 milligrams up to six months; 250 to 750 milligrams to one year; and 325 to 975 milligrams to three years.

Iodine Iodine is an essential mineral for the maintenance of the body processes by its role in the functioning of the thyroid gland. If the activity of the thyroid is too slow, the body will store up energy as fat. If the thyroid is overactive, the body will burn up food and energy reserves too quickly.

Iodine is present in:

Cod liver oil	Saltwater fish
Iodized salt	Shellfish
Meats	Vegetables

If you live in an inland area, a small amount of iodized salt can be added to your baby's food as a source of iodine. Be sure to check the label on table salt to make certain that iodine has been added.

The advisable daily intake of iodine is 6 micrograms (birth to six months) and 10 micrograms (six months to three years).

Phosphorus Phosphorus is essential for the growth of strong bones and teeth and also many bodily processes. It is especially important to the rapidly growing infant.

This mineral is present in large amounts in these foods:

Brown rice	Fish
Cheese	Liver
Corn	Peanut butter
Cow's milk	Soybeans
Dried peas, beans, lentils	Whole grain cereals
Egg yolk	

The advisable daily intake is 240 milligrams to six months; 360 milligrams to one year; and 800 milligrams to three years.

SUPPLEMENTS

It seems that nearly all the vitamins and minerals are readily available in some form of supplement—powder, liquid, or pill. With all the attention given these days to the importance of good nutrition, these supplements seem to many people the answer to staying healthy. Let's face it—it's often easier to get a child to chew a colorful flavored pill than to convince him to eat whole wheat bread and vegetables.

The danger with supplements is that you can easily fall into the trap of thinking, "If some is good, then more is better." The American Academy of Pediatrics warns that "vitamin and mineral supplements are widely abused by the general public, occasionally to the point of toxicity." Not only can some vitamins accumulate in the body to dangerous levels, a large increase in one nutrient can upset the balance of the way vitamins and minerals work with each other.

What supplements, if any, does a normal-term baby really need? Here are the academy's recommendations assuming an infant has an adequate milk intake and is eating a variety of solid foods after six months of age. (Breast-fed infants of strict vegetarian mothers and children on vegetarian diets have special needs and a doctor should be consulted.)

From birth to six months:

- All infants should receive one injection of vitamin K shortly after birth. This is required in many states.
- Breast-fed infants should be given vitamin D. It isn't necessary for formula-fed infants since commercial formula is fortified with vitamin D, as well as other vitamins and minerals.
- Breast-fed or formula-fed infants rarely need iron supplements before four to six months because they are born with an adequate supply of iron.
- Since teeth are being formed, fluoride supplements are recommended by the American Academy of Pediatrics for all infants if the water supply contains less than 0.3 parts per million of fluoride.

From six months to one year:

- Breast-fed babies still require vitamin D supplements. Those drinking commercial formula or fortified milk do not.
- Since iron stores are depleted at four to six months, breast-fed babies need an iron supplement, preferably in the form of iron-fortified infant cereal. For babies still on formula or cow's milk, iron fortified formula and/or iron-fortified infant cereal are convenient sources of iron and are preferable to iron supplements.
- Fluoride supplements should be continued if the water supply contains less than 0.3 parts per million fluoride.

After one year:

- Routine vitamin and mineral supplementation in normal children is not recommended.
- The exception is fluoride if the drinking water doesn't contain 0.3 parts per million fluoride.

Of course, these recommendations assume an infant or child is eating adequate amounts of milk and/or a variety of good food. What if you're like many parents and are concerned your child just doesn't seem to be eating enough?

Don't start stuffing him with vitamins, minerals, and protein powders. *Do* discuss your child's diet with your doctor. If specific supplements are advised, remember *never* to give more than the recommended amounts. An overdose, especially of vitamins A, D, E, and iron, can be dangerous. Also, many of the flavored chewable pills may seem like candy. So don't call them candy and keep them out of your child's reach.

Fiber Our consciousness has certainly been raised about the importance of fiber—but what exactly is it and how should it be included in our children's diet?

First of all, dietary fiber, in the form of cellulose, pectin, and other compounds is part of every plant, including the stem, leaf, root, skin, and seeds. Some high-fiber foods are whole wheat cereals, brown rice, wheat germ, broccoli, carrots, beets, spinach, peas, winter squash, apples, prunes, pears, raspberries, peanuts, and legumes (lentils, lima beans, and pinto beans).

Because fiber can't be digested, it isn't a nutrient. So what does it do? The current interest in fiber was stimulated by research that suggested high-fiber diets might help prevent certain diseases like cancer of the colon. Because fiber produces softer, more frequent stools, there is less time for potential carcinogens to be in contact with the intestinal system. There is also evidence that fiber may reduce the levels of cholesterol and triglycerides in the blood and so reduce the chance of coronary heart disease.

There seems to be no question that American adults can benefit from eating more fiber, but what about infants and children? There are indications that the intake of fiber is low for as many as 75 percent of the children in the United States.

The American Academy of Pediatrics advises, "Fiber probably is not needed in infants less than one year old. For older infants and children, the diet should include whole grain cereals, breads, fruits, and vegetables. However, a diet that places emphasis on high-fiber, low-calorie foods, to the exclusion of the other common food groups, is not recommended for children."

In other words, use moderation. Needless to say, you should not be adding fiber supplements, like bran, to your baby's food.

Potassium Chloride Potassium chloride is a substance that may be sold as a supplement, but its use can result in high levels of potassium in the blood, a potentially fatal condition. The Food and Drug Administration warns, *"No one should use potassium supplements without medical supervision. The practice is particularly dangerous to children."*

FOOD AND CANCER

Research has shown that the food you and your children eat may affect the chances of developing some types of cancer. The National Cancer Institute and other experts warn against eating high amounts of fat (including polyunsaturated), and foods that are smoked, salt cured, salt pickled, or preserved with nitrates or nitrites (such as bacon, corned beef, and hot dogs).

On the other hand, certain foods may actually protect you from some cancers. These include high-fiber foods such as whole grain cereals (see "Fiber," in this chapter), and fruits and vegetables that are high in carotene or vitamin C. These include

Dark yellow vegetables (carrots and winter squash) .
Dark green leafy vegetables (spinach and kale)
Members of the cabbage family (broccoli, cauliflower, and Brussels sprouts)
Fruit (orange, grapefruit, tomato, and pepper)

Remember, it is important for your child to get these vitamins and fiber from the foods he eats, not from supplements.

HYPERACTIVITY: FOODS AND ADDITIVES

Infants and children obviously have different amounts of energy. Some are placid and easygoing, while others cry easily and get into everything as soon as they can move around. Most fall within normal levels, but a very small percentage of children have activity levels so high they are considered hyperactive. There are many theories, but little proof, as to the cause of hyperactivity.

Several years ago, Dr. Benjamin Feingold observed that hyperactive children improved when synthetic colors, synthetic flavors, and any food containing salicylates (such as oranges, apples, grapes, plums, cucumbers, and tomatoes) were removed from the diet. Since then, controlled studies have concluded that although the change in behavior was not widespread, a few children do have negative reactions to synthetic food dyes and may be helped by an additive-free diet.

The American Academy of Pediatrics (AAP) notes that it is not a dangerous diet, but it should be used under competent nutritional guidance. So if you feel your child might benefit, ask your doctor before eliminating various fruits and vegetables. Artificial dyes and flavors are unnecessary and controversial and should be avoided anyway by all children.

There is no scientific evidence to support the claim that sugar significantly increases activity levels. Still, that doesn't mean it is a good idea to add sugar to your child's foods.

2

How to Be
a Smart Shopper

NUTRITIONAL COST

Now that you know your baby's nutritional needs, let's look at how to buy foods in terms of their "nutritional cost." That is, how you can get the most food value for your money and also avoid foods, additives, and pesticides that may be harmful for your baby.

Throughout this book I stress the *least expensive* ways to feed your baby. This economy is not the same thing as skimping. We all want our babies to have the best food possible, and we are ready to pay a high price for quality. However, expensive foods are not necessarily the most nutritious and may even be harmful for your baby. For example, prime meats contain more fat and less protein than lower grades, and expensive processed foods may contain additives and fillers and have often lost nutrients.

But you must also keep in mind that some less expensive foods may be poor nutritional buys. For example, unenriched white rice is less expensive than brown rice but has lost many of the nutrients. Fruit "punches" may be less expensive than a juice, but they contain a much higher amount of water and sugar.

Instead, you should select your baby's food by considering its "nutritional cost"; that is, where you can find the most food value for the least amount of money. Look for the

...oods and recipes in this book. They are your best
n... ...onal buys.

If you look back over the lists of foods that are high in
specific nutrients, you will see that the same inexpensive
foods appear on many of the lists:

Carrots	Liver° (beef, lamb)
Dried peas, beans, lentils	Milk°
Egg yolk°	Nonfat dry milk°
Kidneys°	Peanut butter
Leafy greens (turnip, kale,	Poultry°
spinach, collard)	Soybeans°

Fruits and vegetables are always less expensive in season
and in areas where they are easily grown. Near the end of
the season you can prepare and freeze ahead. Fresh fruits
and vegetables are usually less expensive than frozen or
canned.

Meat protein will probably be the most expensive item
on your list, but you can usually find sales on at least one
type each week. Again, you can prepare a few weeks' supply
and freeze.

INEXPENSIVE PROTEIN

Fortunately, there are other ways that you can serve complete protein and still economize. Remember the list of "incomplete" protein foods in the last chapter—cereals, rice,
nuts, legumes (dried peas and beans), pastas, and wheat
germ? They are all very cheap sources of protein. If you
combine these foods with small amounts of the more expensive protein foods in dishes such as beef and rice, or even
serve them at the *same meal*, you will have adequate
amounts of high-quality protein at a lower cost.

Even more economical is the use of "complementary"

°These foods are all excellent sources of complete protein. Some of
them may not appeal to you, but your baby was not born with specific likes
and dislikes.

incomplete protein foods. Each of these foods has some amino acids that are lacking in the others. The trick is to put together the right combination of grains, seeds (nuts), and legumes to end up with complete protein. My rice-and-bean casseroles aren't family favorites, but babies love them! They purée and freeze very well.

In Chapter 10 you will find more ways to combine these foods and specific recipes that your family might also enjoy. For a more detailed description of "complementary" protein foods and enough recipes to satisfy everyone, see books like *Diet for a Small Planet* by Frances Moore Lappé, *Recipes for a Small Planet* by Ellen B. Ewald, *Jane Brody's Nutrition Book*, and *Jane Brody's Good Food Book*.

HOW TO READ LABELS

When you consider the immense variety of foods that are available in a supermarket, shopping becomes a challenging game between you and the food industry. The secret of winning is very easy. Just read and take advantage of all the information that is printed on the labels for the protection of you, the consumer.

The U.S. Department of Agriculture (USDA) and the Food and Drug Administration (FDA) enforce several laws that cover all food that is sold in interstate commerce or is imported, and many states and localities also have their own laws. These acts require that the food be pure, wholesome, and honestly labeled. The label must include (when applicable) the grade; inspection shield; brand name; weight, measure, or count; description; dates; and a list of ingredients.

In 1990, the Nutrition Labeling Education Act was passed, and the FDA is writing specific regulations for new labels. They should begin to appear on products in two to three years and are likely to show the following:

- Serving size
- Number of servings per container
- Number of calories per serving
- Total amount of fat, saturated fat, cholesterol, sodium,

sugars, dietary fiber, protein, total carbohydrates, and complex carbohydrates
- Total amount of important vitamins and minerals
- Percentage of fruit or vegetable juice contained in beverages

In this section I will help you to understand how you can easily use this information in buying the food that you will prepare for your baby. Of course, you will also be able to use your marketing know-how in shopping for the rest of the family. In the Bibliography I have listed additional sources of consumer information.

U.S. Grades These grades are used to classify foods according to their appearance, such as size, shape, color, or by their tenderness. All the grades are equally wholesome, and the lower grades contain the same amount of nutritional value as the highest grade. In the case of meats, the lower grades contain even more protein. These grades are particularly useful in buying food to prepare as purées, since appearance and tenderness is irrelevant once you have puréed the food for your baby. The higher the grade, the more expensive the item usually is, and it is usually an unnecessary expense to use the top grade. Because the names of the grade vary according to the food, I have indicated the appropriate grade for the various foods in the recipe chapters. Here are some examples of grade marks:

You should always look for the initials "U.S." before the grade, because they indicate that it is a USDA grade.

Inspection Shields The shields appear on all meat, on poultry products, and also on many other foods. Their presence means that the food was prepared under federal supervision and inspected for wholesomeness. You should always try to buy foods for your baby that carry these seals. Here are some federal seals:

Products that do not come under federal control may still carry state or local inspection seals, and you should become familiar with them.

Brand Names The label must contain the brand name or the manufacturer's name. You can easily recognize the well-advertised name; however, many supermarkets and other distributors have goods packaged under their own or a private label. Very often, the food is packaged by the same well-known manufacturer, who simply puts on a different label. Usually the private labels are less expensive than the well-known ones, since you do not have to pay for the cost of advertising. Because most of the food that you will buy for your baby comes under government inspection and grading, you can get the same food value and quality from the private-label brands and save money.

For many products, such as mayonnaise, canned fruits, juices, and vegetables, the government has established *standards of identity* that define minimum and maximum amounts of major ingredients. So you are assured of getting "at least" a certain amount of fruit and "not more than" a set amount of water in a can of fruit, regardless of the brand.

Weights, Measures, or Counts This information on content must be printed clearly on the label. Always compare different brands according to their weight in order to get the most for your money. Do not be deceived by larger packages. You can also use these weights to compare different sizes of the same brand in order to see if you really are saving money by buying the larger size.

In many areas, *unit pricing* is required by law and it makes economical shopping easy and fast. Under each item is listed the price per weight or count. Take advantage of it, and if it is not required in your area, support your local consumer organization in passing such a law.

Description of Food The name on the label must clearly and accurately describe the food, such as "sliced green beans," "orange juice," "whole carrots." If there are two main ingredients, the food that is present in the *largest amount* must be listed *first* in the name; such as "beans with pork" instead of the way we usually refer to it, as "pork and beans." Also, if a food resembles a food for which a standard of identity has been set, but does not contain the required ingredients, it must be labeled "imitation." The word *flavored* is also used to identify an imitation food.

Often, descriptions are added to the name of a food, and these are usually a good warning that the basic food has been modified. Cheese is a good example of this type of labeling. The word *food* in the label "pasteurized process cheese food" shows that the product contains less cheese, but added nonfat dry milk and water. The term *spread* in "pasteurized process cheese spread" indicates an even higher moisture content than the cheese food. Instead of "orange juice," you can find cans labeled "orange drink," "punch," or ". . . ade." These beverages all contain more water than those labeled "juice." *In general you will get the most food value for your money and the least additives and fillers if you avoid those products whose names show modification of the basic food.*

There are two words that may be added to the name of a food to indicate added food value. The word *enriched* is added to the name of many cereals, flours, and baked goods. This means that the vitamins riboflavin, niacin, and thiamine and the mineral iron have been added at least in minimum amounts to replace the loss due to processing. Some brands contain amounts that are higher than the minimum, so it is worth your time to look at the amounts or percentages that are listed on the label. The amount of iron in cereals is particularly important since they will be one of your baby's main sources.

The word *fortified* means that vitamins and minerals not normally in the food have been added to the product. It may also mean that the amounts of some nutrients have been increased above the normal amount.

Because these fortified and enriched foods are usually more expensive, read the label to see what has been added and consider if it is necessary for your baby. If not, you are spending money needlessly for nutrients that are naturally present in other foods that your baby eats. For example, fruit drinks fortified with vitamin C may be more expensive than a pure fruit juice and contain less vitamin C than the juice or fruit.

"Natural" Foods It seems that one of the most popular words in food advertising and on labels is *natural*. The manufacturers are aware of consumer interest in unrefined, unprocessed, additive-free foods, and they seize every opportunity to claim in bold letters that their product is "natural." A survey showed that the majority of people believe these foods are indeed better for them. Don't be mislead!

The term *natural* has not been under government control and can mean anything the manufacturer wants them to mean. For example, one "natural" fruit drink contains some natural orange flavor, but is made almost entirely from chemicals and is artificially colored. Some foods contain large amounts of sugars and starches that, although "natural," are not good for you and are a waste of money.

The Federal Trade Commission's proposed definition for the term *natural* requires that in order to be advertised as natural, products may not contain synthetic or artificial ingredients and may not be more than minimally processed.

The agency determined that minimally processed foods could also be considered natural if the process was not far different from what a consumer could do in his own kitchen. Under this definition, minimal processing includes such things as washing or peeling fruits or vegetables; homogenizing milk or fruit juices; canning, bottling, and freezing foods; baking bread; aging and roasting meats and grinding nuts. Highly processed, high-technology procedures such as puffing, extruding, and processes that changed the shape of things are not considered natural. Anything that contains added sugar and salt, highly refined products or oils, other than cold-pressed oils, would not qualify as a natural product.

Read the small print in the list of ingredients to find out what you are buying. Avoid those brands that do not give a complete listing of contents. Many companies are even giving a list of ingredients on foods that have a "standard of identity" such as ice cream and mayonnaise. Do not be willing to pay extra just because a food is labeled "natural"!

Dating Codes Most foods are marked with a code to indicate the packing date. Perishable foods always contain the last date on which the food may be sold. This date is used to help the owner of the store in removing spoiled foods and is often in coded form. However, in many states laws have been passed that require open and clear dating of perishable foods such as milk, eggs, and baked goods. Take advantage of these dates to buy the freshest food possible. Even where the date is coded, you can usually interpret it, because it is a combination of month, date, and, possibly, year. For example, 903 usually means September 3 and 1023 on milk means October 23. Some baked goods use letters to indicate the day of the week. If your area does not have open dating, try asking your local grocer for information on interpreting dates of perishable items that you frequently buy. Where possible, buy brands that are clearly dated and labeled—they have nothing to hide!

RDA Nutritional Information You may have seen the abbreviation "RDA" on a label and wondered what it meant.

RDA stands for Recommended Dietary Allowance and applies to the daily amount of a nutrient that is necessary to *maintain good nutrition* in the average healthy person. Labels usually list RDAs for adults. The amounts are established by the Food and Nutrition Board of the National Research Council. They currently apply to sixteen nutrients.

This information on a label can be very helpful in selecting the product with the lowest nutritional cost and to help you plan a balanced, healthy diet. But keep in mind the specific needs of your baby and look for actual amounts of nutrients that may also be listed on a label. You can compare these amounts with the advisable daily intakes that are described in Chapter 1.

List of Ingredients This list must be clearly printed on the package and it is your most valuable aid in safe and economical food buying. If you read the list, you will know what is in the product and at least the relative amounts. The ingredients are listed in descending order of amount. *Thus the ingredient that is listed first is present in the largest quantity.* If the label on a can of fruit drink reads "water, sugar, and juice," you will be buying more water and sugar than actual fruit juice. Although the drink may be priced lower than a fruit juice, this product may actually be more expensive in terms of its nutritional cost. Whenever you are in doubt about a product, or the name seems confusing, just read the list of ingredients!

HOW SAFE IS OUR FOOD?

In recent years, there has been a growing concern about the safety of pesticides and other chemicals used in growing food as well as the additives used to improve food. People seem willing to pay high prices for anything "organic" or "additive free." Is this really necessary to protect our health?

When a private environmental group reported that the pesticide Alar was found in minute amounts in apples and had the potential of causing cancer in mice, the attention given by the media was enormous. Infants and children were considered to be at greatest risk because of their lower body weight and the fact they consume large amounts of applesauce and juice. Many parents responded by throwing out all apples and apple products. Stores put up signs announcing Alar-free apples.

Alar was quickly withdrawn from the market by the manufacturer. In general, all the concern and publicity caused many farmers to reduce the use of pesticides by 25 to 50 percent. Several states and the federal government are encouraging research for alternate ways to control pests.

"Organic" Foods For a growing number of people, the answer to avoiding even small traces of chemicals is to buy only "organic" produce. This generally means the food was grown by traditional farming methods without synthetically compounded fertilizers, pesticides, herbicides, or fungicides. As of now, less than 1 percent of the produce grown in this country is organic and it's priced two to three times higher than regular fruits and vegetables.

The problem is how can you be sure the produce really was organically grown. Given the small supply and the increasing demand, many of the claims are probably fraudulent. As yet there are no federal controls and only a few state agencies monitor organic farming. However, there are private certification programs like the Organic Crop Improvement Association. You can get a complete list from the consumer group Center for Science in the Public Interest (CSPI) (see "Bibliography").

An alternative to buying expensive organic produce is to prepare fruits and vegetables in ways that remove as much chemical residue as possible. You can always peel skins, but that also removes some nutrients and fiber. Many chemicals and bacteria can be removed from produce by simply washing well with water and dish detergent . . . there's no soapy taste! It's also best to buy American-grown produce because the type and amount of chemicals used are under stricter control.

CSPI recommends peeling skins from the following:

- Carrots
- Cucumbers, if they are waxed
- Apples, peaches, and pears, *if* you get fiber from other

sources (these are the fruits most likely to contain risky residues)

Additives In shopping for prepared foods for your baby, it's important to read the list of ingredients so you check what additives are in the food. There are almost 10,000 officially approved additives and most must be included on the label. However, some additives, such as monosodium glutamate (MSG), which have been used for years have been found to be harmful when they are tested on infant animals. Your baby's low weight and immature digestive system are two important considerations.

Obviously, the safest course is to avoid all foods that contain additives, and one way is to make at home, from basic foods, everything your baby eats. However, if you'll excuse the old expression, you should not throw out the baby with the bath water. You will be very busy with a baby in the house, and this may not be the time to start baking bread. It would be nice if you could take advantage of the convenience of some prepared foods in feeding your baby. Also, some additives are actually nutrients used to improve the value of the food. These can be considered "fortifiers."

The most difficult job for parents is to interpret, or recognize, the long technical names of the various additives in the list of ingredients. The following are the most common ones. Some are harmless and are used to improve or maintain the quality of the food, some are controversial and should never be given to an infant, and others are simply unnecessary—used only to improve appearance or texture or to cover lack of quality. You will find most additives listed on a label either by their specific name or by their type, such as "preservatives."

PRESERVATIVES. Preservatives are used to delay deterioration or spoilage, which is an advantage with some perishable foods. However, they are often added to prolong shelf life of a product for unnecessarily long periods to increase its chances of sale. Some common harmless preservatives are sodium chloride, sodium benzoate, calcium propionate, sodium propionate, sodium carbonate, acetic acid, tartaric acid, lactic acid, sorbic acid, and citric acid. Benzoic acid can cause allergic reactions.

Sodium nitrite and sodium nitrate, found in many prepared meats, have been strongly criticized by researchers because of their cancer-causing potential.

Sulfites can cause allergic reactions, such as difficulty in breathing, in sensitive people, especially asthmatics. Other reactions may be nausea, diarrhea, hives, and flushing. They are often used in dried fruit, dried or frozen potatoes, prepared sauces and gravies, and vegetables. Just look out for the term *sulfer dioxide* or anything with the word *sulfite*, such as like sodium bisulfite. Needless to say, you should not feed your baby any food containing this preservative.

Antioxidents are another type of preservative and some commonly used ones are propyl gallate, butylated hydroxyanisole (BHA), and butylated hydroxytoluene (BHT). BHT has produced allergic reactions and is possibly related to cancer. It has been banned in many countries.

EMULSIFIERS. To improve the texture or consistency of foods emulsifiers are added. These include monoglycerides, diglycerides, and disodium phosphate. Lecithin is an organic compound found in egg yolks, soybeans, and corn and is also accepted as harmless.

STABILIZERS. Stabilizers or thickeners, are also used to add texture and consistency to food. They make food nutritionally expensive, because you are paying for and filling your baby up with a large percentage of nonnutritious fillers instead of the actual food. Some commonly used fillers are the vegetable gums agar-agar, gum arabic, gum tragacanth, and pectin. Gelatin is a thickener that does contain a little protein. Some cellulose compounds used are methyl cellulose and carboxymethyl cellulose. Food starches, such as tapioca, cornstarch, and rice starch, are nonnutritious. Flour, when enriched or unbleached, can thicken while adding some nutrients; however, the terms *white, bleached,* and *wheat* flour indicate that the flour is merely a filler.

ARTIFICIAL COLORS. Colors consist of coal-tar dyes and have long been controversial. These are completely unnecessary in food you will be serving your baby. Some natural food colors are annato, betain, caramel, carotene, chlorophyll, and saffron. These are just as unnecessary, but are less controversial.

ARTIFICIAL FLAVORS. Flavors, or enhancers, are

widely used and are also unnecessary in your baby's food. MSG is an example of an organic-based additive that has been identified as potentially harmful to infants. Hydrolyzed plant protein is also used, and this is an early step in the production of MSG. Salt is a natural flavoring that can be dangerous when it is overused. Some artificial flavorings are amyl acetate (banana), benzaldehyde (cherry, almond), and citral (lemon). One wonders about the basic quality of the food when such enhancers, or added flavors, are considered necessary.

SWEETENERS. There are also many forms of sugar, which may be called cane sugar, sucrose, corn syrup, sugar syrup, fructose, and dextrose. These are empty nutrition additives that can depress the appetite and contribute to dental decay. It is not considered harmful to occasionally use prepared foods that contain these sugars, but you must be careful not to serve these foods as a steady diet or select foods that contain them as major ingredients. Artificial sweeteners such as cyclamates, saccharin, and as partame should not be part of an infant's diet.

For easy reference, CSPI lists the following as additives to avoid:

- acesulfame K (a sugar substitute)
- artificial colors
- aspartame (artificial sweetener)
- BHA and BHT (antioxidants)
- caffeine
- monosodium glutamate (MSG)
- sodium nitrite and sodium nitrate
- saccharin (artificial sweetener)
- sulfites

Fortifiers Vitamins and minerals are added to many foods, and in a sense, they are additives. However, their purpose is to replace those vitamins and minerals that have been removed through processing or to add nutrients that are not readily available in food. They are an attempt to improve the quality of our diet. Some common fortifiers are iron, thiamine, riboflavin, niacin, iodine, potassium iodide, and vitamins A, C (ascorbic acid), and D.

A recent development in food processing has been the use of low-cost protein fortifiers in various foods, especially those with incomplete proteins such as cereals, baked goods, noodles, spaghetti, soups, etc. This is an inexpensive means of improving the protein quality of foods with vegetable and grain proteins. They are either composed of nutrients found in foods or are essential amino acids. They will be listed in the list of ingredients on the label and include the following:

Animal protein sources are nonfat milk solids, cheese whey, egg white solids, sodium caseinate, fish protein concentrate, whey solids, and hydrolyzed milk protein.

Vegetable sources are soybean flour, soybean protein, brewer's yeast.

Essential amino acids are lysine, methionine, threonine, and tryptophan.

When you prepare your own baby food, you also have the opportunity to add your own fortifiers. Molasses, rich in iron, can be used as a mild sweetener. Wheat germ, high in vitamin E and B vitamins, can be used as a thickener. Nonfat dry milk powder can be added to almost any food. Lemon and orange juice supply vitamin C and can be used instead of water in some recipes.

So, if you read the list of ingredients, you will be able to select foods without *unnecessary* or *potentially harmful additives*. You don't have to memorize these difficult names; instead copy down the ones that you want to avoid, and take the list shopping. You can even practice at home with labels on foods that you have already bought. If you are in doubt about any additive or see a long list of long names, just don't buy the food.

In general, the whole process of label reading is less time-consuming than you might think. Because you tend to use the same foods, once you have identified the best ones in terms of safety and nutritional cost, you can simply keep buying them. This is the best way to convey your preferences and objections to the food industry. It really can be an easy job and a rewarding one!

You'll find more detailed information, in the book *Safe Food*, published by the consumer group Center for Science in the Public Interest. (Bibliography)

A MONEY-SAVING CHECKLIST
- Buy fresh fruits and vegetables in season.
- Buy other foods on sale or specials.
- Buy store or "no-name" brands.
- Buy lower grades when appearance or tenderness is unimportant.
- Read dating codes to buy fresh foods.
- Use unit pricing to buy the lowest priced brand or size. Larger amounts are usually, but not always, a better buy.
- Read the list of ingredients to ensure that you are not paying for unnecessary or harmful ingredients. Remember: fortified, natural, enriched, or organic foods may not be your best nutritional buy!
- Do not buy highly refined and processed foods.
- Use "fresh" leftovers that might have been thrown away; the baby won't know the difference!
- Combine inexpensive incomplete protein foods in the same dish or meal.

Throughout the book I have indicated with a dollar sign ("$") those foods or recipes that are inexpensive in terms of their "nutritional cost." Under most foods you will also find specific "best buy" information.

There is simply no reason for any baby to grow up nutritionally deficient, regardless of family income. It is also unnecessary to deprive the rest of your family by buying expensive foods for your baby. You will be able to save money while giving your baby the best possible start in life. This, I believe, is the best reason for you to prepare your own baby food!

3

Feeding Your Baby

As you read books, consult doctors, and talk with other mothers, you will find that everyone seems to have their own specific ideas on breast feeding versus bottle feeding, the age to start solids, which solids, schedules, sterilization, and so on. If you have other children you will already have your own way of feeding your baby. In spite of wide differences of opinion on the various aspects of feeding, babies seem to thrive. They are really very adaptable!

Most experts do agree that the important factor in successful feeding is a relaxed and confident mother. You will be able to maintain this attitude if you try to follow whatever methods are most convenient and comfortable for you. In this chapter, I have tried to show the various choices that you have among the methods that are generally recommended. Of course, if you regularly consult a doctor, he will give you specific advice. Just don't be afraid to ask questions!

BREAST FEEDING OR BOTTLE FEEDING

The first choice that you will make is whether to nurse your baby or use a formula. You should decide *before* you go to the hospital, because soon after your baby is born, you will receive medication to prevent the milk from coming if you will not be nursing. This is not the time that you will feel like making the decision.

Breast Feeding The American Academy of Pediatrics states, "Human milk is unquestionably the best source of nutrition for full-term infants during the first months of life." If you aren't already convinced of the advantages, here they are.

- Most important, human milk is designed by nature to supply specific nutrients in the amounts that are best for human infants. Cow's milk, the basis of most formulas, may be fine for calves, but it doesn't have the same composition as human milk.
- Human milk is more easily digested than formula and that means less chance of spitting up.
- Infants are rarely allergic to breast milk, and those who are breast-fed for at least two months may be less likely to develop food allergies. This is important if allergies seem to run in the family.
- Breast-fed infants are also less likely to develop infections, especially respiratory and intestinal ones, as all formulas lack antibodies.
- Studies indicate that breast feeding may contribute to straighter teeth. Nursing infants use their tongues differently and suck more vigorously with their mouth muscles.

There are also several advantages for you, personally, in nursing. This is really the most convenient, economical, and easy way to feed your baby. The milk is always available and sterile. You don't have to buy or mix formulas, sterilize bottles, or store them. Some women object that nursing may tie them down, but after nursing is going well, a daily relief bottle can be given and that gives you up to eight hours between feedings. If you feel that you may be too busy to nurse, remember that it also gives you a good excuse to retreat by yourself for a while and relax.

Then there is the all-important job of regaining your figure. You will do so faster because nursing naturally causes the uterus to contract. You will be supplying extra calories in the milk you produce, so you can eat great amounts without gaining weight and can even lose any extra pounds easily. Really a pleasure if you have been calorie watching for the past nine months!

Considering all these advantages, it's surprising that breast feeding seems to be on the decline. In 1989, only 52 percent of mothers breast-fed their newborn infants, compared to 62 percent in 1982. After three months, only 31 percent were still breast-feeding, dropping to 18 percent at six months.

This decline may be due to the fact that more mothers are now working, and they tend to go back to work sooner. But with good planning, many mothers have found they can work and continue breast-feeding.

Even before your baby is born, it is essential to get information from other mothers who have successfully nursed their babies. Contact La Leche League, which distributes information on nursing and often has women on call to give advice on specific problems. They also have a toll-free hotline, 800–LA-LECHE for questions and referral to local groups. You can also write to their main office (see Bibliography).

Here are some recommendations:

- Nurse as soon after delivery as possible, then whenever the baby is hungry. This will help establish the milk supply.
- Under normal conditions, supplemental bottles of formula or even water should not be given for the first two weeks. An infant may be confused by a rubber nipple and also may take less from the breast, causing decreased milk production.
- Eat good amounts of a balanced diet.
- Drink at least 2 quarts of fluid daily.
- Remember, what you eat and drink will show up in your milk.
- Watch out for allergic reactions in your baby to foods that you are eating, and avoid them. These are also the foods that may cause a reaction when the baby eats them.
- Avoid excessive caffeine: Cut down on coffee and tea, including herb teas, which are apt to contain stimulants.

- Nicotine may affect your baby and can reduce your milk supply—so don't smoke.
- The general opinion is that a small amount of alcohol (one beer or glass of wine a day) is harmless.
- Although many drugs are safe, check with your doctor before taking even nonprescription drugs. For example, aspirin has caused significant effects in some nursing infants.
- Don't worry about how much milk your baby is getting. At least six feedings and six wet diapers a day usually indicates adequate nourishment. (If a baby doesn't regain his birth weight by three weeks, or continues to lose weight after ten days, consult your doctor.)
- If you begin to have pain in a breast, stop nursing on that side and call your doctor.
- Get as much rest as possible.
- Relax!

Bottle Feeding What if you can't breast-feed for some reason or decide to stop before your baby is six months old? Don't feel guilty! Commercial infant formulas are designed to be as close to human milk as possible and comply with the amounts of nutrients as recommended by the Committee on Nutrition of the American Academy of Pediatrics. Each ounce supplies 20 calories. *(Do not use home-prepared formulas or give regular cow's milk for the first six months. They do not meet the minimum levels of many important nutrients and their composition can cause problems.)*

Most commercial formulas are prepared from modified cow's milk. Some infants (estimated at 0.4 to 7.5 percent) are allergic to the protein in cow's milk and may be given soy-based or other specialized formulas. But let your doctor decide if your baby needs this type. The same goes for the "iron-fortified" formulas. Here are some of the basics of formula feeding.

Formulas come in various forms:

- Ready-to-feed is obviously the easiest to use, but it is also the most expensive. The small bottles are very

convenient when traveling—all you need to do is
screw on a nipple.

- Concentrated liquid must be diluted with water.
- Concentrated powder must also be diluted with water
  and has the advantage of being easy to carry and easy
  to store.

At least for the early months, dilute the concentrated form
with water that has been boiled for five minutes. You can
save time if you boil all the water you need for the day and
keep it in the refrigerator. The most important thing to remember when using a concentrate is to dilute it exactly according to directions—usually equal parts formula and
water.

- *do not add more formula because you think your baby
  will be getting more nutrition.* The higher concentration will just put more strain on his digestive system
  and could result in dehydration, kidney stones, and
  other serious problems.
- *do not add more water because you are tying to save
  money or you feel your baby is overweight.* He needs
  the exact concentration of nutrients in each bottle of
  formula.

BUYING AND STORING FORMULA. All infant for-
mula containers carry "use by" or "use before" dates to ensure that the contents are fresh and high quality. Do not
buy formula that is past the expiration date, or store it so
long at home that it becomes outdated.

- Keep unopened formula in a cool (below 72°F), dry
  place. Warm temperatures can affect quality and even
  curdle formula.
- Opened cans of liquid formula should be kept tightly
  covered, in the refrigerator, no more than forty-eight
  hours.
- Formula that has been prepared from concentrate can
  be stored in the refrigerator up to forty-eight hours.
- Freezing formula is not recommended because it may
  cause physical separation.

- *do not keep any formula left over from a feeding—
microorganisms have multiplied and could cause intestinal infections.* If your baby rarely finishes his bottle,
you're probably giving too much.

STERILIZATION. This is important if you are preparing
a day's supply of formula that you will be storing in bottles.
Sterilization will slow down the growth of bacteria that can
cause intestinal illness. However, most doctors don't require
sterilization of the bottles or nipples if the formula is prepared less than three hours before each feeding. Of course,
everything (including your hands and the can opener)
should be washed thoroughly.

You may find it more convenient to prepare enough formula for a full day's feeding (it is easier at 2:00 A.M. to just
grab a bottle). Then it is necessary to boil the bottles and
nipples for twenty minutes. Fill the sterile bottles with prepared formula and refrigerate.

Check with your doctor to find out when you can stop
sterilizing.

BOTTLES AND NIPPLES. There are various types of
bottles. The clear glass or plastic ones allow light to enter,
and that can reduce the amount of riboflavin in the formula.
So the colored and opaque ones seem a better choice.

The most convenient bottles are the disposable, sterilized liners that fit inside an opaque plastic holder. There
are also advantages for the baby. Because the plastic bag
collapses as he drinks, there is less chance of swallowing air.
Also, the nipple is shaped so that it does not collapse and
prevent milk from flowing—very frustrating to a baby. The
only disadvantage is their expense—currently four to five
cents apiece.

Of the various nipples, the orthodontic type are designed to simulate a mother's nipples. So if you are breast-
feeding and giving a supplemental bottle or weaning your
baby, he might adapt more easily to this nipple.

TEMPERATURE. It can be very frustrating listening to
your baby cry while you wait for the bottle to warm. Or
you've gotten it too hot and you're waiting for it to cool
down. In fact, it's not necessary to warm a bottle at all.

There is no reason, physical or psychological, not to give

your baby formula that is room temperature or straight from the refrigerator. By the time it is part way to his tummy, it will be warmed by his own body heat. And if you're traveling, it is certainly more convenient not to have to warm bottles.

If you do choose to warm formula, a microwave can really speed up the process. But be careful.

- *Never* heat the disposable bottles in the microwave. Because heated air continues to expand, the bags might break during a feeding. Babies have been scalded this way.
- Formula in a rigid bottle can be heated on a low setting, with the top off.
- Put the top on and shake to distribute the heat, since there can be very hot areas.
- As with any method, *always* test the temperature on the inside of your wrist—it should feel barely warm.

GIVING THE BOTTLE. First of all, don't be tempted to prop the bottle—it could cause choking. Besides, your baby still needs the close body contact.

- It's best to hold him in your lap, supporting his head in the bend of your arm, so his head and shoulders are slightly raised.
- Don't feed him flat on his back. In that position, some formula might be forced into the inner ear canal and cause infection.
- Tilt the bottle so the neck is always filled with formula. This helps prevent swallowing air.

Whether you decide to nurse your baby or use a formula in a bottle depends on your own situation. Either way your baby will be well nourished. Most important is for you to have a confident and relaxed attitude toward the whole process. Your baby will respond to this more than to where his milk is coming from. You also may find that feeding was going well in the hospital but becomes unsettled when you first come home. Or the reverse may happen. Your baby may have difficulty feeding in the hospital and then settle down at home. Most feeding problems are usually resolved within the first two weeks, so just try to be patient and relax.

HOW MUCH FORMULA? If you are breast-feeding, you have no way of knowing exactly how much milk your baby is getting. If you are bottle feeding, the best thing you can do is ignore the markings on the bottle. Otherwise, the tendency is to encourage your baby to finish the bottle "to the last drop." Studies have shown that formula-fed infants tend to gain more weight than breast-fed infants, probably due to overfeeding. However, your baby doesn't have to be fat to be well nourished.

Some babies also resist being pushed and feedings become tense. So respect your baby's wishes! Remember that needs vary with periodic growth spurts and individual levels of activity. Some babies are more placid and some are constantly active. And just as with older children, the desire for food may vary from day to day.

The following table should only be used as a general guide to how much formula to prepare. To estimate amounts for each feeding just divide the daily recommended ounces by the number of bottles usually given each twenty-four-hour period.

Recommended Amounts of Formula per Twenty-Four Hours

BABY'S WEIGHT	CALORIES°	FORMULA†
6	312	16
7	364	18
8	416	21
9	468	23
10	520	26
11	572	29
12	624	31
13	672	34
14	672	34

°Calories are calculated from the U.S. 1980 Recommended Dietary Allowances for average infants from birth to six months. Individual activity levels may change requirements.

†Most formulas contain 20 calories per ounce.

SCHEDULES

A feeding schedule is more for your convenience than for your baby's needs, and fortunately for everyone, the days of keeping to a strict schedule are long past. It must have been so frustrating to watch the clock and listen to a baby cry.

If you are breast-feeding, it is important to nurse frequently to establish your milk supply. If you are giving formula, your baby will still need frequent feedings in the early weeks. However, because formula is digested more slowly than breast milk, he may go longer between feedings.

The usual interval is a minimum of three hours and a maximum of four hours. Most babies settle into this within a few weeks. You can gradually shift your baby to the intervals most convenient for you—for example: 7:00 A.M., 11:00 A.M., 3:00 P.M., 7:00 P.M., 11:00 P.M., and 3:00 A.M. If you like to stay up late and sleep late, try to start the day at 9:00 A.M. It's comforting to keep reminding yourself that by three months, most babies will sleep through the night. By the way, as to the idea that solid food will help—it's just an old wives' tale.

Now, if your baby cries well before a scheduled feeding, or is on demand feeding and seems to be too demanding, it may be that he is not hungry. Instead, he may be wet, uncomfortable, or just plain lonely. So check everything out before you rush to give a breast or bottle. And remember, you can't spoil a young baby with too much cuddling!

When you begin feeding your baby solids you will space them out so that they roughly fall into breakfast, lunch, and dinner. Again, this is for your convenience. We happen to live in a three-meal-a-day society, but some research has shown that it may be healthier to eat more frequent, smaller meals. So you should not hesitate to give midmorning and midafternoon snacks, such as juice, fruit, or crackers if your baby is hungry. If he is eating healthy snacks, you really can't spoil his appetite.

One thing to avoid is the "strung-out" meals, which last a half hour or more as you try to get down one more bite. You can end up spending much of your day with a spoon in your hand, and your baby will never get the idea of specific meals. He may even come to resent spending so much time eating! Try to remember that if your baby does not eat much at one meal, he will be hungrier for the next one.

WHY, WHEN, AND HOW TO INTRODUCE SOLID FOOD

The next major decision, after whether or not to breast-feed, is when to introduce solid foods. The American Academy of Pediatrics and other experts on infant nutrition strongly recommend that you *do not introduce solids, even cereals, until your infant is at least four months old and preferably not until six months.*

In spite of all the reasons, both physical and psychological, in favor of waiting, solids are still often given well before this age! Perhaps this is done from an urge to show that the infant is developing rapidly, from the mistaken belief that solid food will enable the infant to sleep through the night, or from concern that the infant is not getting enough breast milk. Whatever the reason, introducing solid food before four months is unnecessary for nutrition, creates extra work, and has possible harmful effects.

By four to six months, an infant is developing the neuromuscular mechanisms needed for recognizing a spoon, swallowing nonliquid foods, and appreciating the taste and color of foods. The intestinal tract is developing immune or defense mechanisms for protection against foreign proteins, and has an increased ability to digest and absorb other proteins, fats, and carbohydrates. The kidneys are better able to process larger amounts of protein.

Some doctors advise delaying solids until much later than the four to six months recommended by the American Academy of Pediatrics. This might be important if there is a family history of allergies. However, there are some disadvantages in delaying too long. Solid foods do provide a wide range of nutrients that may be required by an older baby; a larger baby might require more milk than the mother is able to produce; and the older a baby is, the more difficult it might be to adjust to a form of feeding other than the breast or bottle.

The specific age that you begin feeding solid foods depends on the individual rate of growth, stage of development, and level of activity of your child. This is a decision that should be discussed with your pediatrician. However, there are some guidelines that can be useful:

- Your infant is able to sit with support and has good control of his head and neck. This allows him to indicated desire for food by opening his mouth and leaning forward and to indicate disinterest or fullness by leaning back or turning away.
- The extrusion reflex has disappeared and the infant can easily swallow solid foods ... although this may take a few messy practice feedings.
- Your infant's weight has reached 13 to 15 pounds.
- Your infant requires more than a quart of formula a day. (The AAP recommends that daily intake of formula should not exceed 1 quart at any age.)
- A breast-fed baby feeds more than eight to ten times a day (except in the first weeks).

The "When to Introduce a Food" table was created from the recommendations of several pediatricians and from personal experience, as a practical *order* for introducing the different foods. After your baby is seven to eight months old, you have leeway of a month or so for any specific food, so don't consider this list as the last word. If a food shows up whole in a bowel movement, the baby's system is not mature enough to digest that food—just delay it for a month.

Many foods are included that you may not have considered "baby food"; however, they are nutritious and often economical. Also, don't feel that you have to feed your baby every food that is listed here, and don't be afraid to try foods that may have been left out.

When to Introduce a Food

AGE (MONTHS)	CEREALS	FRUIT	VEGE-TABLES	PROTEINS
4	Rice (dry infant cereal)			
4½	Other infant cereals: Oatmeal Barley	Banana (raw) Apple-sauce		
5	Enriched: Cream of rice Pearl bar-ley	Cooked: Pears Apricots Peaches Prunes Plums Nectar-ines		Yogurt
6	High-protein Farina, Cream of Wheat Wheat germ	Cooked: Pineap-ple Guavas Man-goes Papayas Kiwi	Cooked: Green beans Winter squash Peas Toma-toes	Yogurt (with any intro-duced fruit)
7	Whole Grains: Oatmeal Whole wheat Brown rice Wheatena Ralston	Cooked: Cherries Grapes Raw: Pears	Cooked: Aspara-gus Summer squash Celery Corn Potatoes Carrots	Egg yolk Egg yolk custard Cottage cheese Grated cheese Chicken Turkey

AGE (MONTHS)	CEREALS	FRUIT	VEGE-TABLES	PROTEINS
8	Enriched: Noodles Spaghetti Macaroni	Raw: Apple Plums Apricot Grapes Melon Avocado Mango Papaya Guava Kiwi	Cooked: Broccoli Beets Spinach Green leafy vegetables Rutabaga Turnip Parsnips Okra Legumes Peanut butter	Veal Liver Kidneys Beef Lamb Lean fish
9	Any cooked fruit Raw: Pineapple Citrus	Any cooked vegetable Raw: Greens Tomatoes	Ham Pork Duck Soybeans Lentils	
10	All table foods			Whole egg (if not allergic)

How to Introduce New Foods The way that you introduce a food is really more important than the taste or texture. Always offer a new food with a smile and some encouraging words. Your baby soon becomes an expert at interpreting your expression and can acquire your own likes and dislikes of specific foods. Here are some other suggestions:

- Give a new food in the morning or at lunch. If you give it at dinner and he has a reaction, you may be in for a sleepless night.
- Always start with a small amount—about 1 teaspoon for the first time—then increase daily.
- Never offer thinned foods in a bottle. A baby may choke on food sucked through a nipple. Also, eating from a spoon is one more skill a baby needs to learn, and he can only do it through practice.
- Introduce one food at a time and wait four days before giving another new food. Then if he has an allergic reaction, you will know which food caused it (see "Food Allergies," in this chapter).
- Your baby is most likely to accept a new food if you offer it at the beginning of a meal when he is most hungry. You can also mix it slightly with a favorite food such as a fruit. This is especially good for introducing meats and foods with coarser textures.
- When your baby first begins to taste solid food, his natural sucking response may cause most of the food to spill out. Do not feel that he is spitting out the food because he dislikes it; he will soon learn how to swallow. Some babies find it easier to manage a fairly thick purée, so you can always try different consistencies of food.
- There is always the question of whether you offer solid food before or after the bottle or breast. Obviously, if he has just finished a full feeding, he will not be interested in solid food. But if he is starving, he will not be in the mood to experiment. The best time to offer solids, at least in the early months, is after he has finished about half a milk feeding.
- If your baby shows an obvious dislike of a specific food after you have offered it at several meals, forget it for a month or find a substitute. Other than milk, no one food is really essential.
- If your baby starts coughing or decides to sneeze just as you have given him a mouthful of food, hold your hand an inch or so away from his mouth. A wet hand is easier to clean than a shower of puréed food all over you!

How to Introduce Coarser Foods It is to your own advantage and your baby's that he begin eating regular family foods as soon as he can. You will save preparation time and your baby will be getting the most nourishment from foods that have not been thinned. Also, when he is eating food that he can pick up and feed himself, he will have a feeling of independence and you will have the freedom from feeding him every bite. Since you can control the consistency of baby food that you prepare yourself, your baby will make the switch easily at an early age. An extra bonus from making your own baby food!

When your baby is seven to eight months old, or easily eating fine purées, you can begin to gradually accustom him to coarser purées, then finely chopped food, then finger foods. Don't worry about how many teeth he has or doesn't have; he will be able to manage most foods very nicely with his gums.

Here are some general suggestions that I have found practical.

- Introduce your baby to each new consistency or texture very gradually—one food a day. Do not force them.
- Start with foods that are particular favorites—fruits and vegetables are good ones.
- If you have a blender or food processor, you can make a coarser texture by using a slower speed or a shorter blending time. It is very easy to make gradual changes.
- You can also begin mashing many foods with a fork.
- If you are thinning a food, start using less liquid.
- When you are giving a coarser food such as ground meat, mix it with a little smooth fruit or vegetable purée.
- Most important—do not look anxious; *serve with a smile!*

PLANNING A BALANCED MENU

The most important part of feeding your baby is to make sure that you offer him a balanced menu of the foods that he requires. Experiments have even shown that, from a variety of foods, a baby will choose those that contain the necessary nutrients. Because your baby's basic needs are similar to those of the rest of your family, this menu planning will require very little additional time. It really is very simple— just become familiar with the four basic food groups and the number of servings from each group.

This book is designed to help you, with the recipe chapters divided into the three main food groups—cereal grains, fruits/vegetables, and protein foods. The other important group, Dairy, will be satisfied by your baby's daily intake of formula or milk.

You can then select any food from within the basic group. This allows you considerable room for substitution in order to take advantage of foods that are available and convenient at a particular time, especially those that fit in best with family meals. For example, a serving of cereal grains does not always have to be cereal, you can also use rice or spaghetti. Or if you don't have meat prepared, you can occasionally give an extra egg. Fruits and vegetables can be interchanged, and you don't have to serve a different one at each meal, or even each day. If your baby becomes tired of one food, he will let you know!

A balance among the food groups will give you the best nutrition, and it is unnecessary and time-consuming to try to offer a wide variety each day. Of course, too much of any one food should also be avoided, no matter how nutritious that food is. Even milk should be limited to 1 quart a day. *Just remember that there is no "wonder food"!*

The following "Menu Planning Guide" indicates the daily servings of each food group and the sequence in which they are usually added to make up a complete menu. Although protein and calories are essential each day, many other nutrients can be stored so that you can also balance your baby's menu over a few days. The day is divided into breakfast, lunch, and dinner mainly for convenience, but you can serve these foods at any time during the day.

A "serving" is really whatever your baby will eat. In order to plan, you can count an average serving, for a six- to twelve-month baby, *as 1 to 2 food cubes or 3 to 6 tablespoons.* A "food cube" is the amount that can be frozen in the form of an average ice cube, or about 3 tablespoons (see "Food Cubes," in Chapter 5). Do try to give equal amounts of the various foods. If you are serving an "all-in-one" meal such as a stew, increase the amount to 3 to 6 food cubes.

Menu Planning Guide

AGE (MONTHS)	BREAKFAST	LUNCH	DINNER
4	Cereal		Cereal
5	Cereal	Fruit	Cereal
	Fruit		Fruit
6	Cereal	Fruit	Cereal
	Fruit	Vegetable	Fruit
7	Cereal	Fruit	Cereal
	Fruit	Vegetable	Fruit
	Egg yolk	Cheese	
8	Cereal	Fruit	Cereal
	Fruit	Vegetable	Fruit
	Egg	Protein	Vegetable
9	Cereal	Fruit	Cereal /protein
	Fruit	Vegetable	Fruit
	Egg	Protein	Vegetable
	Also snack of extra juice, crackers, etc.		

So, from nine months on, your baby's daily menu will include

3 protein foods (including one egg)
2 cereal grains

five fruit/vegetable (including one serving of juice, one dark green or yellow)

3 to 4 cups milk (24 to 32 ounces)

This is the balanced diet that your baby should continue eating for several years!

FEEDING EQUIPMENT

You will not need any special or expensive equipment to feed your baby. The important thing is to use whatever is most practical for you.

Feeding dishes can range from any small dish to an electric three-compartment feeding dish. The latter is the most expensive and is designed to keep the food at a constantly warm temperature. This can be a disadvantage if you leave the food in the dish for any period, since it is an ideal temperature for bacteria to grow. It will also accustom your baby to eating food that is always the same temperature and this can be a problem if you find yourself without this dish. There is no medical reason for your baby to eat food at a constant warm temperature.

The big advantage in using any warming dish is that you can quickly heat your baby's food without creating an extra pot to wash. You can use the inexpensive plastic dishes that can be filled with hot water; or a small heatproof dish that can be put in the oven or in a pan of hot water (a custard cup, heavy dish, or a small blender jar can be used). You can also wrap any food in aluminum foil and heat it in the oven. This is a fast way to heat a frozen food cube. Microwaves are faster, but you must stir and test the food. Hot "pockets" can form while heating and can burn your baby's mouth.

Of course, there is no reason why the food has to be warmed at all. Your baby will adapt to any temperature and you just have to learn to ignore the cries of outrage from other mothers and grandmothers!

A spoon should be small, narrow, and shallow—it does not have to be silver! A demitasse spoon is perfect if you have one and the small plastic picnic spoons are also a good size. When you first offer solid foods, try using a wooden tongue depressor, a dull butter knife, or a well-washed Popsicle stick. These flat sticks are also good for your baby's early attempts at feeding himself.

A bib is a feeding necessity. Use a big plastic bib, with a catch-all pocket (see Chapter 4 for instructions on making one), and a snap fastener. Since a baby does not have much of a neck, it can be a real problem to tie a bib on. The plastic bibs can be easily wiped off, dry quickly, and are more practical than the terry cloth or cotton bibs.

A feeding chair is not a necessity, but it is a great convenience. You won't have to juggle a wriggling baby and a spoon. An infant recliner seat is fine at first. Just don't walk away, leaving the baby alone, if the seat is on a table. It can easily tip over.

When your baby is five to six months old, he may outgrow or become very restless in a recliner, and it will be time to switch him to a high chair. Select one that is easy to clean, has a removable tray with a raised edge to catch spills, and a wide base so it won't tip over when your baby starts leaning over. I would have preferred a decorative antique cane high chair, which would have tipped easily and been impossible to clean. Luckily, I was talked out of it! If you do not have the room for a high chair, there are several seats available that either fasten to a regular chair or onto the edge of the table. Your baby then sits right at the table. These seats are less expensive than a high chair and are very practical for traveling.

WHEN YOUR BABY WON'T EAT

After you have planned balanced menus, carefully bought the food, and prepared nutritious dishes, you still have to get the food into your baby. This is probably the subject of greatest concern among mothers, yet you will have the most success if you can just relax and not worry about it. Again, serve with a smile!

Feeding is your baby's earliest contact with another person and just as food is essential for his physical growth, happy mealtimes will help him get the idea that people are really very nice. At one time, the thought was that a baby should consider eating as serious work, so playing was discouraged. The result was often a problem eater. There is no reason why you can't sing, make faces, or give your baby a toy to play with while you are feeding him. Most important is for your baby to look forward to mealtimes with pleasure.

You must not allow feedings to become a battleground over the choice of foods or the amount. If your baby dislikes one food, there is always another from the same food group that you can substitute. Your baby's appetite will also vary with each meal or each day. Since the baby food that you prepare will be inexpensive, you should not mind throwing out any uneaten portions.

It will also be easier for you to maintain this casual attitude if you can forget the idea that a baby must be fat to be healthy, and that it is a sign of success as a mother to have a fat baby, or stuff in as much food as you can.

Your baby is not a turkey and there is even a limit to how many nutrients he can use. So be ready to resist advice from grandmothers and even total strangers on how to "fatten up" your baby.

There are some subtle ways that you can encourage your baby if he starts to show a lack of interest in eating.

- You can offer him some different foods or prepare foods with a coarser texture.
- Or he may be ready for finger foods as an attempt at feeding himself.
- If he seems restless in a reclining seat, change the position so he has something else to look at; or move him to a high chair.
- You can try feeding him at the same time the rest of the family is eating, although this may take some organization on your part.

You may encounter real stubbornness, and your baby may decide to give up eating completely for a day or so. Remember that a baby has very few ways that he can assert himself and not eating is one of them. If you show that it bothers you and you make a feeding a major battle, you can have a problem eater.

Doctors also point out that it is normal for a baby to become less interested in food around his first birthday. That's the time the tremedous growth of the first year begins slowing down and a decrease in a child's appetite is normal.

Your baby will probably still continue to drink milk and this will supply him with enough nutrients for a while. You can fortify his bottle (see Homemade Fortified Milk, page 273), but be careful not to give him more than 1 quart of milk a day or he may not become hungry enough to begin eating again. You may also not even attempt to feed him for a meal or two, and the chances are that he will forget why he stopped eating in the first place. This may be hard to do, but remember that babies do not want to be hungry and there has never been a case of a baby choosing starvation. Sooner or later he will begin eating again.

SELF-FEEDING

There will come the day when your baby begins to grab for the spoon, try to hit it out of your hand, or put his hands in the food. This means that he has the idea of feeding himself. If you discourage him and don't allow him to try, you may be feeding him for the next year. So, try cheerfully to accept the mess that is about to begin and consider that it is a step toward the day when he will be neatly feeding himself. There are some ways that you can at least control the mess.

- At first, you can give your baby a spoon to hold and play with while you are feeding him. This may satisfy him for a week or so.
- At the end of a meal give him a spoon or Popsicle stick and let him practice with a thick purée such as bananas. If he tries to feed himself when he is hungry, he may become very frustrated and discouraged.
- If he begins fingerpainting on the tray with food, allow it for a few meals so that the novelty will wear off,

then gently discourage it by removing the tray and
ending the meal.
- If your baby feeds himself with his fingers, it is a step
in learning. Keep offering a spoon, but remember, fingers came before silverware.
- Put newspaper under the high chair.
- If he refuses to allow you to feed him altogether, but
cannot manage a spoon well enough to eat an adequate amount, start serving finger foods (see Chapter
14).
- In general, do not discourage self-feeding, but do not
force your baby into it.

GIVING UP THE BOTTLE

Parents often fear their child may never give up his bottle—
that he will still be carrying one when he walks up to accept
his diploma. While this is unlikely, there's no question that
many toddlers and preschoolers still insist on a bottle.
When is the best time to make the switch from bottle to
cup?

Many doctors feel that until a baby is nine months or so,
he really needs to satisfy his sucking instinct. Until then,
milk or formula should be given in a bottle. However, if you
wait until a child is over a year old, he's more likely to give
you a real battle. So the best time to start weaning is around
nine to eleven months. Here are some suggestions to make
the process easier:

- Do it gradually. Doctors advise giving juice only in a
cup and that can be started well before nine months,
as soon as a baby can handle a cup. Use a training cup
with a cover and give only a small amount at a time.
- Take away the lunchtime bottle first and serve milk in
a cup. Then every few days, abandon another bottle.
You can give a cup of milk as a snack if he is not
drinking enough at mealtimes.
- Insist that your child drink his bottle while sitting in
your lap. At this age, his interest in moving around

will become stronger than his interest in his bottle. Don't let him carry the bottle around on crawling adventures.

- Never give a bottle in his crib, to help him fall asleep easily. Milk is likely to stay in his mouth and it can cause cavities. Also, if he is accustomed to going to sleep with a bottle, he may cry for one if he wakes up during the night.
- Never use a bottle as a pacifier.

DIGESTIVE DIFFICULTIES

Since your baby's digestive system might take a while to start working properly, he may have digestive problems. Here are some common ones to look out for, and some suggestions. Of course, you should consult your doctor.

COLIC. The American Academy of Pediatrics defines colic as "severe abdominal discomfort in a young infant." It's not an illness or disease, but rather a definite set of symptoms:

- A baby begins crying more around the age of two to four weeks.
- The crying follows a pattern, occuring every day at the same time, often in the evening. At other times, the baby seems content.
- He may fall asleep easily, then wake up crying intensely.
- He draws his legs up, his abdomen may be bloated and he may pass gas.
- Nothing seems to comfort him for long, and the crying may continue for an hour or two until he falls asleep.

Colic isn't as common as parents may think. Unfortunately, there is no positive proof of the cause. One theory is that the baby swallows lots of air during a feeding. But doctors point out it would then be likely to occur after every meal. The same logic rules out an allergy to formula. (There is no evidence that hypoallergenic formulas relieve colic.) Other theories blame it on an immature neurological or digestive system. Or it may be that crying (for any reason) results in air being swallowed, which then causes a cycle of pain and more crying.

What can you do once your doctor has eliminated other reasons, such as illness or food allergy, for the crying? Try the usual methods of soothing—music, rocking, or swaddling. Some parents say it helps to warm the crib with a heating pad, then lay the baby on his tummy. (Always remove the heating pad first.) The doctor may prescribe medication if the colic is severe, but *never* give medicine or sedatives without your doctor's advice.

Sometimes nothing seems to help and that can be very frustrating. Just remember—it is not your fault, it is not something you did or didn't do—so don't feel guilty. The good news is that colic usually disappears by three months!

DIARRHEA. This can be a sign of teething, an oncoming illness, a reaction to a specific food or a spoiled food. If it continues more than a day, your baby may become dehydrated, so you should definitely contact your doctor. The recommendation for mild cases is to increase the amount of liquid the baby drinks. If he is eating solids, some foods that may help are rice cereal and bananas.

Celiac disease is a form of diarrhea in which the bowel movements are frothy and foul-smelling and contain undigested food. It is usually a result of an inability to digest and absorb food properly. You should contact your doctor, who will plan a special diet for your baby.

CONSTIPATION. This is usually not a serious problem. It is not necessary for your baby to have a bowel movement every day. You should watch out for hard dry movements that are painful. They may be softened by feeding him barley cereal, prune juice, or stewed prunes or by adding a little molasses to his bottle. *Do not give your baby an enema or laxative* (unless prescribed by a doctor), *or mineral oil.* Don't add bran to his food.

VOMITING. This is a forceful throwing up of a large amount of food. It may be caused by oncoming illness, a reaction to a specific food, or eating spoiled food. If it occurs frequently, it may be a sign of a more serious problem. In any case, contact your doctor.

A less serious but very annoying problem is when your baby "cheeses" or spits up a small amount of food as he burps. It may be caused by a difficulty in digesting fat or by just overeating. Most babies outgrow it in several months, so be patient and always have a towel handy. Some studies have shown it may help to place the baby on his tummy after a feeding.

IS YOUR BABY ALLERGIC TO MILK?

When your baby shows symptoms of abdominal pain, diarrhea, vomiting, or gas after every feeding, it's natural to suspect the milk.

The least likely cause during the first year is a rare congenital intolerance to the lactose in milk. The lactase enzyme that is essential to the digestion of the lactose in milk is usually present at birth through the first year or two, then it may begin to decline. This is most common among native American, black, Mexican-American, Jewish, Asian, and Middle Eastern children.

A temporary intolerance to lactose may also be the result of gastrointestinal disorders that are viral, bacterial, or parasitic in origin. There is a standard lactose tolerance test that is based on the observation of the syndrome of abdominal pain, diarrhea, gas, and bloating after the ingestion of lactose. If an intolerance to lactose is diagnosed, a lactose-free formula is available. For older babies who are no longer on formula, you can buy the enzyme lactase in liquid form and add it to milk the day before the milk is consumed, so that most of the lactose is predigested. Milk with lactase is also available.

A more likely cause of adverse reactions to milk in infancy is a hypersensitivity (or allergy) to the protein in milk, especially cow's milk. *This is not related to, and should not be confused with, lactose intolerance.* If an infant's digestive system is too immature to properly digest milk protein, he or she may develop a sensitivity. Infants with a family history of food sensitivities may also be more susceptible. One or more of the following symptoms may appear as soon as two days after birth, and usually by four months:

Vomiting	Asthma
Diarrhea	Canker sores
Cramps	Eczema
Hives	Chronic runny nose

Do be alert to the persistence of any of these symptoms, especially after a feeding, and bring them to your doctor's attention. *Don't assume it's just gas or "normal colic."*

There is no laboratory test or skin test that can diagnose hypersensitivity to milk protein. The only method is to observe whether symptoms subside within forty-eight hours after removal of milk from the diet, and consistently reappear within forty-eight hours after milk is reintroduced. This should be done under a doctor's supervision. There is some question as to how many such challenges are necessary to confirm a diagnosis. Milk-free formulas based on soy protein can be given and are nutritionally adequate. (There are even soy-free formulas for the infant who is also sensitive to soy protein.)

Human breast milk has a protein composition different from cow's milk and is much less likely to cause an adverse reaction. This is another good reason to nurse your baby, especially if there is a family history of food sensitivities.

However, a breast-fed infant may still show symptoms. Some studies have shown that nursing infants can react to large amounts of cow's milk in the mother's diet.

Remember that any diagnosis of lactose intolerance or sensitivity to milk protein must be made by your pediatrician, who will prescribe the necessary changes in your infant's diet. Later, when your child is eating a variety of foods, you will have to read the list of ingredients and avoid any foods and ingredients that contain milk protein or lactose such as:

MILK PRODUCTS LIST

Butter	Lactoglobulin
Buttermilk	Lactose
Cheeses	Milk solids
Condensed milk	Nonfat dry milk
Curds	Skim milk
Custards, puddings	Sodium caseinate
Frozen custard	Sour cream
Half-and-half	Whey
Ice cream	Whole milk
Lactalbumin	Yogurt°

FOOD ALLERGIES

Foods other than milk may cause allergic reactions in infants and children. They may occur on the first exposure or after several feedings, when the system has become sensitized to a particular food. To help identify such foods, new foods should be introduced one at a time and given for four days before introducing another new food. Sometimes small amounts are tolerated while larger amounts of the same food cause a reaction.

These reactions are not only the digestive ones—vomiting, abdominal pain, and diarrhea. They may also be respiratory—runny nose, sinusitis, ear infections, coughs, wheezing. Or they may affect the skin as rashes, hives, and eczema. The reaction could be immediate, but could take up to two days to show up.

The potential for food allergies does seem to run in families. It is also greater for infants who are fed solid foods before four to six months of age, since their immature intestinal walls allow food proteins to enter the circulatory system.

The problem is that many parents are too quick to blame food allergies for symptoms that may be caused by a

---

°Might be acceptable in cases of a moderate intolerance to lactose.

cold, intestinal infection, or a more serious problem. In fact, allergies are much less common than many think, with a small number of foods responsible for the majority of reactions. These can only be confirmed through careful medical evaluation. So do not start long-term elimination of foods (especially valuable ones like milk, wheat, and eggs) from your child's diet without consulting a doctor.

The American Academy of Pediatrics recommends that exclusion of a food for two to four weeks should serve to evaluate it as a source of symptoms, and that, for children, a diet free of milk, eggs, and wheat can be used as a trial treatment for up to a month without concern. For longer periods, the diet will have to be supplemented, under a doctor's supervision, with calcium, iron, and vitamins. The actual intake of protein and calories should be periodically monitored. Substitute fruits and vegetables can be easily selected in place of those that cause symptoms. The following listings are organized by food group.

HIGH-ALLERGY FOODS LIST

Cheese	Citrus fruits
Egg white	Raspberries, blueberries
Ice cream	Strawberries
Milk°	Tomatoes
Chocolate	Buckwheat
Fish	Corn†
Nuts	Semolina
Pork	Wheat
Shellfish	

°See also "Milk Products List." Read the list of ingredients on any processed food.

†Corn products also include corn syrup, dextrose (corn sugar), cornstarch, and corn oil. Read the list of ingredients on any processed food.

LOW-ALLERGY FOODS LIST

Barley	Asparagus	Chicken
Oatmeal	Beets	Lamb
Rice	Carrots	Olive oil
Rice cereals	Fruits	
Tapioca	Apricots	
	Cranberries	
	Peaches	also juices
	Pears	
	Pineapple	
	Sweet potatoes	
	Lettuce	

FEEDING YOUR BABY AWAY FROM HOME

We all travel around with our babies, and we are likely to be away from home at a mealtime. Here are some suggestions that may be helpful.

- If your baby is on formula, you can carry the individual bottles of commercial formulas that do not require refrigeration until they are opened. You just screw on a clean nipple. These formulas are also available in small cans, which are less expensive.
- If you are using bottles with the canned formula, or for water and juice, use the plastic disposable bottles that fit inside a holder. You won't have to worry about washing or sterilizing bottles.
- If your baby is off formula and drinking regular milk, just carry the nonfat dry milk powder for emergencies. It does not need to be refrigerated and you can mix each disposable bottle as you need it, right in the bottle. Use 2 ounces of dry milk for an 8-ounce bottle. Even if your baby is regularly drinking whole milk, an occasional bottle of nonfat milk will not disagree with him.
- Solid food is not really necessary at every meal, and your baby probably won't mind having just a bottle for

one meal. If you do want to feed him solid food you can look for an "instant" food (see Chapter 13). *Do not introduce new foods when you are away from home.*

- You can also carry the frozen food cubes with you. Place enough cubes for a meal in a plastic bag, and they will defrost in time without any need for special storage. Some cooked fruits will keep for several hours. You can then feed your baby out of the plastic bag and throw it away. If you are carrying milk, the cubes will also help keep the milk cold.
- Be sure to accustom your baby to eating cold food and milk when necessary. This will be most convenient when you are traveling.

4

Equipment for Easy Cooking and Puréeing

I have been saying, throughout this book, that it is easy as well as nutritious to prepare your own baby food. Your mother and grandmother might doubt this, but they did not live in our gadget-conscious modern world. You have a wide choice of equipment for easy cooking and puréeing of baby food. Some of these things you may already own.

COOKING WITH STEAM

Now, you probably have your own favorite cooking methods and utensils, but keep in mind that many of the vitamins and minerals are water soluble and thus are lost in the cooking liquid. Many nutrients are also destroyed by high heat, long cooking time, and cutting food into small pieces before cooking.

There is unanimous agreement among nutritionists that the steam method of cooking best preserves the vitamins and minerals in food. One study showed that, in steam cooking, only 6 percent of the vitamins were lost, whereas pressure cooking resulted in a 12 percent loss. Boiling in water caused a loss of 29 to 39 percent. Vegetables are most often the victims of the water-boiling method.

In the steam method, the food is held above rapidly boiling water and cooks in the rising steam. While it is especially important that the food your baby eats is as nutritious as possible, this method also produces food that retains its natural flavor and color. Your entire family will appreciate these steamed fruits and vegetables that are both nutritious and flavorful. This method is also the easiest and simplest way of cooking. You can choose from a variety of low-cost utensils or improvise one of your own.

A steamer/blancher is a good utensil for the steam method. It consists of a deep pot with a tight-fitting cover and another pot that is completely perforated and fits inside the first pot to within 1 inch of the bottom. It is similar in appearance to a double boiler. The water in the bottom will boil and the food will cook in the rising steam without being immersed in the water. This utensil is sometimes called a blancher because it is used to quickly immerse fruits and vegetables in boiling water before freezing. It sells for as low as $6 and is available in many stores, especially those that carry home canning and freezing equipment, such as a hardware store. An imported, more expensive heavyweight steamer is sold in some stores that carry gourmet and professional cooking equipment. Because you may use the steamer daily, the extra cost may be justified; however, the inexpensive steamer is quite adequate.

Steam baskets are also sold for use in steam cooking. There are several types available for $3 to $8. Most are adjustable to fit inside any pot you already own to convert it into a steamer by raising the food out of the cooking water. You must be sure that the steam basket fits well inside the pot so that the cover will fit tightly. One disadvantage of the steam basket is in removing it from the pot. Since all parts are inside the pot, it is easy to burn yourself. Also, if you have a full pot, the basket may tip while removing it.

Chinese cooking has become very popular and you can easily find an inexpensive Chinese bamboo steam basket. This flat round basket with a cover can be set in a wok or over a pot. It holds a good amount of food and can be handled easily.

Since the main principle in the steam method is to keep the food supported about 1 inch above the bottom of the pot, just out of the water, you can improvise in creating your own steam basket. A small colander might fit inside a large pot or you may have a round wire rack of the kind used in baking. Remember, whatever you use as a platform, it must have holes in it to allow the steam to come through.

A double boiler is a common utensil that will give almost the same results as a steamer for some foods, and is also useful for making custards and cooked cereals. Since the food cooks at a temperature below boiling, some of the bacteria that cause spoilage may not be destroyed. You should be especially careful in storing foods cooked this way.

If you already own and are familiar with the use of a pressure cooker, you may wish to use it to prepare your baby's food. This method of cooking with steam under high pressure has the advantage of reducing the cooking time; however, you must be careful not to overcook the food. Look for the Underwriters Laboratory Seal as a check on quality and follow the manufacturer's instructions. An improperly used or malfunctioning pressure cooker can be dangerous.

An electric crockpot is also useful. This is a heavyweight, tightly sealed utensil that maintains a low heat. The food simmers slowly, steaming in its own juices for 10 to 12 hours. This slow cooking retains the vitamins and minerals and tenderizes the food. Thus it is especially good for meats and poultry. Several foods may be combined, and it is suitable for making large quantities.

Aluminum foil offers a simple means of nutritious cooking of almost any food. The food is tightly sealed in a double layer of foil and bakes in a slow (325°F) oven. The cooking time for most food is slightly longer than with the steamer. This is a very good way to cook meats, because the slow moist heat will soften the tough fibers for easier puréeing. The cooking time for meat is about the same as with potting or braising. There is no need to add any water since the food will steam in its own juices. The tight seal will prevent the loss of those vitamins that are destroyed by air.

If your oven is already in use in preparing the family

meal, it is very convenient to use foil to cook baby food at the same time.

Instead of foil, you can also use a heavy baking dish with a tight-fitting cover. Unless the food is very juicy, it will be necessary to add a little water when you begin cooking.

In general, here are the points that you should remember when selecting and using any steaming equipment.

- Buy a large utensil so that you can cook a large amount of food, or combine different foods, at the same time. This will save you cleanup and preparation time.
- Make certain that the lid is tight fitting and heavy enough so that the steam cannot lift it. You can add curtain weights if necessary.
- Steam food whole and in the skin whenever possible. It is most nutritious and saves you cutting and peeling time. It is even easier to remove skin or pits of fruits and vegetables after cooking.
- Be careful not to let the water in the bottom of a steamer boil away during a long cooking time.
- Rinse the pot immediately after use for easy cleaning.

MICROWAVE OVENS

A microwave oven is expensive ($100 and up) and definitely not something you need to buy just to prepare baby foods. However, microwave cooking is efficient in terms of time and nutritional value for most of the foods you prepare for the rest of the family. I know skeptics who, once they began using their microwave ovens, now say they couldn't live without them.

How Do Microwaves Work? First of all, microwaves ovens, when used properly are absolutely safe. And that goes for any food cooked by microwaves—even for infants.

Microwaves are not a form of radiation that contaminates the food. They are simply a source of heat energy, just like gas and electricity, except they don't heat the air or cooking containers. Instead microwaves move directly to the fat, sugar, and moisture molecules in food and cause them to vibrate very quickly. This vibration generates heat energy that cooks most food much faster than other methods.

In fact, microwave cooking is actually steam cooking because foods require little or no added water. So it preserves the most vitamins and minerals.

What about microwave energy escaping from the ovens? They are carefully designed to meet federal safety standards; however, it is important to follow these commonsense precautions:

- Do not attempt to operate an oven with the door open or tamper with the safety interlocks on the door.
- Do not place any object between the front face of the oven and the door. Keep these surfaces clean of any food residue. Be sure the oven door seals tightly.
- Do not operate the oven if the door does not close properly or if there is any damage to the door seals.

What Size and What Power? If you don't already own a microwave, there is a variety of sizes, power levels, and, of course, prices. A full-power oven has 650 to 700 watts; a medium-power oven, 500 to 600 watts; and a low-power oven, 400 to 500 watts. In general, the small-capacity ovens have the lowest power levels.

The difference in power affects how quickly the food is cooked. *The times given in the recipes are for a power level of 650 to 700 watts.* If you have a low-power oven, increase the cooking time by approximately one-half (50 percent). For example, allow 6 minutes instead of 4 minutes, 7½ minutes instead of 5 minutes, 9 minutes instead of 6 minutes, and so on. A low-power oven will also not cook large amounts of food as evenly.

Even the small, low-power ovens are perfectly adequate for making baby foods and they are the least expensive. However, if you plan to be using a microwave as a regular alternative to preparing family meals, a midsize or large high-power oven might be a better investment. As to the size, it really depends on how much room you have in your kitchen.

Cooking Utensils There are many types of "microwave-safe" cookware for sale, but it is not really necessary to go out and buy a complete new set of pots. One advantage of a microwave oven is that you can use many things you already own.

- Glass bowls, dishes, baking pans, etc. are microwave safe.
- Pottery or ceramic dishes without metallic glazes or trim can be used.
- Sturdy china without metal trim is okay, but do not use fine china.
- Microwave-safe plastics and thinner plastic containers (also foam cups and dishes) are fine for heating, but become distorted if used for cooking foods at high temperatures.
- To test any glass, pottery, or china container, place it in the oven, next to a cup of water, and heat on the highest power for 15 to 20 seconds. If it feels warm, it should not be used. Melamine ware tends to absorb energy and should also be tested.
- Do not use metal dishes or aluminum foil because they reflect microwaves and the food will not cook. Metal can also cause arcing, which can damage the oven (do not use metal twister ties). (Small pieces of aluminum foil can be used to cover parts, such as turkey legs, which seem to be cooking too quickly.)
- Metal skewers and clamps are usable when the proportion of food is much greater than the metal.
- Foil trays can be used if no more than ¾ inch deep.
- Wood containers should not be used because they will become dry and crack as moisture in the wood evaporates during cooking.

GENERAL TIPS FOR MICROWAVING
- Most food should be cooked covered with a tight-fitting lid or plastic wrap. Remember that steam builds up, so remove the cover carefully—open a lid by tilting it away from you; prick plastic wrap to allow steam to escape.

- Even though cooking containers do not absorb heat from microwaves, they can become very hot from the food cooking. So handle them carefully and use pot holders if necessary.
- Microwaves only penetrate about 1½ inches into the food, the rest heats by conduction. So evenly shaped foods cook most evenly, and foods cut into small pieces cook more quickly. Foods also cook better if arranged around the outside of a dish, not concentrated in the middle.
- When food varies in shape or size, place the larger, tougher parts near the outside. For instance, arrange broccoli with the stems facing out.
- The amount of time required to cook a food depends on the amount of food. If you increase the amount specified in the recipes, it will take proportionately longer to cook.
- Foods continue to cook for a few minutes after the microwave stops. This is called "standing" time and is allowed for in the recipes.
- Standing time is especially important in heating formula in bottles. (Always use the lowest setting, wait 2 to 3 minutes, then test the temperature of the food before feeding it to your baby.
- Unless otherwise specified, standing times given in recipes are for *covered* dishes.
- If you plan to purée a food you've prepared in the microwave, let it cool slightly first.
- *Never* heat disposable bottles in the microwave.
- Frozen food cubes can be thawed, covered, on the *medium* setting. Allow about 1 minute for each cube. Stir well.

THE ELECTRIC BLENDER

In the old days, food had to be scraped and strained in small quantities. No wonder people thought that making your own baby food was difficult and time-consuming! Fortunately, electric blenders and food processors have revolutionized the preparation of baby food.

The modern high-speed blenders can quickly and easily purée almost any food, even meats and poultry, into the finest consistency for the youngest infant. The blenders range in type from four speed to sixteen speed, and some have specialty features or solid-state controls. The prices will vary accordingly.

Selecting a Blender Here are some features that should be considered:

• Solid-state controls, which ensure even processing at the lower speeds regardless of the load factor, are not a necessity in processing baby food where you will usually use the higher speeds. This feature does cost more.

• It will be necessary with most blenders, when puréeing a heavy consistency, or a small amount, to move the food carefully from the sides of the container into the blade area with a rubber spatula. It is safer to stop the blender.

• Some blenders (Oster and Hamilton Beach, for example) have small jars available either in heavy glass or plastic. These are very efficient for processing small amounts (1 cup or less), such as leftovers or food from the family meal. You can save time and effort by blending, feeding, and storing in the same jar. If you have difficulty finding these small jars, check a hardware store or call the manufacturer.

• Do not use the small drink blenders or coffee mills to process baby food. Hand-held food blenders are adequate for puréeing soft foods and are very convenient for small amounts. Food processor attachments are also available.

• Other heavy, small jars, such as home canning jars, with a 2½-inch neck and the proper screw thread, can be used, but may be less efficient in blending. Be careful not to use a light jar since the action of the food and the blades may cause it to break. In using any jar, do not fill it more than three-fourths full to allow for expansion of the food during processing.

• The cycle or pulse feature on some blenders is useful in chopping foods evenly. The blender will stop at intervals during processing. This is an advantage in controlling the coarseness of purées that you are preparing for an older baby. However, it is not a necessity and may add to the cost of the blender.

• Another advantageous feature of a blender is the ability to add ingredients through the top while it is operating, without removing the entire lid.

Using Your Blender Your blender will easily process baby food if you use it properly and care for it. If you are not satisfied with the blender you already own, you may not be following the manufacturer's instructions. In general, these are the important things to remember in using any blender:

• Read the instruction book carefully. If you do not have one, you can write to the manufacturer, giving the model number.
• Set the blender on a clean, dry, solid surface.
• Be sure the cover is firmly in place before starting, and add ingredients through the top if possible.
• Do not remove the container from the base while the motor is running. Never leave the blender while processing.
• When using an older or less powerful blender, start the motor on a slower speed before adding ingredients, then switch to a faster speed.
• If liquids are used, pour them in before adding the dry ingredients.
• If the blender has a small base, cut the food, especially meats, poultry, and cheese, into 1-inch cubes.
• Allow boiling or steaming foods to cool slightly before blending.
• If you are puréeing a small quantity and it disperses along the sides, stop the motor, push the food down with a rubber spatula, and restart. It may be necessary to repeat this several times.
• Do not allow the motor to labor when processing a heavy or thick load. Either stir to introduce air, add liquid, or switch to a higher speed. If the mixture is very thick, make only a small amount at a time.
• If there is any burning smell, shut the motor off im-

mediately, clean the blades, and check the repair directions.

- Clean your blender immediately after use by adding some detergent and water and running the blender on a medium speed for a few seconds. Finely puréed foods can stick like glue if they are allowed to harden. Eventually the turning ability of the blades will be slowed.
- Do not put the blade assembly in the dishwasher because the lubricating oils will wash away and the blades will not turn easily, thereby putting strain on the motor.
- Remember that most blenders will not mash potatoes, grind raw meat or poultry, or extract juices from fruits and vegetables.

The way that you use your blender for preparing your baby's food depends on the speed selectors and the general condition of your particular blender. In general, you will be using the highest speeds (blend, frappé, purée) to process food for the younger infant. These speeds will produce the finest consistency. As you prepare various types of food, you will soon find the proper speeds.

As your baby becomes accustomed to solids, and after a food has been introduced, you can begin reducing the blender speed or processing time or using the cycle feature for a coarser consistency. If the baby has difficulty swallowing or digesting a particular consistency, it is easy to thin or reblend the food. However, your aim should be to accustom your baby to eating increasingly coarse food until he can chew and swallow small bits of ordinary table food at family meals. An electric blender will give you the most control and ease in regulating the consistency of your baby's food.

Repairing Your Blender When you are regularly using your blender to process your baby food, any breakdown is a major inconvenience. There are several faults that you can test for and repair yourself before you surrender your blender to the repair shop.

1. If the blender will not start and makes no sound: Plug another appliance into the outlet. If that does not start, then the outlet is at fault, not the blender.

If the other appliance does start, then check the electric cord and the plug on the blender. If these are disconnected, you can buy a replacement plug at any hardware store.

2. If the blender hums and tries to start: *Stop the blender.* Remove the blender container from the motor base, start the blender to see if the mechanism that turns the blade assembly now turns. If it does not, then the fault is in the motor itself, and you will probably require professional repair. If you have access into the blender base, you can try to clean any encrusted food, then oil.

If the motor is turning, then your problem may be the common one of a frozen blade assembly. Food has probably become lodged around the blades or under the turning axle. Soak the blade assembly in detergent or a penetrating oil, then clean with a brush and thin thread or dental floss, then lubricate. If the problem persists, you may be trying to process too heavy a load.

3. If the motor overheats or smokes: *Stop the blender.* Clean out any dust and food to allow for better cooling. Lubricate any parts of the motor you can reach. Clean the blade assembly as in the preceding paragraph.

4. If the blender is very noisy or vibrates: *Stop the blender.* Check the blades for accidental bending and straighten them. Lubricate the blade assembly and gearbox. If the problem persists, you will need professional repair.

Used carefully, the electric blender is a valuable aid in processing your baby food. It is fast, effortless, allows you to make large or small quantities, and gives you control over the consistency of the food. A blender or a food processor is also the only way you will be able to prepare many raw foods, such as citrus purées, that are highly nutritious. If you do not already own one, it is a good investment. Aside from substantial savings in making your own baby food, the blender offers many uses and savings for the entire family.

THE FOOD PROCESSOR

A food processor has all the advantages of a blender—plus some! The only things it doesn't handle as well are very small amounts of some foods and large amounts of liquid (it will leak out through the center shaft). A food processor is more effective in handling large amounts and thick purées; it will purée just about anything you would use as baby food, except mashed potatoes.

This is an expensive item just to prepare baby foods, but it will have a long and useful life in your kitchen. For example, you can whip up two loaves of bread in five minutes and easily save money on a staple food!

Selecting a Food Processor The original food processor is the Cuisinart®, available in improved and larger models. There are now many other manufacturers that sell less expensive food processors and there is a running argument among users as to which is better. Some people report that slicing, chopping, and the ability to handle heavy loads suffers on the less expensive processors. Before you make a purchase you should talk to some owners and check a consumer comparison survey. The lowest priced model is adequate for preparing baby foods and for most kitchens. Some features that should be included are

- A warranty
- A pulse switch to give you more control over processing
- The ability to knead bread, if you're a home baker
- An automatic circuit breaker to protect against overload and motor burnout
- A safety feature that prevents use when cover or bowl is not secured properly

Using Your Processor Before you use a food processor, carefully read the manufacturer's instruction book. The following suggestions are applicable to most processors:

- Insert the metal blade before adding food.
- Handle the blades very carefully and keep out of children's reach.
- Before processing, cut most food into cubes 1½ inches square; hard vegetables and tough meats should be cut into smaller cubes. Soft fruits and vegetables can be added in large pieces.
- Do not overfill the food processor bowl.
- If the motor labors, stop and remove some of the food.
- If the blade jams on a hard lump of food, unplug machine and remove lump. In fact, it is safest to unplug the processor when not in use or when changing parts.
- For purées, begin with little or no added liquid, then add a tablespoon at a time as necessary.
- For coarser purées, cut food into same-size cubes so it all ends up the same coarseness. Watch your time!
- Remove pits and seeds before processing.
- Rinse the food processor immediately after using.
- To soak the processor bowl, leave the blade in place and the bowl will fill to the top.

OTHER WAYS TO PURÉE

As handy as blenders and food processors are, there are alternative methods of processing food, which are still adequate, although slower. Some of these utensils are even more practical for processing small amounts. Also, they are easy to carry or are readily available if you go away from home.

Food mills can be purchased in small or large sizes. The food is placed in the basket, and as you turn the rotary handle the blade presses food through holes in the bottom of the basket. It is actually a more automatic version of the spoon-and-strainer method. It is, however, considerably faster and requires less effort. The food mill strains most cooked foods, with the exception of meat, to a smooth consistency acceptable to even the youngest infant. It also works well with soft, raw fruits such as bananas, pears, and plums. Meat and poultry will require more effort and will be processed more coarsely. The mill will purée liver or organ meats to a strained consistency that is fine enough to serve as a first meat food. You may also prefer to use a mill to remove seeds, skin, and fibers from fruits or vegetables. If you do not have an electric blender or food processor, you will find the food mill is a very adequate utensil for processing your baby food, either in large or small batches.

One indication of the increasing popularity of home-prepared baby foods is the appearance of inexpensive food mills that are sold specifically for puréeing baby foods. They are compact and a very convenient way to purée small amounts of food from family meals or when away from home. Some mills prepare a finer purée than others, but all can prepare at least the consistency of junior foods.

Also available are electric food mills with different blades for puréeing baby foods of various textures. They are very effective; however, they process small amounts at a time and are expensive in terms of their limited usage.

Graters come in a wide range of types, sizes, and prices. Most will process food suitable for an older baby, with similar consistency to the junior foods. If you own one, experiment with various foods to see if you can achieve the right consistency for your baby. You may even use it for grating some raw fruits and vegetables. A grater is particularly useful in processing small amounts, so if you have an electric blender that does not work well with small loads, you may also want to use a grater.

A rotary grater, such as a Mouli, is especially efficient for making small amounts. The food is placed in the small magazine and is grated as you rotate the handle of the drum. By varying the pressure on the cover of the magazine, you can grate a fine or coarser consistency. Mouli brand graters come with a variety of drums which can be used to produce different consistencies. It is safe, easy to clean, and small enough to carry when traveling.

Strainers are probably the oldest means of processing baby foods, but they require time and effort for most foods. The food is strained by pushing it through holes in the strainer with the back of a spoon. This is impractical for making large quantities. Strainers vary in size and in the fineness of the holes. A fine strainer will purée fruits and vegetables comparable to the strained foods for the youngest infant. They are not usable for any meat or poultry.

The one strainer that you should keep handy, even if you are using a blender for other foods, is a small, very fine strainer to strain juices for your baby's bottle. You can carry it when traveling to prepare small servings of soft fruit and vegetables.

Forks and spoons are the most available and least expensive means of preparing baby food. You will find them adequate for mashing some soft foods to a coarse texture. Some foods, such as bananas, egg yolks, or canned pears, can be mashed finely enough for the youngest infant. If a fork or spoon is the only means available at a particular mealtime, don't be afraid to experiment. A hungry baby can become very adept at swallowing!

MISCELLANEOUS UTENSILS

There are also several ordinary household utensils that you should use in preparing baby food. You probably already own them.

- A stiff brush for cleaning fruits and vegetables. The most nutritious method of cooking produce is in the skin, but it must be free of dirt.
- A good sharp paring knife with the slot in the middle of the blade. If it is necessary to remove the skin on produce, this knife will take the thinnest layer.
- A juicer for preparing fresh citrus juices. A manual juicer can be bought for around $3, while an electric juicer costs $20 and up. A juice extractor, sold through health food stores, can be used for any fruit or vegetable juice. They are very expensive, starting at $60, and not necessary.
- An egg beater, if you do not have a blender, for preparing fruit or egg beverages.
- A potato masher for mashed potatoes, winter squash and similarly textured foods.

As you can see, the type of equipment that you will use in preparing your baby's food depends on the amount of money, time, and effort you want to spend. You may already own many of these utensils or suitable substitutes. If you can coordinate preparation of your baby's food with that of the rest of the family, using the same equipment, you will save both money and effort. Just look at any piece of equipment and ask how you can use it. Discovering new uses for common utensils can be fun!

RECOMMENDED EQUIPMENT LIST

Aluminum foil

Double boiler

Electric blender—varying speeds, good quality, with small jars—or food processor

Food mill

Hand juicer

Paring knife

Potato masher

Rubber spatula

Small, fine strainer

Steamer/blancher, six-quart size (or microwave oven)

Vegetable brush

5

The Safe
and Healthy Way
to Store Foods

Nutritious, well-balanced meals may be planned for your baby, and the freshest and best-quality foods purchased. However, you may still end up with food that is lower in vitamins. Storage is very important in the preservation of vitamins that can be destroyed by exposure to air and light. Improper handling and storage can also be dangerous to your baby's health, since bacteria, which are present in all food, can grow to harmful levels in just hours.

HOW SPOILED FOOD
CAN AFFECT YOUR BABY

Babies are particularly susceptible to digestive upsets and when you notice "something" did not agree with your baby, what may really have happened is that bacteria in poorly kept foods were causing the upset. The discomfort usually takes the form of gas or diarrhea. Other forms of bacteria can produce toxins that can be more harmful and even fatal. You should be aware of the dangers of improper handling and storage. The U.S. Department of Agriculture has published the following information on these bacterial illnesses:

Salmonellosis is caused by bacteria that are widespread

in nature and live and grow in the intestinal tracts of human beings and animals. The bacteria grow and multiply at temperatures between 44° and 115°F. The symptoms are severe headache, followed by vomiting, diarrhea, abdominal cramps, and fever. These bacteria in food can be destroyed by heating the food to a temperature of 140° and holding for ten minutes, or to a temperature even higher for less time. Refrigeration at 45°F or below inhibits the increase of these bacteria, but they remain alive in the refrigerator, in the freezer, and even in dried foods.

Much of the raw poultry in this country is contaminated with salmonella bacteria; however, it is usually destroyed by *thorough* cooking. *Never* serve poultry that is rare or pink. *Always* wash your hands and any surfaces and utensils used in preparing raw poultry (use hot water and soap), before handling any other food to be eaten uncooked, such as salad.

Raw eggs can also carry salmonella. Because this illness can be severe, and even fatal, with infants—they should not be fed raw or underdone eggs.

Perfringens poisoning is caused by bacteria that grow in cooked meats, gravies, and meat dishes that are held without the proper refrigeration. The symptoms are nausea without vomiting and acute inflammation of the stomach and the intestines. To control the growth of surviving bacteria on cooked meats that are to be eaten later, you must cool the meats rapidly and refrigerate them immediately at 40°F or below.

Staph poisoning produces mild symptoms of vomiting, diarrhea, and abdominal cramps that are often attributed to other causes. The growth of bacteria that produce the toxin is inhibited by keeping hot foods above 140°F and cold foods at or below 40°F.

Botulism is caused by a toxin that is produced in cans or sealed containers where there is an absence of oxygen. The toxin produces severe symptoms of double vision, inability to swallow, speech difficulty, and progressive respiratory paralysis, with possible fatality. The bacteria can be destroyed by the high temperatures obtained only in a pressure canner. This form of poisoning can occur through improper home canning methods, especially with meats and vegetables. If you suspect a food is contaminated, throw it away without tasting.

You should always contact a doctor if anyone in your family shows signs of the above-listed symptoms.

Signs of Spoilage Although it is not always possible to detect—by taste, smell, or appearance—when food has become spoiled, some common signs are

- Off odors
- Mold (green or white fuzzy spots)
- Fermented odor of fruit juices
- Rancid odor or flavor
- Slime on meats or poultry
- Sour tastes in bland foods
- Cans that are bulging, leaking or spurting liquid when opened. *These conditions may be caused by botulism and the contents should be thrown away without tasting.*

GENERAL RULES OF HANDLING AND STORING FOODS

If this introduction to the various types of food poisoning frightens you a little, that's good! If you are familiar with the possibilities of food poisoning, it need never occur with your baby or the rest of your family so long as you follow the basic rules of proper preparation and handling. Time and temperature are the important factors and the danger lies in holding foods for any length of time at temperatures above refrigerator temperature and below serving temperature of hot food. Remember:

- Work with clean hands when preparing food.
- Work with clean utensils, especially grinders, blenders, can openers, and cutting boards. The bacteria on wooden surfaces can be destroyed by rinsing with chlorine bleach (⅛ cup to 1 quart water). Utensils

should be washed in hot water and soap or in the dishwasher.

- Cook or prepare a food immediately after removing it from refrigeration. If you use an automatic oven, remember not to hold the food in the oven more than three hours before cooking.
- Cooked food, if not served immediately, should be cooled as quickly as possible. Put the dish in cold water if it cannot be put immediately in the refrigerator. Keeping the food cold will inhibit the growth of food-poisoning bacteria.
- The temperature range of 60° to 120°F is the most dangerous zone; one in which bacteria multiply quickly.
- When you are using leftovers as baby food, purée and use the recommended storage time from when they were first prepared or cooked.

Purées Need Special Care Prepared baby food is particularly susceptible to spoilage, because the food is usually creamed, puréed, or ground. More important, you probably serve your baby food warm, instead of hot or cold, and this is the temperature at which bacteria grow rapidly. The electric warming dishes are designed to hold food at this dangerous temperature. How often have you warmed food in preparation for a feeding, and then spent half an hour or more preparing your baby? Many babies are also notoriously slow eaters and a feeding may last another half hour. If he does not eat, you may feel the baby is not hungry just now, and put the food aside for a while. **Remember that from the time the food is taken from the refrigerator, or out of the fresh jar, bacteria can be growing.** If there is leftover food, you can put it back to use at the next feeding, but the new refrigeration will only slow the bacterial growth that has occurred while the food has been out. Instead, follow these basic habits:

- If you prefer to warm your baby's food, do it immediately before his feeding.
- Only warm as much food as he usually eats, then throw away the leftovers if it has been out for more

than a half hour. (Since your homemade food was not as expensive as the commercial, you won't feel so guilty if you waste some.)

- Serve cold foods that adults usually eat cold, such as fruits, custards, and puddings. In addition to the lessened danger of food poisoning, you will find it very convenient when traveling or in a hurry.

Now, let's go into some detail on the various ways you can store your baby's food, both before and after you prepare it.

PANTRY STORAGE

While most of the foods that you will use in preparing your baby food will require at least refrigeration, some foods can be stored in the pantry. The pantry or area used for storage should be in the coldest part of the kitchen, and away from the oven and refrigerator exhaust. A basement, where the temperature is 60° to 68°F, is a good place for storage of certain vegetables and for long-term storage of canned goods. While most of the pantry foods will not spoil to a harmful degree, they will lose quality and texture. In general, keep most pantry foods, other than vegetables, covered, preferably in airtight containers, and dry. The following list (ordered by food group) gives suggested storage times for those foods you are most likely to use in preparing your baby's food.

FOOD	STORAGE TIME
Cereals—ready to eat	4 months
dry	6 months
Flour	1 year
Rice	2 years
Pastas	2 years
Bread	1 week
Crackers	3 months

FOOD	STORAGE TIME
Evaporated milk	1 year
Nonfat dry milk	6 months
Fruits, dried	6 months
Vegetables, dried	1 year
Bananas	Until yellow with brown spots
Oranges, grapefruit, other citrus fruits	1 week
Melons	1 week
White potatoes, sweet potatoes, onions, hard squash, eggplant, rutabagas	1 week at room temperature / 5 months at 60°F
Peanut butter, unopened	9 months
Honey, molasses	1 year
Sugar—brown granulated	4 months / 2 years
Soups, dried	1 year

REFRIGERATOR STORAGE

Most fresh and perishable foods and all cooked foods require proper refrigeration. The low temperatures will retard spoilage by slowing the growth of bacteria and will also prevent the loss of essential nutrients. When storing food in your refrigerator, you should be aware that different areas can vary in their temperatures.

- The temperature range in the middle of the refrigerator should be 38° to 42°F.
- The chill tray, or meat keeper, should be the coldest area, about 32° to 35°F.
- Milk, cheese, and other dairy products should also be kept in the coldest area.

Note: Storage for canned foods is covered in the section "Canned Foods."

- The temperatures at the bottom of the refrigerator and in the door are the highest.
- Heavy frost on the freezer unit and warm weather can cause temperatures to rise several degrees. At those times it may be necessary to use a colder temperature setting.
- Frost-free refrigerators and freezer combinations usually have more uniform temperatures, but different makes can vary.

The only way that you can be sure of setting your refrigerator controls to the proper setting is to check the temperature with a refrigerator thermometer or a common outdoor thermometer. At night, place the thermometer in the area of the refrigerator that you want to test so that it does not touch any metal surface or grill. In the morning, read the thermometer when you open the door for the first time. If the temperature in the center of the refrigerator is 42°F or above, change your control to a lower setting, and check again in a day or so.

Your refrigerator should be kept clean and any spoiled food should be removed immediately, because bacterial decay can be passed to other foods. The movement of air in the refrigerator will cause drying and loss of vitamin C, so tightly wrap, or cover, all foods, using plastic wrap, plastic bags, airtight containers, or foil. Beware of the practice of using aluminum foil to wrap small amounts of leftovers. Because you can't see the contents, it's easy to forget about these little packages until they have spoiled. Raw meat, poultry, and fish should be loosely covered to retard the growth of bacteria. (The only exceptions to covering are fruits, including tomatoes, which keep longer uncovered.)

Because you often do not know how fresh the food is when you purchase it, use it as soon as possible and look for signs of spoilage before using. These approximate storage times are based on the proper degree of refrigeration.

FOOD	**TIME**
DAIRY	
Butter	1–2 weeks

FOOD	**TIME**
Cheese—cottage, ricotta	5 days
cream, Neufchâtel	2 weeks
American, Cheddar,	2 weeks, if
Swiss, etc.	sliced, 3–4
	weeks,
	whole
Custards, puddings, etc.	4 days
Eggs—in shell, raw, fresh	4–5 weeks
cooked yolks and whites	1 week
Margarine	4–5 months
Milk—liquid, reconstituted	4–5 days
evaporated, in open can	4–5 days

FRUIT

Apples	2 weeks
Apricots, avocados, grapes,	1 week
nectarines, pears,	
peaches, plums, rhubarb	
Berries, cherries	1 week
Cooked purées	2–3 days
Pineapples, ripe	4 days
Raw purées	1 day

VEGETABLES

Asparagus, broccoli,	3 days
Brussels sprouts	
Cabbage	1–2 weeks
Carrots, beets, radishes	1–2 weeks
Cauliflower	3–5 days
Cooked purées	2 days
Green peas, limas, corn	1–2 days
Lettuce and green, leafy	3–14 days
Other vegetables	3–5 days

MEATS, FISH, POULTRY

Cold cuts, cured meats	3–5 days
sealed	2 weeks
vacuum packages	
Cooked meats and meat	3–4 days
dishes	
Cooked purées	1–2 days

FOOD	*TIME*
Fish—fresh or cooked	1–2 days
Frankfurters	4–5 days
Gravy, broth, or stuffing	1–2 days
Ham—whole, halves, steaks	5–7 days
canned, unopened	6 months
Poultry—uncooked	2–3 days
cooked	3–4 days
Uncooked meat	3–5 days
chops, roasts, steak,	1–2 days
stew, ground liver, kidneys, etc.	1 day

OTHER FOODS (opened)	
Cooking and salad oils	3 months
Honey, molasses	1 year
Peanut butter—commercial	6 months
homemade	10 days
Wheat germ	2 months

FREEZER STORAGE

The freezer gives you the best opportunity to feed your baby conveniently with home-prepared foods. One of the most common reasons that women give for using commercial foods is that it takes too much time to make and purée food for each meal. The freezer enables you to prepare and store several weeks' supply of food at one time—baby food that is fresh and ready to feed to your baby at a minute's notice.

Freezing preserves the nutritive value of food better than canning, and the value is nearly equal to that of fresh foods. The protein, fat, and carbohydrate content of food is not affected by freezing. There is little loss of vitamin C in frozen fruits and other vitamins and minerals are well retained.

Freezing foods will also prevent the growth of bacteria when the food is stored around 0°F and used within the recommended time. The organism that produces the botulism toxin in canned nonacid and protein foods does not grow in frozen foods.

How to Check Your Freezer Temperature While we usually think of freezing temperatures as anywhere below 32°F, the long-term storage of high-quality foods requires a temperature of 0°F or below. Storage temperatures above 10°F will result in a rapid loss of nutritional value and quality. You can check your freezer temperature with an outdoor thermometer in the same way that you check the temperature of your refrigerator. Do not rest the thermometer on the freezer coils; instead place it on a frozen package in the middle of the freezer. Leave it in overnight and take a reading in the morning. If your freezer temperature is above 5°F, and you cannot set it lower, plan to store the frozen baby food for less than the recommended times. In side-by-side refrigerator/freezers, there are often areas in the freezer that are above 10°F. These shelves should not be used for long-term storage.

What and How to Freeze You can freeze almost any raw or cooked food that you have prepared as baby food. You can save time and money by buying seasonal or sale foods and preparing large quantities of baby food. You can also save time and money by puréeing and freezing small quantities of food that are left over from family meals. Here are some basic principles of proper freezing that will give you a ready supply of safe and nutritious foods for your baby.

- Cook or prepare food as soon after buying as possible, to prevent loss of nutrients and spoilage.
- After cooking, chill the food quickly in the refrigerator.
- It is safe to freeze cooked purées that have been prepared from frozen raw meats, fish, poultry, fruits, or vegetables.
- However, *do not freeze* any baby food that has been prepared from ingredients *already cooked, frozen,* and *thawed* (see the section in this chapter on refreezing).
- If you are using leftovers from family meals, don't al-

low them to sit at room temperature for too long. If possible, purée and freeze the leftover food immediately after the meal.

- It is important not to stir air into the puréed mixtures before freezing, so purée the food, then allow it to settle. Watch out for this if you are using a blender.
- Freeze the food as quickly as possible to preserve the quality. Place the food directly on the freezing coils for fast freezing. If possible, lower the freezer temperatures below 0°F when freezing large amounts.
- Wrapping materials are also very important in terms of preservation and time saving. Because the dry air of the freezer can produce a loss of moisture and nutrients, you must use a wrap that is moisture resistant and as airtight as possible. Rigid containers of aluminum or plastic and flexible freezer wraps, such as aluminum foil or plastic freezer bags, can be used. The flexible wrapping requires that the ends be sealed with tape, and bags should be closed. One type of storage bag even allows you to freeze food, then heat it by placing the entire bag in boiling water. Ordinary paper, waxed paper, and thin plastic wraps are not suitable. A plastic wrap designed especially for freezing is now available.

These storage times are based on a freezer temperature of 0°F. The food may not spoil when kept longer or at higher temperatures, but it may lose nutritional value and quality. The following USDA times are given for fresh food that you may freeze before preparing and for raw and cooked baby food. Many people have reported that they have successfully frozen baby foods for one to two months longer than these recommended times.

FOOD	TIME
FRESH	
Chicken	1 year
Fish, lean	6 months
Ground beef, lamb, veal	4 months
Ground pork	3 months

FOOD	TIME
Roasts, steaks	
beef	1 year
lamb, veal	9 months
pork	6 months
Liver, kidneys, etc.	3 months
Turkey, duck	6 months
Citrus-juice concentrates	1 year
Fruit	1 year
Vegetables	8 months
Butter, margarine	9 months
Cottage cheese	3 months
Cream cheese	1 month
Eggs, whites, and/or yolks	1 year
Ice cream, ice milk, sherbet	1 month
Milk	3 months
Other cheese	3 months

COOKED OR PREPARED

FOOD	TIME
Bacon	1 month
Baked goods	1–2 months
Fish	2 months
Frankfurters	1 month
Ground beef, lamb, veal	4 months
Ground ham	1 month
Ground pork	2 months
Liver, kidneys, etc.	1 month
Luncheon meats, cold cuts	1 month
Poultry	3 months
Fruit purées	1 year
Vegetable purées	1–2 months
Combination dishes with gravy, sauces, etc.	1 month
Soup—bean, split pea, lentil	2 months
Frozen desserts	1 month
Steamed pudding	6 months

Refreezing Food You may want to refreeze food that has become accidentally thawed because of power failure. If the power fails, most freezers will maintain temperature below freezing for at least two days if the door is not opened. Or you may begin to thaw food and then decide not to use it. It would be wasteful to have to throw the food away and you should be aware of when you can safely refreeze food.

• If there is any off-odor to the food, throw it away.
• Any food that is partially thawed and still contains ice crystals may be refrozen.
• Uncooked foods that are completely thawed, but are held at refrigerator temperature for no longer than one day, may be refrozen. If the food has warmed above refrigerator temperature, do not refreeze.
• Cooked foods that are completely thawed cannot be refrozen. This applies to many baby foods.
• Commercially frozen fruits, vegetables, and red meats can legally be thawed and refrozen if they have been held at refrigerator temperature for a day. Try to avoid buying any frozen foods that have been refrozen because there may be a loss of texture and flavor. Signs to look for are frost inside the package, boxes that are solid on the bottom with space at the top, and sweating or battered packages.

Food Cubes Since puréed and frozen baby food will spoil quickly after thawing, it is most efficient to freeze baby food in individual portions that can be taken out for a day's meals or, even better, before each feeding. I strongly recommend the following method of freezing your baby food as both convenient and safe.

1. Cool the puréed food quickly.
2. Pour it into ice-cube trays. The plastic type is better than the metal trays (with dividers) for keeping purées seperate. Cover with wrap.
3. Freeze the food cubes quickly.
4. For long-term storage, transfer the frozen food cubes to plastic freezer bags, cover and seal.
5. *Date and label the containers. Frozen baby food*

purées all look the same. In general, keep the protein foods, cereals, vegetables, and fruit in separate containers. It's easier to select a meal.

6. Before a meal, take out the food you want to serve. Allow half an hour to thaw at room temperature, or you can thaw and heat the cubes quickly in the oven or microwave. (Always stir and test the food.)

You will find this method is really the key to feeding your baby easily and conveniently with food you have prepared yourself. You can always keep an adequate supply on hand and you will never need to rush to prepare food for a hungry baby.

CANNED FOODS

Canning is a widely used form of preserving food. Commercially canned foods are usually safe from food poisoning and retain a large amount of vitamins and minerals, although less than frozen foods. Many of the foods that you will feed your baby can be prepared directly from cans, so it is important to know how to buy and store canned goods.

- Do not buy or use cans that are leaking, have bulging ends, or spurt liquid when opened. These may be signs of botulism and the food should be thrown out without tasting.
- When buying vacuum-packed jars, be sure the lid has not been opened.
- The ideal temperature for storing canned goods for more than one month is 65°F. At this temperature vitamins are well retained for as long as a year.
- In general, the longer the storage period and the higher the storage temperature, the greater the loss of nutrients.
- Read the labels carefully to select brands of canned goods that have the fewest additives and are without unnecessary sugar or salt.
- Remember that ingredients are listed in *descending*

order of amount. Thus the ingredient that is listed first is present in the largest amount.

- Where possible, buy food that is packed in its own juices. *About one-third of the water-soluble vitamins and minerals in canned food and vegetables will be in the liquid.* To get the full nutritive value, use this liquid or juice as a thinner when preparing your baby's food. Or strain it and serve it as a beverage.
- Wash the top of a can before opening. If you are opening a vacuum-packed jar with a turn-off lid, rinse under the edge of the lid. The air rushing in when you open the jar will pull in any dirt under the lid. When you open a vacuum-packed jar, listen for the *pop* sound. If you do not hear it, the jar may have been previously opened and the food spoiled.
- Opened canned food can be covered tightly and stored in the refrigerator in the original jar for the recommended time.

The maximum storage times for opened canned food that is stored in the refrigerator at 35° to 40°F are as follows:

Citrus juices	3 days
Evaporated milk	4–5 days
Fish	2 days
Fruit	1 week
Meats	3 days
Poultry	2 days
Soups	3 days
Tomato-based sauces	5 days
Vegetables	3 days

Home Canning Canning your own baby food is an alternative to the frozen food cube method, especially if you do not have adequate freezer space. If you are already an experienced home canner and you own the necessary equipment, canning your prepared baby food is convenient and safe. You may do your baby food purées at the same time you are canning food for the family. You can use the smallest size jars.

Unless you are already doing your own canning, it will not be worth the time and expense to start for the few months that you will be preparing baby food. It can also be dangerous. Improperly canned foods can allow the growth of the toxin that causes botulism—the most harmful of food poisoning. If you are interested in learning how to can all types of food, send for the booklets published by the USDA that are listed in the Bibliography or buy a good canning cookbook.

6

The Baby Food System

Since you probably want to spend as little time as possible preparing your own baby food, in the following recipe chapters you will find everything you may want to know about any food you choose to prepare for your baby. You should not have to refer to any other cookbook. But first, here are the essentials of the easy baby food system, and it really is easy if you know how.

HOW TO PLAN

The most important fact to remember in preparing your own baby food is that you must *plan ahead*. The last thing that you want to do is to cook and purée your baby's meal while he is shrieking with hunger. Just as you would buy a supply of the commercial baby foods, you should plan to keep on hand a supply of frozen food cubes (see "Food Cubes," in chapter 5) or fresh, canned, or frozen "instant foods" (see Chapter 13). This supply is particularly important when your baby is young and eating only a limited variety of foods. Even when your baby is older and is eating more family foods, this planning is very convenient.

You can also save money by preparing large amounts of foods that are in season or are on sale. You don't have to worry about a large variety, just make a balanced selection of a few highly nutritious foods (see Chapter 1) and use the simplest recipes. Or prepare a large supply of all-in-one meals, such as stews.

Just remember not to make more food than your baby will eat in the recommended safe freezing or storage time. Also, do not make a large amount of a food until you have successfully introduced it to your baby. This is especially important with the foods that tend to cause allergies.

You can plan to feed your baby entirely from this store of home-prepared or instant foods as conveniently as if you were buying baby food. Of course, if a family dish is ready and suitable, you can always purée it and serve it to your baby.

HOW TO SAVE TIME

The easiest and most convenient time for you to prepare baby food is when you are already in the kitchen making your family's food. You will also save time and effort by making large amounts of various foods at the same time. To save preparation and cooking time:

- Prepare the same kind of food for your baby that you are making for your family. The recipe section is designed so you can easily look up any food. For example, if you are cooking fried chicken, steam a few pieces for Chicken Purée. This will also save you time marketing.
- Use the cooking method that fits in with the way you are already cooking. (But never fry foods for your baby.) If you are using your oven for roasting, then use a recipe for baking or aluminum foil steaming. Microwave cooking is fastest for most foods.
- Whenever possible, use leftovers from family meals.

To save cleanup time:

- Cook your baby's food in the same pots or steamer that you have used for your family's vegetables.
- Cook several fruits, vegetables, meats, etc., in the

same pot, baking dish, or steamer. You can then purée them separately or in any combination.

- Purée different foods, one after another. You will only need to rinse quickly between processing each food. It is always easier to use equipment when it is already out.

HOW TO USE LEFTOVERS

One of the easiest and most economical ways to prepare baby food is to combine leftovers from family meals. The cooking is already done. You can use any food that you have already introduced, as long as it is not highly seasoned or fried. Just be sure that the food, especially the meat, poultry, or fish, has not been kept for more than a day. *Use "fresh" leftovers!*

You can even *plan* to have leftovers from the family dishes that your baby can eat. If you make a large batch, you can freeze enough for a month or two and always have a nutritious meal on hand. Or you can purée just a few servings with a small food grinder. It's even easier if you have a blender with small glass or plastic jars—you can blend, store, warm, and serve the meal and only wash one jar.

Meal-In-One Leftover Purée

Here is a well-balanced, all-in-one meal that you can prepare from any leftovers. This recipe will help you use the right amounts and types of food, but you can use your imagination and the "Food-Combination Guide" in this chapter in combining other foods.

> 1 **cup (or less) liquid (cooking juice, vegetable, or fruit juice)**
> 1 **cup cubed cooked poultry, meat, organ meat, fish**
> ⅔ **cup vegetables or fruit (raw or cooked)**
> ½ **cup cooked rice, noodles, or cereal**

1. Place liquid in blender or food processor. Add other ingredients.
2. Purée to desired consistency.
3. Freeze in food cubes at once.

STORAGE: In freezer for up to 4 months, depending on the type of food used (see Chapter 5).

YIELD: 3 cups or 15 food cubes or 4–5 meals.

HOW TO PURÉE

The type of equipment that you use to prepare purées depends on what is available, as well as the consistency that your baby will swallow. In general, you should gradually increase the coarseness of the food so that your baby easily makes the transition to finger and family foods at an early age. This is one of the advantages in making your own baby food. If you make a food too coarse and your baby rejects it, you can just go back to a smoother texture.

Under the specific foods, I have suggested the best equipment to use in preparing purées of different textures. Here are some general guidelines.

- Use an electric blender for almost any food. You can vary the speed and blending time for a smooth or coarse purée. The only foods that should not be puréed in a blender are those with fibers, such as raw celery, and seeds.

- A food processor can be substituted for a blender in all recipes unless otherwise indicated. As with a blender, do not process raw celery or seeds. To purée small amounts of food, you will have to stop the processor once or twice to push down the food from the sides of the bowl.

A food processor will more easily prepare thick, heavy purées—just start with a few short chopping pulses, then let it run, checking consistency at five-second intervals. To prepare the smoothest purées, process the solid food first until it is thoroughly chopped, then add liquid as necessary.

Fruits and very tender vegetables will need little or no additional liquid. Harder-textured vegetables (raw or slightly cooked) and some meats can be puréed into a texture smooth enough for most babies; however, they will not be as smooth as when puréed in a high-speed blender. This should not be a problem because your baby will be older when introduced to these foods and should not mind a coarser purée.

You can also experiment with some family foods in a processor that can't easily be prepared in a blender or food mill. I quickly turned pancakes, quiche, and even oatmeal bread into purées!

- Use a food mill for most foods except meats and poultry. Organ meats can be puréed, but it is a very slow process. The food mill is an excellent way to purée while removing skins, fibers, and seeds of either raw or cooked foods. (You will find it is easy to cook a food unpeeled or cored, such as apples, and then strain with the food mill after it has been cooked.) The mill also produces a very smooth purée.
- A hand grater can be used to grate small amounts of raw vegetables such as carrots or beets. These foods will not be as smooth as those made with a blender. Chilled meats and poultry can also be grated very fine. A rotary grater is the easiest to use.

- A strainer is a slow version of a food mill. It will make a very fine purée of most foods but is not suitable for meats and poultry.
- A fork or spoon is adequate for preparing coarser purées or for mashing smooth foods such as egg yolks or bananas. You can also use a spoon to scrape smooth purées from some raw fruits or cooked meats.

Thinning—Thickening Many of the purées that you will make will need some kind of thinning, a few will require thickening. I have found that the terms "a little" and "enough" liquid are not satisfactory. If you make a mistake in preparing a large amount of baby food, you will end up with either soup or glue. So in all the recipes I have given specific amounts for thinning and thickening your purées. Depending on your own baby's preferences, you can change the amounts. *Remember that the thicker a purée is, the more original nutrients the specific food serving will contain.*

One of the advantages of making your own purées is that you can thin purées with more nutritious liquids than plain water, and thicken them without using refined flour or food starch. *This is where you can make every bite count!*

NUTRITIOUS THINNERS

Cooking or canning water (boiled down, without salt)

Evaporate milk (undiluted)

Fruit juice

Milk (whole or skim)

Vegetable juice

NUTRITIOUS THICKENERS

Cooked whole grain cereal—oatmeal, rice

Dry infant cereal

Egg yolk (hard boiled)

Nonfat dry milk powder

Soybean purée

Wheat germ (whole or ground)

Whole wheat or soy flour (in cooked purées)

A specific thinning liquid or thickener may be mentioned in a recipe. If you do not have it on hand, you can pick a substitute from the above list.

Food-Combination Guide Here is another way to change the consistency and flavor of your baby food dishes without using liquid thinners or sweeteners. You can combine foods according to their tastes and juiciness, either when cooking or during a feeding. The following guide is useful as a quick reference, and you can have some fun in making up some unusual, but nutritious combinations. Your baby may love peanut butter and bananas, or peaches and lima beans, or fish and oranges.

THIN	MEDIUM	THICK
SWEET		
Apple, sweet, cooked	Apple, sweet, raw	Parsnips
Apricots	Banana	
Banana	Beets, raw	
Beets, cooked	Carrots	
Cherries, sweet	Corn	
Grapes, sweet	Peas	
Guava		
Mango		
Melon		
Nectarine		
Papaya		
Peaches		
Pears		
BLAND		
Asparagus	Artichoke	Cereal
Cucumber	Avocado	Chicken
Mushrooms	Beans, green	Cooked dried peas, beans, lentils

THIN	**MEDIUM**	**THICK**
Squash, summer	Beans, wax	Egg yolk
	Cauliflower	Fish
	Squash, winter	Meat
		Potatoes
		Rice

SOUR OR STRONG		
Apple, sour, cooked	Apple, sour, raw	Ham
Berries	Brussels sprouts	Peanut butter
Cherries, sour	Broccoli	Wheat germ
Eggplant	Leafy greens	
Grapefruit	Pineapple	
Kiwi	Rutabagas	
Lemon	Turnips	
Okra		
Onions		
Orange		
Peppers		
Rhubarb		
Tomatoes		

HOW TO USE AND MODIFY THE RECIPES

The recipes in the following chapters contain specific details and you can "go by the book." I have also shown how you can modify any recipe to *your* convenience. This is more important than using the exact ingredients or cooking methods and is really the key to the easy preparation of baby foods. Please feel free to substitute as shown in the previous section, "How to Purée." Just keep in mind the general principles of healthy simple cooking.

Cooking Methods and Times One thing to avoid is *overcooking*. Just because you will purée a food does not mean that you have to cook it to a pulp. Many foods even become tough and stringy when they are overcooked. I have also found that the longer you cook a food, the more likely you are to forget and leave it on the heat. Burned liver has a powerful smell, and it is almost impossible to clean the pot! In general, cook your baby food to a minimum, just until it can be easily puréed and digested.

Fortunately, *the most nutritious cooking is the simplest*. Many vitamins and minerals can be lost in water, air, or high heat. So try to steam your baby food in a tightly covered container, with little or no water. The cooking times given in the recipes, especially for fruits and vegetables, are minimum times for whole food. You can decrease cooking time by cutting food into smaller pieces, but you will lose nutrients. You may have to increase the time if you are using equipment other than a blender or food processor.

Salt and Seasonings Most of the recipes are also simplified in the use of salt and seasonings. Although babies are born with preference for sweet tastes (breast milk is sweet), studies suggest that they do not have a taste for salt. In fact, even at two years of age, children preferred plain water instead of salted.

In the United States, much more than the minimum amount of salt is consumed, and this might be a factor in the development of hypertension that affects one in five adults. While there is no conclusive evidence that a high-salt intake during infancy and childhood leads to later hypertension, the American Academy of Pediatrics states, "There is no need to add salt (or sugar) to fresh or frozen foods when they are used for home preparation of infant foods. Canned foods which contain large amounts of salt (and sugar) are unsuitable."

If you are preparing food for the family, and they are accustomed to salt, add it after you've taken out the baby's portion. Of course, it's best for everyone to reduce the amount of salt added to foods and cut down on prepared foods that are high in salt. You can use leftovers as baby food if they are only lightly salted.

The same logic applies to highly spiced food that might

irritate a baby's digestive system. If your family likes chili that makes steam come out of their ears, don't feed it to your baby.

Blander seasonings such as herbs are fine if they are an essential part of a family dish, and you want to purée some for the baby. There's no reason to go to the trouble of adding elaborate seasonings when you're just making baby foods. Some parents might feel this is the way to develop a gourmet palate, but there's no evidence that infants can taste the difference. You do want to teach your baby to enjoy the natural flavors of foods that can be simply and easily prepared.

Sweeteners Even though infants are born with a preference for sweets, there are very few foods that will require sweetening with sugar for your baby to eat them. You can always combine naturally sweet fruits and vegetables with the more sour ones.

Once again, here are some nutritional reasons not to add refined sugars:

- They are simply "empty calories," which means they don't supply any protein, vitamins, or minerals. If your baby consumes more calories than needed, the extra will be converted to body fat. You will have a chubby, but not necessarily well-nourished baby. The added fat cells will stay forever and may make it more difficult to maintain a healthy weight in later years.
- A baby can develop a taste for highly sweetened food that will become an increasing problem as he becomes older and is able to chose his own foods. This is the time to start preventing a sweet tooth.
- Speaking of teeth, sweet foods also contribute to dental cavities, and even the first baby teeth are important.
- There is one area where sugar does not seem to be the culprit. The early studies that linked high sugar intake with hyperactivity have not been supported by further research.

If you believe sweeteners like brown sugar, honey, and maple syrup are significantly more nutritious than refined white sugar, you're wrong. (However, blackstrap molasses is comparatively high in some nutrients.) The following table shows the small amounts of nutrients, all of which can be adequately supplied by fruits and vegetables.

Comparison of Sweeteners

NUTRIENTS	WHITE SUGAR (100 GM)	DARK BROWN SUGAR (100 GM)	BLACK-STRAP MOLASSES (100 GM)	HONEY (100 GM)	MAPLE SYRUP (100 GM)
Calories	385	370	213	306	252
Calcium (mg)	Trace	76	579	5	104
Phosphorus	1	37	85	5	8
Iron	0.1	2.6	11.3	0.5	1.2
Sodium	1.0	24	96	5	10
Potassium	3.0	230	2,927	.50	176
Thiamine	0	0.01	0.28	Trace	—
Riboflavin	0	0.03	0.25	0.05	—
Niacin	0	0.2	2.1	0.5	—

Sources: "Nutritive Value of Foods," *Home & Garden Bulletin* #72 (Washington, D.C.: USDA, 1981); C. Adams, "Nutritive Value of American Foods in Common Units," *Agricultural Handbook #456* (Washington, D.C.: USDA, 1975); B. K. Watt and A. L. Merrill, "Composition of Foods—Raw, Processed, Prepared," *Agricultural Handbook #8* (Washington, D.C.: USDA, 1963).

If you do want to add some sweetening to family foods, and prefer using brown sugar or molasses, here are some suggestions:

- In most recipes you can substitute brown sugar in place of white sugar.
- Molasses can be substituted for up to half of the amount of sugar that the recipe calls for. Decrease liquid by ¼ cup for each cup of molasses.

Warning: Honey should never be given to babies under one year. It may contain spores that can cause botulism, a serious, even fatal, form of food poisoning. By the time a baby is a year old, the acids in his digestive tract will be able to destroy the spores. After your baby is older than one year, honey can be used in recipes with the following substitution: ¾ cup honey for each cup of sugar and decrease liquid by ¼ cup.

In shopping for prepared foods, you should keep an eye out for the various forms of sugar. It may appear on labels as sucrose, total invert sugar, corn syrup, corn sugar, dextrose, glucose, levelose, and fructose. Although fructose occurs naturally in fruit and sounds healthier, it is just as empty nutritionally as any refined sugar.

Now it may seem that the noncaloric sweeteners, like aspartame and saccharin, are good alternatives to sugar. However, there are no long-term studies on their effects on infants and should definitely *not* be used in baby foods.

The bottom line is that sugar is not harmful used in moderation, but it also is not really necessary.

Measurements Since you may want to change any recipe to make either a single serving or a month's supply, these equivalent measures are useful.

3 teaspoons	=	1 tablespoon
⅛ cup	=	2 tablespoons
¼ cup	=	4 tablespoons
⅓ cup	=	5 tablespoons + 1 teaspoon
½ cup	=	8 tablespoons
⅔ cup	=	10 tablespoons + 2 teaspoons
¾ cup	=	12 tablespoons
1 cup	=	16 tablespoons
	=	5 food cubes
2 cups	=	1 pint
4 cups	=	1 quart
1 food cube	=	about 3 tablespoons

Substitutions Here is a handy list to use with any recipe, showing how to substitute a more nutritious ingredient or what to use if you do not have a certain food on hand.

1 whole egg	=	2 egg yolks
1 cup buttermilk	=	1 cup milk + 1 tablespoon vinegar or lemon juice
1 cup whole milk	=	½ cup evaporated milk + ½ cup water
	=	1 cup skim milk + 2½ teaspoons vegetable oil
1 cup skim milk	=	⅓ cup nonfat dry milk powder + 1 cup water
1 part corn starch	=	2 parts flour
	=	4 parts dry infant cereal
1 cup white flour	=	¾ cup whole wheat flour + 1–2 tablespoons more liquid

1 cup white or whole grain flour: replace 3 tablespoons with soy flour

1 cup dry cereal: add up to ½ cup wheat germ

The following recipes are divided into chapters according to their main nutritional food group—cereal grains, fruits, vegetables, and protein foods. I have arranged the recipes in this way so that you can easily select a balanced diet for your baby (see "Planning a Balanced Menu," in Chapter 3). Some recipes, such as desserts, stews, leftovers, custards, etc., are combinations of different food groups.

You will see there is a very wide variety of foods, including some you may not have thought of as baby food. You can easily look up any food that you have on hand, or are preparing for your family, to see if and how you can serve it to your baby. Please do not feel that you have to try every food or recipe.

Most of the recipes give very basic and easy instructions on how to prepare a food in the most nutritious way, and, short of puréeing, *they can be used to prepare plain food that anyone can enjoy.* There are also some recipes that are often family favorites and that only require puréeing for your baby to enjoy them.

In selecting and using any of these recipes, remember always to keep in mind what is most convenient for *you!* Remember that those foods and recipes marked "$" are the best "nutritional buys."

7

Cereal Grains

The various cereal grains are highly economical sources of protein (incomplete), carbohydrates, minerals, the B vitamins, and vitamin E. They also contain trace elements that are essential in a balanced diet. You should include two to three servings in your baby's daily menu. The grains are processed into many products that your baby can eat—cereals, flour, pastas, baked goods, rice, etc. The different grains are

Barley (slightly laxative)

Corn (corn meal and grits)

Oats (highest in protein, iron, and fat)

Rice (lowest in protein, good for treatment of diarrhea)

Rye and buckwheat

Wheat (used mainly for flours and cereal, possible source of allergy)

The amount of nutritional value in any cereal grain depends in large part on the way it was processed or refined. All cereal grains start out as whole grain. If they are processed, the bran, which is the outer covering, is removed and a large amount of the B vitamins and minerals is lost. Often the germ, or heart of the grain, is removed. This is the most nutritious part of the grain and contains the highest amounts of protein, minerals, vitamin E, and the essential fatty acids. If the bran and germ are removed, the resulting grain is mostly starch, highly refined, and should *not* be counted as a *cereal* serving, since it lacks the iron, protein, and other nutrients that are essential to your baby.

The federal government, in order to prevent deficiencies, has set minimum levels (which manufacturers must meet in order to describe their products as "enriched") for four of the nutrients lost in the refining process—thiamine, riboflavin, niacin, and iron. The other B vitamins, vitamin E, and many minerals are still missing in refined, enriched cereal grains. Do read the cereal label for the term *enriched* and read the list of ingredients on products to identify those that are enriched such as breakfast cereals, baked goods, pastas, and rice. You can also compare the levels of enrichment, because some brands use higher amounts than the minimum levels. In general, the enriched products are more expensive than the original whole grain products, because you are paying for the cost of refining and also enrichment.

In the wide variety of cereal products, it is confusing and difficult to identify those products that are whole grain. Often the label will proudly state "whole grain" or "stone ground," which means the whole grains have been ground between millstones, thus retaining the most nutrients. Some other products are whole wheat flour, rye flour, cracked wheat, barley, oatmeal, oat flour, brown rice, whole wheat cereals, kasha, and whole grain cornmeal. It is worth your time and money to read labels in order to buy whole grain products or at least enriched ones. Remember that these cereal grains are your baby's main sources of many of the essential nutrients.

If you understand and keep in mind the differences between the various grains and ways of processing, you will able to select the most nutritious products, which include cereals; rice; pasta, flours, and baked goods; and wheat germ.

CEREALS

NUTRITION. Cereals are high in incomplete protein and B vitamins and contain fair amounts of vitamin E and minerals.

INTRODUCE. In general, the dry iron-fortified infant cereals can be started as early as four months, enriched refined cereals at five months, and whole grain cereals at seven months. (If your baby is not eating iron-fortified cereals, consult your doctor about other sources of iron.)

BUY. As you have seen, the amounts of the nutrients vary due to the type of processing and enrichment. So it is important to look at the different types of cereal that you can feed your baby.

Precooked dry infant cereals are produced by the major commercial baby food companies They include oatmeal, barley, mixed cereals, rice, and high protein. According to the manufacturers, they are finely milled from whole grains (that's why you may see dark specks in the cereal), then enriched with high levels of niacin, riboflavin, thiamine, and most important, iron. For some cereals, a ½-ounce serving (4 tablespoons of dry cereal) supplies 45 percent of the U.S. RDA of iron. Others supply 35 percent of the RDA for infants.

It is important to read the nutritional information on the packages since the amount of enrichment may vary among the types of cereal and the companies. You may as well get the most for your money.

These infant cereals are very smooth to introduce as a first solid food and they do offer a much higher level of iron than adult cereals, even the whole grain kinds. So you should serve them to your baby, at least until he is eating a variety of solids that include those high in iron (such as egg yolk, organ meats, and green leafy vegetables).

The jars of cereal and fruit combinations may be convenient for travel, but are a more expensive form of cereal. Remember, you're paying for the water.

Whole grain cereals are more difficult for young babies to digest, but they can be introduced by seven months. *They should not be given to a baby who has diarrhea.* These cereals supply all the fiber; B vitamins, especially B_6, B_{12}, and folic acid; plus the other minerals that are in the original cereal grains. Their iron level is not as high as the dry infant cereals.

You can easily purée the same types of whole grain cereal that you serve your family, such as oatmeal, Wheatena, kasha, and barley. "Granolas" that contain a high percentage of sugars should not be used.

The refined enriched cereals include enriched farina (wheat), enriched cream of wheat, and enriched cream of rice. Again, read the labels and select the brand with the highest level of enrichment. Some may be fortified with vitamins A and D, and calcium; however, they are usually more expensive and these vitamins are supplied in other foods that your baby is eating. The level of their iron enrichment varies and may be lower than that of the dry infant cereals. Read the label to make certain that ½ ounce of the uncooked cereal or 3½ ounces of the cooked cereal supplies at least 6 milligrams of iron. These cereals can be used if no other cereal is available, but you may as well serve the dry infant cereals until your baby can eat the whole grain cereals.

STORE. All cereals should be kept in tightly covered containers at cool room temperature. They may be kept for several months. Cooked cereals can be covered and stored in the refrigerator for one to two days. If your family does not regularly eat cooked whole grain cereals, and you want to feed them to your baby, you will find it convenient to cook a quantity and freeze the cereal in food cubes for up to one month. Two cups of cooked cereal will make about 10 food cubes or servings.

Preparing Cereal In general, when preparing a specific cereal, you should follow the instructions that are printed on the box. Here are some suggestions to increase the nutritional value or save time.

- The usual dilution of dry infant cereal is one part cereal to three to four parts milk or formula. You can gradually increase the amount of cereal as your baby becomes accustomed to thicker solids.
- You can fortify the dry infant cereals by mixing in grated or regular wheat germ (see "Wheat Germ," in this chapter). Use about ½ teaspoon wheat germ for each tablespoon of dry cereal.
- In a blender or processor you can grind regular oatmeal very finely so that it is smoother. One part of the

ground oatmeal can be mixed with three parts hot milk. This ground oatmeal can also be used as a nutritious thickener.

- Pearl barley can be cooked, then mashed with a small amount of milk. It is one of the more digestible whole grain cereals.

- You can always use milk instead of water when you are cooking any cereal. The milk is important in supplementing the incomplete cereal protein. Reconstituted nonfat dry milk is an inexpensive milk to use in cooking.

- Cooked cereals will be creamier and smoother if you put the cereal into the cold water, or milk, and then bring them to a boil together.

- You can use any instant cereal as a nutritious thickener for juicy fruits and vegetables. Add ¼ to ½ teaspoon dry cereal to each ¼ cup of purée (or 1 to 2 teaspoons per cup).

- You can also save any cooked cereal that is left over from the family breakfast, or even make some extra, to use as a thickener.

- Purée cooked cereal, adding milk 1 tablespoon at a time.

FLOUR, PASTA, BAKED GOODS

NUTRITION. Flour and products made from flour—breads, noodles, spaghetti, crackers, etc.—have the same nutritional value as the grains that they are made from. They can be substituted for a cereal serving; for example, 1 slice whole wheat bread = ½ cup oatmeal. As with any cereal grain, the nutritional value depends on the amount of processing and enrichment. Durum flour, often used in pastas, contains the most protein.

INTRODUCE. Baked goods like hard crackers and toast can be introduced around nine months as a teething food, but your baby will not eat enough at first for this to count as a cereal serving. Spaghetti and noodles can be added around eight months. Unbleached or whole wheat flour can be used as a thickener at any time.

BUY. It is very important for you to read labels on flour and flour products in order to buy those that are whole grain or enriched. *Do not buy* or use any refined flour or product that lists as the main ingredient: "flour," "wheat flour," "white flour," "rice flour," or "bleached flour." These cannot be counted as a cereal serving. Remember that if it is enriched, it will read "enriched flour."

Whole grain flours are often listed as "whole wheat flour," "buckwheat," "graham flour," or "rye flour." You should avoid the whole grain breads that contain entire pieces of grains, because these will be difficult for a young baby to digest. They can be served from nine to ten months on. Soy flour contains the largest amounts of many nutrients and the protein is also complete. It can be substituted for one-eighth of the flour in any recipe. Unbleached and whole wheat flours can be substituted in most recipes calling for "flour," with the exception of cake flour. Other whole grain flours are available in special stores, but these require the use of recipes that are designed for them.

STARCHES. You should not confuse starches with flours. Starches are extracted from cereal grains and they are almost completely carbohydrate. They do not contain protein, vitamins, or minerals that are present in flours. Starches are widely used as thickeners in prepared foods, and in some commercial baby foods.

You can recognize these starches in the list of ingredients by the names "cornstarch," "rice starch," "tapioca," and "modified food starch." *Do not buy* any prepared food that contains these as major ingredients. *Do not use* these to thicken any of your home-prepared baby foods.

STORE. Flours should be stored in tightly covered containers in the refrigerator for long periods or in hot weather. Breads and pastas should be placed in plastic bags and stored at room temperature.

Using Flour Besides the common use of flour in recipes for baked goods, there are other ways that you can use enriched, whole wheat, and soy flour.

- You can use a small amount of flour to thicken cooked fruits and vegetables.
- You can substitute flour for cornstarch (nonnutritive) in most recipes if you use twice the amount.
- Supplement the protein in flour by adding nonfat dry milk powder to any recipe. You can add at least 2 tablespoons of nonfat dry milk powder for each cup of liquid that is used. Mix the powder in with the dry ingredients.
- Substitute 2 tablespoons of soy flour in each cup of flour called for in a recipe.
- You can use whole wheat bread crumbs, finely ground in a blender, as a thickener for juicy fruit and vegetable purées.
- You can soften graham crackers, arrowroot cookies, and other enriched baked goods that will absorb milk into a soft mush. These are a change from the regular cereals and are a good instant food. Do read the labels on these products to avoid those with additives, especially the controversial preservative BHT.
- Whole grain or enriched breads can be sliced and baked in a very slow oven (250°F) until they are very hard. The slices make excellent teething foods and snacks.
- Using your food processor, you can make an easy cereal purée from family foods such as pancakes and breads—especially good is oatmeal bread!

Pancake / Bread Cereal

> 1   **medium pancake or slice of bread**
> 1–2   **tablespoons milk**

1. Place pancake in food processor and process until you have fine crumbs.
2. While food processor is running, add milk until desired consistency is reached.

STORAGE: In refrigerator for up to 3 days. Or freeze for up to 1 month.

YIELD: 2 servings.

Using Pasta

- When pastas are combined with small amounts of protein foods, such as in spaghetti and meat balls, they make economical cereal/protein dishes that are filling dinner dishes (see Noodle and Cheese Pudding, page 122).
- Do not wash noodles or spaghetti before cooking. After cooking, drain the noodles of most excess water but do not rinse them. You can use a small amount of the cooking water as a thinner and add some nonfat dry milk powder as a protein supplement.
- You can also easily purée any pasta dish that you have cooked for your family as long as it is not highly seasoned and does not contain foods that you have not already introduced.
- You can even plan to cook an extra amount and take out your baby's food before adding seasonings or foods that he is not accustomed to.
- Pasta dishes can easily be mashed and puréed, using a strainer, food mill, food processor, or blender. You may have to add a little more milk or juice to thin, about ¼ to ½ cup for each cup of pasta.
- These puréed foods may be frozen in food cubes for up to one month.
- You can use any of the canned pasta dishes and you will save preparation time. They are almost instant foods since they require only a blender or food mill for smooth puréeing. Read the label carefully to avoid those with additives, and high amounts of salt and sugar.

Noodle and Cheese Pudding

This is a good family dessert that you can serve your baby as a cereal/protein dish at any meal, especially for a light, nourishing supper.

    1   box (16 ounces) broad noodles
    2   cups cottage cheese
    1   cup sour cream or yogurt
    ½   cup brown sugar
    ¼   cup raisins
    2   tablespoons melted butter or margarine
    2   tablespoons fresh lemon juice (optional)
    1   teaspoon cinnamon (optional)
    2   eggs, beaten (egg yolks alone may also be
          used)

1. Preheat oven to 350°F. Lightly butter medium-size casserole.
2. Cook noodles according to package directions for use in baking. Drain and cool slightly.
3. Mix noodles and other ingredients together in casserole. Bake for 50 minutes.
4. Purée for baby with any equipment, adding a small amount of milk to thin, if necessary.

STORAGE: Freeze the casserole or purée for up to 1 month.

YIELD: 6–8 servings (adult).

• **MICROWAVE METHOD**
Cover the prepared casserole tightly and cook on medium-high for 10–12 minutes. Let stand for 5 minutes. Continue as directed.

Macaroni and Cheese

This is a good family dish that you can serve your baby as a purée or a finger food.

- **1 package (8 ounces) macaroni (shells, twists, etc.)**
- **¼ pound mild American cheese, thinly sliced or grated**
- **2 tablespoons butter or margarine, cut up**
- **¼ cup nonfat dry milk powder (optional)**
- **2 cups milk (whole or skim)**

1. Preheat oven to 350°F. Lightly grease a casserole or several small individual baking dishes or cups.
2. Cook macaroni according to package instructions for use in baking. Drain the macaroni (do not rinse).
3. Arrange macaroni in casserole in layers with the cheese and bits of butter.
4. Mix the nonfat dry milk powder with the milk. Pour over the casserole, cover and bake for 45 minutes.
5. Prepare as a purée in strainer, blender, or food mill. You can also mash a small amount with a fork for a coarser purée. You should not need any additional thinning. Or serve whole pieces as a finger food.

STORAGE: In refrigerator up to 4 days. Or freeze for 1 month.

YIELD: 3 cups or 15 food cubes.

- **MICROWAVE METHOD**

Cover the prepare casserole tightly and cook on medium-high for 8–10 minutes. Let stand for 5 minutes. Continue as directed.

WHEAT GERM

NUTRITION. Wheat germ is the most valuable part of the wheat cereal grain, yet it is often removed during the refining of wheat in cereal and flour. It contains the greatest amount of protein, minerals, all the B vitamins, and linoleic acid (an essential fatty acid). Wheat germ is also one of the few good sources of vitamin E, which many doctors feel is very valuable in an infant's diet and is found in lower quantities in cow's milk than breast milk.

INTRODUCE. Wheat germ can be introduced around six months after you have introduced wheat as a cereal. Because wheat is a possible source of allergies, you should begin with a very small amount. If your baby has no reaction, it can be an important addition to his diet.

BUY. You may think of wheat germ as a "health" food and difficult to find. However, it is available in most supermarkets either plain or sweetened with honey. You should avoid using the latter.

STORE. Wheat germ should be stored in a tightly covered container in the refrigerator for two to three months. Because it contains oils, it is likely to become rancid if left at room temperature.

Using Wheat Germ The texture is fairly hard and mixed with milk it is a difficult consistency for a young baby to swallow. You will get the smoothest texture by grinding it in a blender and cooking it with milk for 5 minutes or allowing it to soak until soft. Raw wheat germ, if you can find it, is more tender.

- The best way to introduce and use wheat germ is to grind it, then mix it with a food that has a smooth consistency, such as bananas.
- When you mix wheat germ with another food, always add extra liquid, about twice the amount of wheat germ. Allow the purée to stand a few minutes to soften the wheat germ.
- You can add wheat germ, either ground or whole, to juicy fruits and vegetables as a thickener. Use about 1 tablespoon for each cup of purée.
- You can also mix ½ teaspoon ground wheat germ to 1 tablespoon dry infant cereal.

As you can see, you will be able to use your imagination in finding ways to use wheat germ in your baby's food. You may find nutritious and tasty combinations that your entire family will also enjoy.

RICE

NUTRITION. Rice is a cereal grain that can be used as a cereal or in many main dishes and desserts. It can also be used as a nutritious thickener. It contains less protein than the other cereal grains, but it is a good source of the B vitamins, especially niacin. The amount of nutrition depends on the type of processing.

Brown or natural rice contains all of the nutrients in the rice—it is a whole grain. You can find this in most supermarkets and should use it whenever possible.

Converted or parboiled has been processed so that some of the B vitamins are carried into the grain before the bran or outer part is removed. It is a white rice, easily digestible, and is the next best rice nutritionally. If the converted rice is also enriched, it may be even higher than brown rice in iron and thiamine.

Enriched polished rice has had many of the vitamins and minerals removed during processing. Thiamine, riboflavin, niacin, and iron have been added according to government standards. It is lower in protein than converted or brown rice. I can see no reason to use this instead of the converted rice.

Polished white rice that has not been enriched should not be used since it has a very low nutritional value. Rice flour is often made from this highly processed rice and is usually unenriched.

Unenriched, precooked, or instant white rice is the least nourishing and the most expensive rice, so don't use it.

Wild rice is actually a grass. Although it is expensive, it is a highly nutritious grain.

INTRODUCE. Converted or enriched rice can be introduced as a cereal as early as five months. Because of the bran, you should not introduce brown rice until your baby is around seven to eight months old. Wild rice can be introduced around eight months.

STORE. Rice should be kept in a tightly covered container at cool room temperature (60° to 70°F) for up to two years. Cooked rice may be covered and kept in the refrigerator for two to three days. You may also freeze it as a purée for one month. This is convenient for rice that requires longer cooking times.

Cooking Rice

- To retain the nutrients, especially thiamine, do not wash the rice before cooking and do not drain or rinse the rice after it is cooked.
- Use only as much liquid in cooking as can be absorbed by the time the rice is soft, usually two to three times the amount of rice.
- You may use milk as the cooking liquid to supplement the quality of the rice protein. When you use milk, do not cover the pot or else the milk will boil over.
- If you cook rice in a double boiler, you can cover the pot and it will require very little watching or stirring.
- A nutritious time-saving way to cook rice is to use the same pot and cooking water in which you have just prepared a vegetable, or stewed chicken, etc. Just measure the desired amount of liquid, bring to a boil, and add the rice.
- The cooking times given here are for brown or converted rice.

Basic Rice Purée

This makes a good substitute for a serving of cereal.

   1   **cup brown or converted rice**
   3   **cups water, vegetable juice, or milk**
   ¼   **cup milk**
   ¼   **cup nonfat dry milk powder (optional)**

1. Place rice and water in medium-size saucepan and bring to a boil. Reduce heat and simmer uncovered for 30–45 minutes or until the rice is soft. Add more liquid if necessary.

2. Cool and purée with any equipment, adding milk, and nonfat dry milk, if desired.

STORAGE: In refrigerator 3–4 days.

YIELD: 2 cups purée or 10 food cubes.

- **MICROWAVE METHOD**

Place rice and water in medium-size bowl and cover tightly. (Prick plastic wrap.) Cook on high for 18 minutes for converted rice and 28 minutes for brown or wild rice. Let stand for 5 minutes. Continue as directed.

<u>VARIATIONS</u>

Rice and Wheat Germ Purée. Add ¼ cup of wheat germ during the last 10 minutes of cooking.

Leftover Rice Purée. Use any rice that is left from a family meal and thin with 2 tablespoons of milk for each cup of rice.

Rice Cheese. Purée with ¼ cup grated cheese or ½ cup cottage cheese.

Soybean / Rice Purée

This dish is high in protein and can be used as an economical substitute for a serving of meat. Double the amount for a cereal/protein serving.

½	cup soybeans
1½	cups water
1	cup skim milk (or water)
½	cup brown or converted rice
½	cup skim milk (approximate)

1. Soak soybeans overnight in water in a large-size saucepan or bring to a boil, cover, and allow to sit for 2 hours.

2. Boil soybeans rapidly for 1 hour, uncovered. Reduce heat to simmer.

3. Add 1 cup of milk and the rice and simmer uncovered for 45 minutes. Stir occasionally and add more water or milk if necessary.

4. Cool and purée, using any method, adding about ½ cup of milk to thin.

STORAGE: In refrigerator 3–4 days.

YIELD: 2½ cups or 12 food cubes.

Rice Pudding

This is a nutritious dessert that counts as a cereal and is also high in protein. The rest of your family can enjoy it as a dessert or an unusual breakfast food.

> 1 **cup rice, brown or converted**
> 4 **cups milk (whole or skim)**
> 2 **eggs beaten (you may also use only the yolks)**
> ¼ **cup sugar (optional)**
> 1 **teaspoon vanilla extract (optional)**
> 1 **teaspoon salt (optional)**
> 1 **teaspoon cinnamon (optional)**
> ¼ **cup raisins (optional)**

- **OVEN METHOD**
  1. Preheat oven to 325°F. Butter medium-size casserole.
  2. Mix rice and milk in casserole and bake uncovered, stirring every 15 minutes, for 1 hour or until rice is soft.
  3. Let cool, then mix a little of the rice mixture with the beaten eggs. Thoroughly mix the eggs and any optional ingredients into the casserole. Bake for 15 minutes longer.

- **DOUBLE BOILER METHOD**
  This will require less watching.
  1. Bring the rice and milk to a boil in the top of a double boiler placed directly on a burner. Bring water to a boil in bottom half of the double boiler. Place the top half over the bottom half of the boiler. Cover and steam for 45 minutes.
  2. Remove top half of double boiler from bottom; let water continue to simmer. Stir some rice or milk into the beaten eggs, then mix the eggs into the rice and milk. Add any optional ingredients.
  3. Replace over bottom of double boiler and stir until

the spoon becomes coated. Cool pudding and purée with any equipment. No additional thinning should be necessary.

• MICROWAVE METHOD

1. Combine rice, 1 cup of milk, and salt (if desired) in medium-size casserole. Cover tightly and cook on high for 6 minutes.

2. Uncover and stir in 1 cup milk and sugar and vanilla (if desired). Cover and cook on medium for 8 minutes.

3. Stir in 1 cup milk, cover, and cook on medium for 8 minutes.

4. Stir in the last cup of milk and the eggs. Cover and cook on medium for 4 minutes.

5. Remove and let stand, covered, for about 30 minutes or until most of the milk is absorbed.

VARIATION

Rice/Fruit Pudding. Add ½ cup of fruit purée (apricot, peach, plum, berry, or banana are good) after the rice is cooked and before mixing in the eggs.

Purée baby's portion, using any method; thin with milk if necessary.

STORAGE: 3–4 days in refrigerator.

RICE AND MEAT DISHES

If you prepare meat dishes with rice for your family, you can easily use them as baby food as long as they are not highly seasoned and your baby has already been introduced to all the main ingredients. The protein of the meat will improve the quality of the rice protein and you will have an economical and nutritious dish for your baby.

- For each cup of rice and meat dish, purée with about ⅓ cup of milk or tomato juice as a thinner.
- These are good dishes for introducing your baby to a coarser texture in preparation for eating ordinary family meals.
- If you purée these dishes the same day they are made,

you can freeze the purée in food cubes for up to one month.

Sautéed Rice

This is a nutritious, easy, and economical all-in-one dish that can be made from leftovers. You can use it as a main dish for your family and purée some for your baby's dinner.

½ **cup chopped onions (optional)**
½ **cup chopped leafy greens such as spinach, collard, etc. (optional)**
2 **tablespoons butter or margarine**
1 **egg, beaten**
2 **cups cooked brown or converted rice**
½ **cup cooked diced chicken, liver, beef, or pork**
2 **tablespoons soy sauce**
¼ **cup milk (approximate)**

1. Sauté onions and leafy greens in butter in a medium-size skillet over medium heat until soft.
2. Add egg and scramble lightly.
3. Stir in rice, meat, and soy sauce. Cook over low heat for 5 minutes.
4. Purée with a blender, food processor, or food mill, adding about ¼ cup milk to thin.

STORAGE: Freeze for up to 1 month, or store in refrigerator 3–4 days.

YIELD: 4 cups or 20 food cubes.

8

Fruits

Fruits are among the first solid foods that you will feed your baby. They are high in natural sugar, an easily digested source of carbohydrates, and many contain good amounts of minerals, especially phosphorous and iron. Some fruits are major sources of vitamins A and C. By the time your baby is ten months old, he should be eating daily one serving of citrus fruit (or others high in vitamin C) and at least two servings of other fruits.

Fruits are also the easiest and most economical baby foods that you can make yourself. Many fruits can even be served raw and mashed only with a spoon. Most do not require any thinning or added sweetening, so every bite will contain the most nourishment. You can choose from among the wide variety of fresh, frozen, canned, and dried fruits.

Fresh fruit is inexpensive, flavorful, and highly nutritious when it is selected and stored properly. Many fruits are given grades based on appearance and size, such as U.S. Extra Fancy, U.S. Fancy, and U.S. Extra #1. You can save money by buying the lower, but equally nutritious, grades for use as baby food. You should select those fruits that are in season, because they are inexpensive and the best quality. You should also take advantage of specials on very ripe fruit that you will use immediately or freeze.

Ripe fruit contains the most sugar and vitamins and is easiest for your baby to digest. You can buy unripe fruit and ripen it at home if it was mature when picked. Fruit is mature if it was fully grown when picked. If fruit in immature when picked, it will not ripen properly and will be lacking in flavor and nutrients. (The signs for recognizing mature fruit are given under the specific fruit.) Fruit will ripen at room temperature and should not be placed in the refrigerator or in the sun.

Before storing fruit, sort out any bruised or decayed pieces, because they will cause the other fruit to spoil more quickly. Whether or not you should wash a fruit before storing depends on the specific fruit. You should always wash fruit before using to remove any pesticide residue and dirt. Use dish detergent and warm water and rinse well.

Raw fruit has the highest nutritional value and will require the least preparation—it is one of your best "instant foods." Most babies can eat raw fruit at quite an early age and really enjoy the taste.

- The skin of raw fruit is more difficult to digest and should not be included in the purée until your baby is at least eight months old and the fruit has been introduced.
- You can remove the skin with a sharp knife, with a parer, by blanching, or by using a food mill or strainer to purée. For an individual serving of some fruits, such as peaches, you need only to cut the fruit in half and scrape out the pulp.
- Always cut or peel the fruit just before using to help prevent the loss of vitamins.
- Most raw fruit can be frozen either whole or puréed in food cubes for as long as one year and this is very practical for seasonal fruits.
- Raw fruit purées spoil quickly so you should plan to use them within two days or freeze.

The main purposes of cooking fresh or frozen fruit are to soften the texture and improve the digestibility of less-than-ripe fruit. Most fruit only need to be cooked for the young baby or when first introducing them. The main cooking methods are baking in the skin or aluminum foil, stewing in a little water or in a double boiler (good for very juicy fruits), or steaming (ideal for any fruit with a fairly thick skin that will retain the juice).

The microwave is an ideal way of cooking fruits. It's fast

and most of the nutrients are preserved. Here are some general tips:

- Cook fruits on high, tightly covered with a lid or plastic wrap. Glass containers or special microwave plastics are best because they withstand the high temperatures.
- The cooking times given are for a high-power oven (650 to 700 watts) and are estimates. The size of the fruit may cause the cooking time to vary, so check for tenderness. Remember, less nutrients are lost if fruits are cooked whole and unpeeled.
- For a low-power oven, increase the cooking times by 50 percent.
- For one or two servings, a single fruit (like an apple or a peach) can be wrapped in plastic and will cook in two to three minutes.
- When using a bowl or pot, stir fruit halfway through cooking time so it cooks evenly.
- Because most fruits contain so much juice, there is usually no need to add water for cooking.
- In general, allow about three minutes standing time.
- Remove the cover carefully to avoid being scalded.
- Frozen fruit should be cooked unthawed. Follow times on package.
- Remember to let foods cool slightly before puréeing. Never work with boiling foods when puréeing.

You should choose the cooking method that fits in best with your daily family cooking. For example, if you are roasting, wrap some fruit in aluminum foil and bake it at the same time. In general, fruit should be cooked over low heat for as short a time as possible. If only a fork or spoon is available for mashing, it may be necessary to cook the fruit until it is very tender. If water must be used in cooking, or juice is produced from cooking, use it in the purée or save it as a thinner or beverage. In these recipes, little or no liquid is used in cooking.

Fruit should always be cooked in the skin in order to save the most vitamins and minerals. Cooked skins can usually be puréed with the fruit unless the skin is very thick or sour or there is a large amount of skin, such as with grapes.

Cooking purées can be frozen in food cubes for as long as one year and can be stored in the refrigerator up to three days (see Chapter 5).

Frozen fruit has the same nutritional value as fresh fruit if it has been frozen and stored properly. Select packages that are solidly frozen and not stained. In the case of fruits that are out of season, the frozen fruit may be better quality and less expensive. You will prepare frozen fruit in the same ways as fresh fruit, and it can be substituted in any of the recipes. Because it is usually cleaned, you will even save some preparation time. The cooked purées can be frozen in food cubes.

Canned fruit retains a very high amount of vitamins and minerals, although less than fresh or frozen fruit. It should be stored at cool (60°F) room temperature and used within a year. This is a very convenient form of fruit, since it is already prepared, cooked, and often mashed. They are some of your best "instant foods," with some soft enough to purée with a fork or spoon.

The U.S. Grade B canned fruits are economical for use as baby food. Be careful not to buy cans that are leaking, bulging, or badly dented. If the fruit is packed in a vacuum glass jar, listen for the *popping* sound when you open it to make sure that the jar was not already opened and the fruit spoiled. *Before opening, always wash the top of a can or the underneath edge of the lid of a glass jar in order to remove any dirt.*

Try to buy fruits that are packed in their own juice, or in water, instead of syrup. The juice or water should be used in thinning the fruit or other purées or served as a beverage, since this liquid can contain as much as one-third of the vitamins and minerals. If you can only buy fruit that is packed in syrup, the light syrup will contain less sugar than the heavy syrup. Always drain this fruit and *do not give the syrup to your baby.* This type of fruit should not be served too often. Read labels carefully to avoid canned fruits that contain additives, such as artificial color or flavor.

Opened canned fruit, whole or puréed, may be stored in

the refrigerator for up to one week. It may also be frozen in food cubes for future use.

Dried fruits are a good source of minerals, especially iron. They are high in sugar, but lower in vitamin C than other forms of fruit. Dried fruit can be introduced around five months or at the same time as the cooked fruit. Dried fruits include apples, apricots, dates, peaches, pears, prunes, and raisins. They also make excellent finger foods.

Buy well-sealed, clean containers and try to feel if the fruit is pliable. Many dried fruits have sulfur dioxide added as a preservative and may have a laxative effect. The sulfer dioxide may also cause an allergic reaction (see "Food Allergies," in Chapter 3). Try to buy dried fruits that are packed without preservatives and added sugar. Store dried fruits in tightly covered containers at cool room temperature (60° to 70°F) or in the refrigerator for up to six months.

APPLES

NUTRITION. A well-balanced, good source of vitamins and minerals.

INTRODUCE. Cooked apples may be introduced at four to five months; raw, at eight months. A peeled whole apple, given as a finger food, is useful in cleaning your baby's teeth and massaging sore gums.

BUY. Purchase firm apples of any variety for cooking, ranging from tart to sweet. They are most plentiful in fall and winter months. Avoid apples that have a shriveled appearance from too-long storage, soft apples, and those with large bruised areas.

STORE. Apples can be stored in a cool pantry for several weeks. Or wash, dry, and store uncovered in the refrigerator.

INSTANT USE. Applesauce.

FINGER FOOD. Peeled, whole apple.

Raw Applesauce

Jonathan, Grimes Golden, Delicious, McIntosh, Cortland, and Northern Spy are good varieties to use raw. Always prepare just before using or sprinkle with lemon juice to prevent browning.

> 1 **medium apple (cored, peeled if necessary)**
> 1 **tablespoon fruit juice (if necessary)**
> 1 **teaspoon fresh lemon juice**

> 1. Blend cut-up apple on high speed. (Add fruit juice if apple is very dry.) Or grate with a rotary grater. Add lemon juice.

STORAGE: In refrigerator for 1 day. Or freeze larger amounts up to 1 year.

YIELD: ½ cup purée or 3 food cubes.

Raw Apple / Carrot Purée

> ½ **medium apple (cored, peeled if necessary), cut up**
> ½ **carrot (wash, do not peel), cut up**
> 2 **tablespoons fruit juice**
> 1 **teaspoon fresh lemon juice**

> 1. Purée apple and carrot in food processor or blender, or use grater. Mix with juices.

STORAGE: In refrigerator for 1 day. Or freeze in food cubes up to 1 year.

YIELD: ½ cup purée or 3 food cubes.

Baked Applesauce

---

2 pounds (8 medium) apples

1. Preheat oven to 350°F. Wash and core apples.
2. Wrap single apples in aluminum foil, twisting the corners over the top of the apple so it is tightly sealed. Or place apples in tightly covered baking dish with a little water. Bake ½ hour for softer apples; 45 minutes for harder varieties. Or steam apples over boiling water for 12–15 minutes.
3. Purée with food mill or strainer to remove skin, or scrape out pulp for a single serving with a spoon. Use blender or food processor to purée apple and skin.

STORAGE: In refrigerator for up to 3 days. Or freeze in food cubes up to 1 year.

YIELD: 3 cups or 15 food cubes.

• **MICROWAVE METHOD**
Place unpeeled apples in medium-size baking dish and do not add water. Cover tightly and cook on high for 10–12 minutes or until tender. For 1 medium apple, allow 2 minutes standing time. Continue as directed.

Stewed Dried Apples

---

1 cup dried apples
2 cups water

1. Soak apples in water for 30 minutes.
2. Bring apples and water to a boil in medium-size saucepan, cover and simmer 20–30 minutes. Cool.
3. To purée, the stewed apples should be soft enough to mash with a fork. Use a food mill or blender for large quantities.

STORAGE: As for Baked Applesauce.

YIELD: 2 cups or 10 food cubes.

- **MICROWAVE METHOD**

Place soaked apples and water in medium-size baking dish. Cover and cook on high for 12 minutes. Let stand, covered, for 30 minutes. Continue as directed.

APRICOTS

NUTRITION. A very good source of vitamin A.

INTRODUCE. Cooked apricots can be introduced around five months; raw, at eight months.

BUY. Apricots should be plump, with a uniform golden-orange color. Ripe apricots should yield to a gentle pressure on the skin. They are in season during June and July. *Do not buy* apricots that are dull, soft, or mushy (overripe) or very firm, pale yellow, or greenish yellow (immature).

STORE. Unripe apricots can be kept uncovered at room temperature, not in the sun, for several days until ripe. Store ripe apricots uncovered in the refrigerator for three to five days.

FINGER FOOD. See Apricot Leather, in Chapter 14.

Raw Apricot Purée

One apricot is usually adequate for a single feeding.

1 pound ripe apricots

1. Remove skins of apricots by plunging them in boiling water for 30 seconds, then run cold water over them while you rub off the skins. Or remove skins by puréeing pitted fruit in food mill. Remove the pits.
2. Very ripe apricots can be mashed with a fork. For large quantities or the smoothest purée, use a food mill, food processor, or blender.

STORAGE: In refrigerator for 1 day. Or freeze in food cubes for up to 1 year.

YIELD: 2 cups or 10 food cubes.

Stewed Apricots

1 **pound ripe apricots**
2 **tablespoons fruit juice**

1. If it is necessary to remove skin, dip fruit in boiling water, then rub off skin under cold water. Or remove skins by puréeing pitted apricots in food mill.
2. Bring apricots and juice to a boil in a medium-size saucepan. Cover and simmer over low heat for 10 minutes. Or steam over boiling water for 10 minutes; do not add more juice.
3. Let the apricots cool, then pick out pits.
4. Purée in food processor, blender, or food mill for smoothest purée. You can mash with a fork for a coarser texture.

STORAGE: In refrigerator for up to 3 days. Or freeze up to 1 year.

YIELD: 2 cups or 10 food cubes.

- **OVEN METHOD**

  1 **pound ripe apricots**

  1. Preheat oven to 375°F. Place prepared apricots in medium-size baking dish, adding a small amount of juice or water; cover or wrap individual apricots soaked in juice or water tightly in aluminum foil (good for a single serving). Bake for 20 minutes.
  2. Continue as directed.

- **MICROWAVE METHOD**

Place apricots in baking dish and add ¼ cup juice or water. Cover and cook on high 5–6 minutes. Let stand for 3 minutes. Continue as directed.

Stewed Dried Apricots

  1   **cup dried apricots**
1½   **cups water**

1. Soak apricots in water for 1 hour.
2. Bring apricots and water to a boil in medium-size saucepan. Cover and simmer 15–25 minutes.
3. Cool. Mash with fork, or use a blender or food processor for large quantities or a finer purée.

STORAGE: As for Stewed Apricots.

YIELD: 1½ cups or about 8 food cubes.

• **MICROWAVE METHOD**
Place soaked apricots in small-size baking dish. Add water. Cover and cook on high for 10–12 minutes. Let stand, covered, for 30 minutes.

AVOCADOS

NUTRITION. A good source of unsaturated fat, some protein. High in linoleic acid, an essential fatty acid.

INTRODUCE. Raw avocados can be introduced around eight months. They are not suitable for cooking.

BUY. Avocados should be either light green with smooth skins or dark green or brown with rough, leathery skins. Both varieties are good eating. *Do not buy* fruit with dark, sunken spots or cracked surfaces, both signs of decay.

STORE. Unripe avocados can be kept at room temperature, out of the sun, for three to five days until they have ripened, so that they yield to gentle pressure on the skin. Ripe avocados may be held in the refrigerator for three to five days.

INSTANT USE. Most babies will eat avocado purée without any thinning; so that the fruit can be mashed or scraped with the back of the spoon as it is removed from the skin. An avocado is a good food to use when traveling.

FINGER FOOD. Remove skin and cut in pieces or strips.

Raw Avocado

1 very ripe avocado
1 teaspoon milk or fresh citrus juice (if
   necessary)

1. Cut through skin to pit and remove one-fourth of the
   fruit.
2. Peel back skin and mash avocado with a spoon, thinning with milk if necessary.

STORAGE: Leftover purée can be stored in the refrigerator
for up to 1 day, sprinkle with lemon juice to prevent browning and tightly cover. Store the rest of the avocado in the
skin, tightly wrapped, in the refrigerator for up to 3 days.

YIELD: 1 serving.

Frozen Avocados

2 medium avocados
4 teaspoons fresh milk or fresh citrus juice

1. Mash peeled fruit with the lemon juice. If a blender
   is used, push mix down with rubber spatula for
   smooth blending. A food processor is best for this
   thick purée.
2. Pour purée immediately into ice-cube trays; cover
   and freeze.

STORAGE: Frozen for up to 6 weeks.

YIELD: 2 cups or 10 food cubes.

BANANAS

NUTRITION. High in carbohydrates, good source of vitamins A and C. High caloric value.
   INTRODUCE. Raw, very ripe, or baked bananas can be

one of your baby's earliest foods, at around four to five months.

BUY. Fruit should have firm bright skins, either green-ish, yellow, or brown, depending on the stage of ripeness. *Do not buy* fruit that is bruised or shows soft spots, since it will spoil quickly, or fruit with discolored skins or a dull, grayish appearance that shows that the bananas have been exposed to cold and will not ripen properly.

STORE. Unripe bananas (green to solid yellow skins) should be stored at cool room temperature (60° to 70°F), away from sun. They will not ripen in the refrigerator and the cold will cause a loss of quality. Bananas will ripen in three to five days and the best eating quality is reached when the skins are solid yellow with brown spots or streaks. The riper the banana, the more digestible it is for a baby; so you may use bananas with completely brown skins as long as the fruit itself is not spoiled. Ripe bananas should be stored in the warmest part of the refrigerator for up to 2 days.

INSTANT USE. See Raw Banana.

FINGER FOOD. Cut in small pieces.

Raw Banana

This is one of the easiest fruits to prepare, especially if you use a very ripe banana.

1 **banana**

1. Remove the peel from only the part of the banana that you will be using in one feeding. For a very young infant, start with one-fourth of the fruit. Mash the banana with a fork or the back of a spoon until it is smooth. It is not necessary to add any liquid or sugar.

STORAGE: The banana purée should not be saved, since it browns quickly. The unused portion of the banana should be wrapped, in the skin, and can be stored in the refriger-ator for up to 2 days. Ripe bananas can also be peeled, wrapped tightly in aluminum foil, in meal-size portions, and frozen for several months. Thaw in the foil and use immediately.

YIELD: 1 serving.

Baked Bananas

If you must use greenish or yellow bananas that are not yet ripe, they should be baked to improve their digestibility.

> **1 banana**

1. Preheat oven to 450°F. Peel banana and place in buttered small-size baking dish or wrap tightly in aluminum foil. Bake about 10 minutes until tender.
2. Mash enough for one feeding with a fork or spoon.

STORAGE: In refrigerator, tightly wrapped in aluminum foil, for up to 3 days.

YIELD: 4 servings.

• MICROWAVE METHOD
This is a very easy way to cook a banana. Just slit the peel lengthwise and cook on high for 2 minutes for a medium banana. Continue as directed.

• BROILED OR SAUTÉED METHOD
Unripe peeled bananas may also be sautéed in a small amount of butter, or broiled 3 inches from the heat until slightly browned. Prepare and store as for Baked Bananas.

BERRIES

NUTRITION. Blueberries, raspberries, blackberries, cranberries, etc., contain fair amounts of many nutrients and are high in fiber. Strawberries are very high in vitamin C, almost as high as the citrus fruits.

INTRODUCE. Raw and cooked berries can be introduced at about nine months. Since berries sometimes cause allergic reactions, give only small amounts at first.

BUY. Firm, dry fruit is usually less expensive in season

from spring through fall. *Do not buy* berries that are crushed or show a white fuzzy mold. Avoid boxes that are wet or stained with berry juice.

STORE. Whole berries can be kept uncovered in a flat pan, for one to two days in the refrigerator. Remove any spoiled berries, because decay spreads quickly. Do not wash or stem the berries before storing.

FINGER FOOD. Whole berries for babies over one year old.

Raw Berries

1 quart berries (do not use cranberries)

1. Wash berries just before using.
2. For a purée, press the berries through a strainer or food mill to remove the skin and seeds.

STORAGE: In refrigerator, covered tightly, for 1 day. Or freeze in food cubes up to 1 year.

YIELD: 2 cups or 10 food cubes.

Stewed Berries

Cooking will destroy the vitamin C in strawberries.

1 quart berries

1. Wash berries just before using and put in top of double boiler. Cover and cook 15 minutes over boiling water.
2. Cool and mash. Strain out skin and seeds.

STORAGE: In refrigerator for up to 3 days. Or freeze in food cubes up to 1 year.

YIELD: 2 cups or 10 food cubes.

• MICROWAVE METHOD
Put berries in medium-size dish and cover. Do not add water. Cook on high for 2–3 minutes. Continue as directed.

VARIATION

Because berries contain a high proportion of juice, they are good to combine with other fruit or vegetable purées, either raw or cooked. The juice will serve as a natural thinner.

Cranberry Sauce

1 **pound cranberries**
¼ **cup water (or fruit juice)**
½ **cup sugar**

1. Wash and sort cranberries.
2. Bring water and sugar to a boil in a medium-size saucepan. Add fruit, cover, and simmer 5–10 minutes until berries pop.
3. Use food mill or strainer to purée and remove skin.

STORAGE: In refrigerator for up to 5 days. Or freeze in food cubes up to 1 year.

YIELD: 3 cups or 15 food cubes.

• **MICROWAVE VARIATION**
Combine cranberries and sugar in a medium-size bowl. Do not add water. Cover tightly and cook on high for 10 minutes. Continue as directed.

CHERRIES

NUTRITION. Sweet cherries are quite high in natural sugar.

INTRODUCE. Cooked cherries can be introduced at seven months; raw, at nine months.

BUY. Cherries should be firm and dark with shiny skin. They are in season during June and July. *Do not buy* shriveled fruit with dry stems or brown discoloration, which indicates decay.

STORE. Unripe cherries left at room temperature will ripen in three to five days. Put ripe cherries, uncovered, in refrigerator for one to two days. Do not stem or wash before storing.

FINGER FOOD. Sweet cherries are a messy fruit and the pits must be removed; but babies love them. Serve after baby is one year old. Cut in pieces to prevent choking.

Raw Cherries

An easy way to remove the pits is to take the eraser out of the top of a pencil and use the metal end to push out the pits.

1 **quart or 1 pound ripe eating cherries (Royal Anne, Napoleon, Bing, Black Tartarian, Republican, Lambert, Windsor)**

1. Wash cherries and remove stems just before using. If purée is to be prepared with a food mill or blender, first remove the pits.
2. Mash cherries using strainer, food mill, food processor, or blender. The skin is thin enough to be digestible for older babies, if a blender is used.

STORAGE: In refrigerator, tightly covered, for 1 day. Or freeze in food cubes for up to 1 year.

YIELD: 2 cups or 10 food cubes.

VARIATION

Since cherries contain a large amount of juice, they are a good fruit to combine with more solid fruits such as apples or bananas.

Stewed Cherries

Sour cherries are one of the few canned fruits that should be stewed to sweeten them.

> 1 **quart of 1 pound sweet or cooking cherries (Montmorency or English Morello), or 1 can (30 ounces) sour cherries**
> ½ **cup sugar (use only when cooking sour cherries)**

1. Wash and stem cherries just before using. Place sugar and cherries in top of double boiler over boiling water or in large-size heavy saucepan. Cover and simmer, stirring occasionally, over low heat for 15 minutes.
2. Cool. Remove pits with a fork or slotted spoon (easier than pitting raw cherries). Mash well with fork. Use food mill or blender for quantities and when first introducing fruit.

STORAGE: In refrigerator for up to 3 days. Or freeze for up to 1 year.

YIELD: 2 cups or 10 food cubes.

• **MICROWAVE METHOD**
Combine sugar and cherries in large-size bowl. Add ¼ cup water. Cover and cook on high for 5–6 minutes. Continue as directed.

VARIATION

Since cherries contain a large amount of juice, they are a good fruit to stew in combination with a more solid fruit; just omit the liquid recommended for stewing the particular fruit.

CITRUS FRUITS

NUTRITION. All the citrus fruits—oranges, grapefruits, lemons, tangerines, limes—are excellent sources of vitamin

C. The pulp is also a source of certain vitamins, minerals, and fiber.

INTRODUCE. Citrus fruit juice can be given around nine months (see Chapter 12). Raw purées can also be given by nine months. Since vitamin C is destroyed by heat, citrus fruits should not be cooked. To prevent a rash, wash your baby's face immediately after feeding him a citrus fruit or drink. Oranges are a high-allergy food.

BUY. Citrus fruits should be firm and well shaped. Select the heaviest fruits for the size, because the weight indicates the amount of juice in the fruit. Select fruits with smooth skins, another indication of juice. If the skin is rough or wrinkled, the skin is likely to be thicker with less flesh to the fruit and a large amount of pulp. Russeting, a tan or blackish mottling or specking on the skin, does not affect the quality of citrus fruit. These fruits are most plentiful and inexpensive during the winter months. *Do not buy* citrus fruits that show signs of age (dull, dry, or hardened skin) or signs of decay (soft, discolored areas on the peel, water-soaked areas, or punctures).

The Parson Brown, navel (seedless), and pineapple oranges are best for purées or as finger food. The Valencia orange is better for juice. The seedless variety is more convenient for making purées. Oranges are required by state regulations to be well matured before picking, so skin color should not be used as a guide to quality. Oranges with a greenish cast, or spots, are as good as those that show a deep orange color (often more expensive). Some of those oranges with the brightest color have had artificial color added and must be so marked. There is some question as to the health hazards of this practice, but in any case it is unnecessary and may add to the cost of the orange.

As with oranges, grapefruits are picked ripe and are ready for eating. There is little difference between the white or pink varieties. The seedless types will save you some time when preparing purées.

Lemons should have a rich yellow color. Those with a pale or greenish yellow color will be more sour.

Limes must be mature when marketed and should be a dark green color. The small Key limes may have a yellowish color.

Tangerines should have a deep yellow or orange color. Very pale yellow or greenish fruit may be lacking in flavor. This is the one citrus fruit where the skin should feel loose and puffy. Since the skin peels easily and the fruit is usually quite sweet, tangerines make a good finger food.

STORE. Citrus fruits can be stored at cool room temperature (60° to 70°F) for about one week. They may be stored for a short while in the refrigerator.

FINGER FOOD. Wash fruit, such as an orange, and slice into small pieces.

If you own a blender or food processor, the following recipes will allow you to make full use of all the nutrition in a citrus fruit, both in the juice and the pulp.

Raw Apple / Grapefruit

   1   **medium apple**
   ½   **medium grapefruit**

1. Wash, peel, and core apple. Cut rind from grapefruit, remove seeds.
2. Purée apple and grapefruit in blender or food processor (a slightly rougher purée).

STORAGE: In refrigerator for up to 3 days. Or freeze for up to 1 year.

YIELD: ¾ cup or 4 food cubes.

VARIATIONS

Apple/Orange. Substitute 1 orange for the grapefruit. Prepare orange as indicated for grapefruit. Continue as directed.

Banana/Grapefruit. Substitute 1 banana for the apple. Continue as directed.

Banana/Orange. Use 1 banana and 1 orange. Prepare orange as indicated for grapefruit. Continue as directed.

Carrot/Orange. Use 1 carrot and 1 orange. Cut up carrot and prepare orange as indicated for grapefruit. Continue as directed.

GRAPES

NUTRITION. Grapes are high in sugar and low in vitamin C.

INTRODUCE. Cooked grapes can be given at seven months; raw, at eight months.

BUY. Choose well-colored, firm grapes that are strongly attached to the stem. The green seedless variety are sweetest when they have a yellowish cast to them. *Do not buy* soft or wrinkled grapes (indicative of freezing or drying), grapes with bleached areas around the stem end (indicative of poor quality), or leaking fruit (which shows decay). Grapes are most plentiful in late summer and fall. The Thompson variety is thin-skinned, sweet, and seedless, which makes it ideal as a finger food. You can also buy this variety canned.

STORE. Grapes should be kept at room temperature, out of the sun, until ripe. Keep ripe grapes uncovered in the refrigerator for three to five days. Do not wash before storing.

FINGER FOOD. Always cut in half or quarters. Whole grapes can easily slide into a child's windpipe and cause choking.

Raw Grapes

1   **pound grapes**
2   **tablespoons wheat germ**

1. Wash grapes just before using. Purée with food mill or strainer to remove skin. There is so much skin in proportion to the pulp that a blender will still leave pieces of skin in the purée. However, this is fine for an older baby accustomed to coarser foods.
2. Mix in wheat germ to thicken.

STORAGE: In the refrigerator, tightly covered, for up to 2 days. Or freeze in food cubes up to 1 year.

YIELD: 2 cups or 10 cubes.

VARIATION

Grapes contain a large amount of juice and are very sweet, so they are a good fruit to combine with hard, sour fruits.

Stewed Grapes

1 **pound grapes**
2 **tablespoons wheat germ**

1. Follow instructions for Raw Grapes.
2. Stew in top of covered double boiler over boiling water or simmer in covered medium-size saucepan over low heat for 10 minutes.
3. Puree with any method.

STORAGE: In refrigerator 2–3 days, or freeze in food cubes up to 1 year.

YIELD: 2 cups or 10 cubes.

• **MICROWAVE METHOD**
Place grape purée in medium-size bowl. Do not add water. Cover tightly and cook on high for 5–6 minutes. Continue as directed.

KIWI FRUIT

This tart egg-shaped fruit with a fuzzy brown skin, originally from New Zealand, is now readily available in this country. This is a very juicy fruit and is good mixed with sweet thick fruits, vegetables, and also cereals.

NUTRITION. High in potassium and vitamin C. Best served raw.

INTRODUCE. Cooked kiwis can be given at six months; raw, at eight months.

BUY. Ripe kiwis yield to gentle pressure. You can buy them firm and ripen them at home in a paper bag at room temperature. They become sweeter when ripe. Do not buy kiwis that are mushy.

STORE. Ripe kiwis can be kept in the refrigerator for up to three weeks.

INSTANT USE. Simply cut a ripe kiwi in half and mash the fruit with the back of a spoon. It can also be scooped out into a dish and mashed with a fork. Do not include skin.

Raw Kiwi Purée

1   **pound kiwis**
2   **tablespoons instant infant cereal or wheat germ (if necessary)**

1. Remove skins by plunging them in boiling water for 30 seconds, then run cold water over them while you rub off the skins. Or use vegetable peeler to remove skin.
2. For smoothest purée, use a blender or food processor. Thicken with instant infant cereal if too juicy.

STORAGE: In refrigerator for 1 day. Or freeze in food cubes up to 1 year.

YIELD: 2 cups or 10 food cubes.

Poached Kiwi Fruit

1   **pound kiwis**
1   **tablespoon water**
2   **tablespoons instant infant cereal or wheat germ (if necessary)**

1. Remove skins as directed for Raw Kiwi Purée. Place fruit and water in medium-size saucepan and cover and simmer over medium heat for 8 minutes.
2. Mash with fork. Or purée in blender or food processor. Thicken with instant cereal if necessary.

STORAGE: In refrigerator for up to 3 days. Or freeze in food cubes up to 1 year.

YIELD: 2 cups or 10 food cubes.

• **MICROWAVE METHOD**

Place prepared fruit in medium-size bowl and do not add water. Cover tightly and cook on high 5–6 minutes. *To cook one kiwi:* Do not peel, but prick fruit. Wrap tightly in plastic wrap and cook on high for 1 minute. Let cool, then cut in half and scoop fruit from skin. Continue as directed.

MELON / CANTALOUPE

NUTRITION. Cantaloupes are the most common and generally the least expensive of the melons. They are an excellent source of vitamin A and a good source of vitamin C.

INTRODUCE. Raw cantaloupe can be given at eight months. It should never be cooked.

BUY. Cantaloupes should be mature, either unripe or ripe. Because proper selection is considered to be an art, it is worthwhile to go into some detail. A well-chosen cantaloupe is sweet, juicy, and highly nutritious. A mature cantaloupe shows three signs: (1) The stem should be gone, leaving a smooth, symmetrical stem scar. If the scar is jagged or torn, the melon was picked before it was mature. (2) The netting, or veining, should be thick, coarse, and corky and should stand out in bold relief over some part of the surface. (3) The skin color (ground) between the netting should have changed from green to a yellowish gray or pale yellow.

A ripe cantaloupe will have a yellowish cast to the rind, a pleasant odor when held to the nose, and will yield to light thumb pressure on the blossom end (opposite the scar or stem end). An overripe cantaloupe should be avoided, since the flesh will be soft, watery, and tasteless. Signs of overripeness are a strong yellow rind color, softening of the entire melon, or mold growth in the stem scar.

STORE. Mature, unripe melons can be left at room temperature, out of the sun, for two to four days until ripe. Use immediately when ripe.

FINGER FOOD. Sticks of cantaloupe are an excellent finger food, because they are sweet and juicy. It is a good substitute for carrots as a source of vitamin A.

INSTANT USE. Cantaloupe can also be used as an easy single serving of fruit. Just cut a slice and scrape the melon with a spoon as you feed your baby.

Cantaloupe Purée

½ **very ripe cantaloupe**
2 **tablespoons wheat germ**

1. Cut rind from melon, make sure that all the green is removed. Cut melon into cubes and purée in food processor or blender, adding wheat germ.
2. Serve at once or freeze immediately. The purée spoils very quickly.

STORAGE: Frozen in food cubes up to 1 year.

YIELD: 1 cup or 5 food cubes.

VARIATION

Cantaloupe purée is very sweet and thin because of the large amount of juice in a melon; so it is a good fruit to combine with a sour or hard fruit or vegetable.

PEACHES / NECTARINES

NUTRITION. An excellent source of vitamin A.

INTRODUCE. Cooked peaches can be given at two months; raw, at five months.

BUY. Peaches or nectarines should be firm, but beginning to soften. The skin color should be yellow or creamy. The freestone variety are best for raw purées or for eating fresh. The clingstones are used mainly for cooking. Some good varieties are Elberta, Hale, Hiley, and Golden Jubilee. *Do not buy* fruit that is very hard or has a green ground color. These are immature and will not ripen properly. Also avoid very soft fruit or those with large flattened bruises, since these are signs of decay.

STORE. Unripe fruit should be left at room temperature

until ripe. Keep ripe fruit uncovered in the refrigerator for three to five days.

FINGER FOOD. Peel and cut in pieces. Since nectarines have thinner skins, it is not necessary to peel for an older baby.

INSTANT USE. Cut in half and scrape with a spoon.

Raw Peaches / Nectarines

1   pound freestone peaches

1. Wash and remove skin by dipping fruit in boiling water for 1–2 minutes, then rub skin off in cold water. Remove pits.
2. Purée, using any equipment. A blender should be used when making purée for a young infant.

STORAGE: In refrigerator for up to 2 days. Or freeze in food cubes for up to 1 year.

YIELD: 2 cups or 10 food cubes.

Cooked Peaches / Nectarines

1   pound peaches (any variety)

1. If mashing peaches with a fork or blender, remove skin as directed in Raw Peaches/Nectarines. Otherwise, leave skin on. The skin of nectarines is thin enough to purée in a blender.
2. Steam fruit over boiling water 15–20 minutes. Or bake in covered medium-size dish or wrapped in aluminum foil for 20 minutes at 375°F.
3. Cool, remove pits, and purée. (For a single serving, cut one peach in half and scrape with a spoon.)

STORAGE: In refrigerator for up to 3 days. Or freeze in food cubes for up to 1 year.

YIELD: 2 cups or 10 food cubes.

- **MICROWAVE METHOD**

Put unpeeled, whole fruit in medium-size bowl and cover tightly. Do not add water. Cook for 4–5 minutes on high. Let stand for 3 minutes. Continue as directed.

Stewed Dried Peaches

1 **cup dried peaches**
1½ **cups water or juice**

1. Soak peaches in water for 1 hour in medium-size saucepan.
2. Simmer peaches, covered, in soaking water for 30–40 minutes.
3. Purée with any equipment.

STORAGE: As for Cooked Peaches/Nectarines.

YIELD: 1½ cups or 8 food cubes.

- **MICROWAVE METHOD**

Combine water and fruit in medium-size bowl. Cover tightly and cook on high for 10–12 minutes. Let stand 30 minutes. Continue as directed.

PEARS

NUTRITION. Pears are high in sugar and fiber.

INTRODUCE. Cooked pears can be introduced at five months and raw, at seven months.

BUY. Choose firm pears that have begun to soften, so that you can be sure that the pear will ripen. The color of the pear depends on the variety, and the best pears for using raw are Anjou or Comice (light to yellowish green), Bosc (greenish to brownish yellow with russeting), Bartlett (pale or rich yellow, red), and Winter Nelis (medium to light green). These varieties are in season from August until April. *Do not buy* fruit that is wilted, shriveled, has dull skin, or weakening of the flesh near the ends (signs of immaturity). Soft spots on pears indicate that decay has begun and the fruit is overripe.

STORE. Unripe fruits can be left at room temperature until they begin to soften. Keep ripe washed pears in the refrigerator for three to five days.

INSTANT USE. Ripe pears can be halved and scraped with a spoon. Canned pears can be mashed with a fork.

FINGER FOOD. Remove skin and cut in pieces.

Raw Pears

1   **pound (3 or 4) pears (Bartlett, Bosc, Anjou)**
1   **tablespoon fresh citrus juice**

1. If using food processor or blender, peel and remove core. Purée and add citrus juice to prevent browning.
2. Use in 1 day, or freeze immediately.

STORAGE: Frozen in food cubes up to 1 year.

YIELD: 2½ cups or 12 cubes.

Cooked Pears

1   **pound pears (any variety)**

1. Bake whole fruit in a covered medium-size dish with a little water in the bottom or wrapped in aluminum foil for 20 minutes in a 350°F oven. Or steam firm whole pears over boiling water for 20 minutes. Or broil halved pears, adding a little butter or margarine, for 7 minutes (good for single serving).
2. Purée in food processor or blender or mash with a fork.

STORAGE: In refrigerator for up to 3 days. Or freeze for up to 1 year.

YIELD: 2½ cups or 12 food cubes.

- **MICROWAVE METHOD**

Place in medium-size bowl and cover tightly. Do not add water. Cook on high for 4–5 minutes. Let stand for 3 minutes. Continue as directed.

PINEAPPLE

NUTRITION. Pineapple contains a good amount of natural sugar and balanced amounts of several vitamins and minerals.

INTRODUCE. Cooked pineapple can be given at six months and raw, at nine months.

BUY. Pick mature pineapples, either ripe or unripe. Mature fruit will have a pineapple odor and a very slight separation of the eyes, or pips, and the spikes, or leaves, at the top can be easily pulled out. The fruit should also be firm and shiny, with heavy weight for its size. The mature, unripe fruit will be dark green in color, which will change to orange or yellow as it ripens. *Do not buy* fruit with sunken or slightly pointed pips, dull yellowish green color, and a dried look. These are immature and will never ripen properly. Also avoid bruised fruit with discolored or soft spots, or traces of mold—all signs of decay, which will spread quickly.

STORE. Unripe pineapples can be kept at cool room temperature (60° to 70°F) for three to five days until ripe. Never ripen in the sun. Ripe pineapple should be tightly wrapped to contain the odor and stored in the refrigerator for up to two days. Ripe fruit will spoil quickly, so plan its use carefully.

Raw Pineapple

1 **medium pineapple (2 pounds)**
   Sweet grapes or cantaloupe pieces (as needed)

1. Wash and cut off crown end and stem end. Stand upright and cut off skin from top to bottom. Remove the eyes with a sharp knife.

   2. Cut fruit in small chunks and purée in food processor or blender only. (If your blender is not powerful, cook fruit first.) A few sweet grapes or pieces of cantaloupe can be added as sweeteners.

STORAGE: In refrigerator for 1 day. Or freeze at once up to 1 year.

YIELD: 2 cups or 10 food cubes.

Cooked Pineapple

   1   **medium pineapple**
   1. Prepare as for Raw Pineapple.
   2. Place cut fruit in steamer and cover. Steam over boiling water for 10–15 minutes.
   3. Cool and purée in processor or blender only.

STORAGE: In refrigerator for up to 3 days. Or freeze for up to 1 year.

YIELD: 2 cups or 10 food cubes.

• **MICROWAVE METHOD**
Do not peel fruit. Prick pineapple in several places. Place on dish and cook on high for 12–15 minutes. Let stand for 5 minutes. Cut in half and cut fruit away from skin. Continue as directed.

<u>VARIATION</u>

Pineapple contains an enzyme that has some tenderizing action; so combine this fruit or use the juice in cooking any meat or poultry. Canned pineapple that is packed in its own juice is readily available. Since it only requires blender puréeing, the canned fruit can save you time.

PLUMS / PRUNES

NUTRITION. Plums are a good source of natural sugar. The Italian prune plums can have a laxative effect.

INTRODUCE. Cooked plums can be given at five months; raw, at eight months.

BUY. Choose any variety of plum for cooking. For eating, the Red Beaut, Burmose, Laroda, Duarte, President, or Queen Anne are the sweetest and juiciest. Italian prune plums are purplish to bluish black. They are in season from June through October. Look for fruit with good color and shiny skins that are firm but beginning to soften. *Do not buy* fruits with skin breaks, or brownish discoloration. The immature fruit is hard, poorly colored, and often shriveled.

STORE. Plums should be kept at room temperature until ripe, then refrigerate uncovered for three to five days.

FINGER FOODS. Slices of plums are good finger food, but the baby should be old enough to digest the skin, since peeled plums can be very messy. Whole plums should not be given, since the pits are quite small and might be swallowed or choked on. Dried pitted prunes are also excellent as a finger or teething food.

Raw Plums

Some varieties of plums may be very juicy and may require some thickening—use wheat germ or cereal as necessary.

- 1 **pound (about 15) ripe eating plums**
- 1 **tablespoon fresh citrus juice**

1. Remove pits. Purée in food mill or strainer to remove skin. (The skin is usually too sour to eat and too tough to purée in blender.)
2. Add citrus juice to prevent browning.

STORAGE: In refrigerator for 1 day. Or freeze at once, up to 1 year.

YIELD: 2 cups or 10 food cubes.

Cooked Plums

Some varieties may require thickening or cooking down the liquid.

> **1 pound plums—any variety (good for hard fruit)**

1. Steam whole fruit for 15 minutes. Or bake in covered medium-size dish or wrapped in aluminum foil for 20 minutes at 375°F.
2. Cool and remove pits.
3. Purée in blender unless skin is very sour. Any other equipment can also be used.

STORAGE: In refrigerator for up to 3 days. Or freeze for up to 1 year.

YIELD: 2 cups or 10 food cubes.

• MICROWAVE METHOD
Put whole fruit in medium-size dish, prick skins, and cover tightly. Do not add water. Cook on high for 4–5 minutes. Let stand for 3 minutes. Continue as directed.

Stewed Dried Prunes

> **1 cup dried prunes (with or without pits)**
> **3 cups water**

1. Simmer prunes, covered, in water for 30–40 minutes in medium-size saucepan over low heat.
2. Cool and remove pits if necessary.
3. Purée with any equipment.

STORAGE: As for Cooked Plums.

YIELD: 3 cups or 15 food cubes.

• MICROWAVE METHOD
Combine prunes and water in medium-size bowl. Cover tightly and cook on high for 10–12 minutes. Let stand for 30 minutes. Continue as directed.

RHUBARB

NUTRITION. Rhubarb has balanced amounts of vitamins and minerals. It is technically a vegetable, but is served as a fruit. Use only the stalks; the leaves are poisonous.

INTRODUCE. Cooked rhubarb can be given at eight months. Never use raw.

BUY. Choose fresh, firm stems with a bright, shiny look and a large amount of pink or red color. It is most plentiful in May and June. *Do not buy* stalks that are either very thin or very thick (likely to be tough or stringy). Also avoid stalks that are wilted or flabby, since they are not fresh.

STORE. Keep rhubarb in refrigerator for three to five days.

Rhubarb Sauce

pound rhubarb
½ **cup brown sugar**
2 **tablespoons wheat germ or cereal (if necessary)**

1. Cut rhubarb into 2-inch pieces.
2. Place rhubarb in covered medium-size baking dish, or wrap in aluminum foil and bake for 30 minutes at 375°F. Or place pieces in top of double boiler and cook over boiling water for 15 minutes. Or place rhubarb in large-size saucepan with ¼ cup water and cook, covered, over low heat for 15 minutes.
3. Add sugar.
4. Use either strainer or food mill to purée and remove fibers, for the smoothest purée, or purée in blender or food processor. If purée is too thin, thicken with wheat germ.

STORAGE: In refrigerator for up to 3 days. Or freeze for up to 1 year.

YIELD: 2½ cups or 12 food cubes.

- **MICROWAVE METHOD**

Combine cut-up rhubarb and sugar in medium-size dish. Do not add water. Cover tightly and cook on high 5–6 minutes. Let stand 5 minutes. Continue as directed.

VARIATION

Strawberry/Rhubarb Sauce. Replace ½ pound rhubarb with ½ pound strawberries.

TROPICAL— MANGO, PAPAYA, GUAVA

NUTRITION. The tropical fruits are often ignored, yet are highly nutritious. Mangoes and papayas are excellent sources of vitamin A and good in vitamin C. Guavas are as high as orange juice in vitamin C and may be a substitute if your baby is allergic to orange juice.

INTRODUCE. Raw tropical fruits can be given at eight to nine months.

BUY. Mangoes are in season from May to July, and the other fruits vary. Select fruit that is firm and free from bruises.

STORE. Tropical fruit can be kept at room temperature until ripe. Mangoes and papayas should be soft when touched. The ripe fruit can be wrapped in waxed paper and refrigerated for two days.

INSTANT USE. These fruits can be halved and scooped out with a spoon. They are also available canned and can be easily mashed with a fork.

FINGER FOOD. Peel and halve; remove seeds or pit; cut out small pieces or strips.

Raw Tropical Fruit

If you find a quantity at reduced prices, take advantage of it. As with melon, cut in half, scoop out, and purée. Freeze at once for up to 1 year.

9

Vegetables

Vegetables are an essential part of your baby's menu. They supply many vitamins, minerals, and carbohydrates. Fresh vegetables in season have the highest nutritional value, with frozen vegetables almost as high. As with fruits, canned vegetables are lower in some vitamins, but are more convenient and still supply adequate amounts of nutrients. Color is the most essential key to the amount of vitamins in vegetables, with the deep yellow, orange, or dark green vegetables containing the largest amounts. You should include at least one of these vegetables every day, along with a serving of some other vegetable. Carrots, spinach, turnips, collard greens, and beets naturally contain nitrates, which, in *very* large amounts, may interfere with the oxygen-carrying capacity of blood. By eight months, they can and should be a regular part of your baby's diet—in reasonable amounts. *Remember that there is no "wonder" food!*

One of the greatest advantages in preparing your own vegetables is the large variety that you can choose from. Many of the most nutritious vegetables, especially the green leafy ones, are unavailable in the commercial baby foods. If your baby dislikes one vegetable, you will have a wide range from which to select a substitute. The chances are that your baby will love the vegetables that you prepare yourself, with their natural flavors and textures. Since studies have shown that babies have no preference for the taste of salt, it seems logical that babies may even object to highly salted vegetables. These dislikes can continue through childhood and your child may never eat enough of the vegetables that are so important to his health. But if he acquires a taste for natural vegetable flavors as an infant, the battle is over before it has begun. And remember, just because you can't stand certain vegetables, it doesn't mean your baby won't love them!

Another reason to prepare your own vegetables is their economy and ease of preparation. Buying in season and taking advantage of specials can amount to large savings. Very often you will be able to use vegetables that you have prepared for the rest of the family and might have thrown away as leftovers. Only simple cooking is required for most fresh or frozen vegetables and all of the purées can be frozen as food cubes. Most canned vegetables require no cooking, only puréeing. You should spend the most time and care in selecting and storing vegetables, so that you get the most nutritional value and flavor.

FRESH VEGETABLES. You should use these whenever possible for the most nutrition, flavor, and economy.

- Buy those that are in season and freshly picked for the maximum nutrition and flavor.
- Grades on vegetables are not required. Where you do find them, the U.S. Fancy grade is given on the basis of appearance, which is not essential in baby food. The lower and usually less expensive U.S. Grade No. 1 is adequate. Your best guide to quality will be your own judgment on the appearance and maturity of the vegetables.
- If the official USDA grade shield does appear on a package, it indicates that the product was inspected during the packing and that at the time of packing, it met the requirements of the grade shown on the package.
- Plan the use of what you buy, since most vegetables lose their freshness and quality within two to five days.

Most vegetables should be stored in plastic bags in the crisper section of your refrigerator. This will prevent drying and wilting, which causes a loss of vitamins, especially vitamin C. Root and tuber vegetables should be stored at cool temperature (60° to 70°F) for a short while, and in basements for a month or more. Before storing, cut out any decayed parts or sort out spoiled vegetables to prevent the spread of decay.

At ten months of age, a baby can be given many raw vegetables, either grated or chopped. If a baby cannot digest raw vegetables, pieces will appear in the bowel movement and you should then postpone them for a while.

To preserve nutrients, always cut or peel raw vegetables just before serving, and do not soak any raw vegetable. You can use a blender to liquefy the raw vegetable with water or juice. You can also grate small amounts of raw vegetables and moisten them with vegetable oil or juice. Do not serve raw hard vegetables, whole or in pieces, because your baby can choke on them.

COOKED VEGETABLES. There are several ways that you can cook vegetables; however, the ones that are easiest and retain the most nutrients are the steam, bake, and microwave methods. To steam almost any vegetable, use a steamer/blancher or an equivalent (see Chapter 4). The main principle is to suspend the vegetables above a small amount of boiling water in a pot with a tightly fitting cover. Many vegetables can and should be steamed in the skin, and you can combine different vegetables in the same pot. If a vegetable requires lengthy steaming, add water as it boils away.

Bake any vegetable that has a thick skin, such as potatoes or winter squash, in the skin. This is a convenient method when you are already using the oven for a regular family meal. Most succulent or juicy vegetables can be baked at 325°F by wrapping them tightly in foil or by placing them in a tightly covered dish with a tablespoon or two of water. Then the vegetables will steam in their own juices.

To boil some root and tuber vegetables that require lengthy cooking, place them in boiling water that just covers, in a tightly covered pot. If at all possible, bake instead of boiling these vegetables. Do boil down the cooking water and save it as a thinner, since it will contain vitamins and minerals.

The microwave is the fastest form of steam cooking, and it is ideal for vegetables. Because little or no water is needed, most of the nutrients are preserved and the color and taste comes out fresh. The only problem is that it's so easy to overcook vegetables. The specific times for each vegetable are given by weight (usually 1 pound), and are for a high-power oven (650 to 700 watts). Remember to increase the time by about 50 percent if you have a low-power oven. Here are some other tips for best results:

- Vegetables cut in large pieces may take longer to cook.
- When combining vegetables, use longest cooking time.
- Microwave all fresh and frozen vegetables on high.
- Cook in glass containers. Most plastics cannot withstand the high temperatures of the food.
- Arrange spear vegetables, like broccoli, so the part that takes longer to cook (the stalk) is toward the outside.
- If using a plate, arrange vegetables around the outside edge, leaving a space in the middle. They will cook more evenly.
- If using a bowl or pot, stir the vegetables halfway through the cooking period.
- For most fresh vegetables, add ¼ cup water before cooking.
- Prick whole unpeeled vegetables with tough skins, like potatoes and winter squash. This allows steam to escape and prevents vegetable "explosions."
- Always cover food tightly with plastic wrap or a lid.
- In general, allow at least three minutes standing time.
- Remember to be careful removing the lid or wrap.

To preserve nutrients, with any cooking method, do not cut the vegetables. Most of these recipes give cooking times for whole vegetables. If you really are in a hurry, you can usually reduce the cooking time in half by slicing the vegetables. Never add salt or soda to the cooking water. If you must salt your family's vegetables, do it after cooking.

The cooking times given in the recipes are only guides. Remember that you want to *cook to the minimum* for easy puréeing. If you are using a blender, the vegetables may require less time. If you are mashing by hand or with a food mill, you will have to cook them longer so they become more tender. Young or small vegetables will be more tender using less cooking time.

Remember that vegetables that are cooked, saved, and reheated will lose some vitamins, especially vitamin C. They may be stored for up to three days in the refrigerator; however, the best way to store cooked purées is to freeze them in food cubes.

FROZEN VEGETABLES. Frozen vegetables can be substituted for fresh in any of the recipes. You can save considerable time by using them, since the washing and cutting are already done. These are almost as nutritious as fresh vegetables and offer a wide range from which to choose, especially during the winter months when many vegetables are not in season.

They will be more expensive than fresh vegetables in season, but there are several ways that you can save money. Buy cut vegetables instead of whole ones, and avoid fancy cuts or mixtures. Buy Grade B or Extra Standard vegetables, which are as nutritious, but more mature and less uniform than the highest Grade A. Grace C or Standard is the lowest grade, which usually indicates vegetables with the strongest flavor and firmer texture.

Do not buy packages that are damp or sweating (signs of defrosting) or stained (defrosted and refrozen). Frozen vegetables will maintain their quality for as long as eight months if the freezer temperature is kept at 0°F.

In general, you may follow the cooking times on the package, but use your steamer instead of boiling them in water as is usually suggested. Better yet, follow the microwave instructions. Do not defrost the vegetables before cooking.

Most vegetables are sold in 10-ounce packages, which will yield 1 to 1½ cups of purée, or 5 to 8 food cubes. The large bags of vegetables are very economical, and you can either make a large amount or pour out only as much as you need. You can cook raw frozen vegetables, then purée and freeze the purée.

CANNED VEGETABLES. These are not as nutritious as fresh or frozen, but you do have a wide selection, and they are very convenient to use as an instant food. You can save money by buying the cut or diced styles and also the Grade B or Extra Standard for use in purées. Use the low-salt or salt-free type.

Do not buy cans that are leaking, badly dented, or bulging. If you buy the vacuum-pack jars, make sure that there is a *popping* sound when you open one. If not, the jar may have been opened and the food spoiled. Thoroughly wash cans or lids (especially under the rim) before opening.

Canned vegetables will require very little preparation. They are already cooked and only need puréeing. Most will require a food mill or blender for the smoothest consistency, but you can mash them with a fork to the texture of "junior" foods. The important thing to remember in using any canned vegetable is that the *liquid that it is packed in contains one-third the nutrients* in the vegetable. To use this liquid, drain the vegetables, then boil down the liquid. It can then be used to thin the vegetables, or in other purées. You can also strain it and serve it as a beverage. *The exception is the salt brine* that some vegetables may be packed in. Try to avoid buying this style, but if you do use it, discard the liquid. Never boil canned vegetables before puréeing, since you will lose additional vitamins and minerals. You should only warm them slightly, even serve them cold.

For most vegetables, a 15- or 16-ounce can will yield about 1½ cups purée or 8 food cubes. This can be refrigerated for up to two days or frozen for one month.

CONSISTENCY. Most vegetables, when first introduced, will require a little thinning; however, the least amount is the most desirable in terms of nutrition. *You can start with 1 to 2 tablespoons of liquid for each cup of vegetable.* The liquid should be either cooking water or canning liquid (reduced), juice, or undiluted evaporated milk. A small amount of oil or butter, 1 teaspoon for each cup of purée, can be added to any vegetable to improve the consistency. Wherever possible, combine a thin vegetable, such as tomatoes or summer squash, with a thick one, such as potatoes or cooked dried beans. Here is where you can be most creative in selecting vegetable combinations for your baby. You can also combine vegetables with fruits (see "Food-Combination Guide," in Chapter 6).

Very few vegetables will require thickening, but when it is necessary, use about 1 tablespoon of wheat germ or cereal to each cup of vegetable. Or combine it with a thick vegetable.

You will soon find the consistency that your baby prefers. It is important not to thin with water or thicken with starch.

A food processor will not prepare as fine a purée as will a high-speed blender for hard raw or lightly cooked vegetables such as carrots, but it should be smooth enough for most babies.

Since the storage times are the same for many vegetables, I have listed them here for easy reference. Any variations will be given under the specific vegetable.

REFRIGERATOR		**FREEZER**
Raw	*Canned or Cooked*	*Fresh*
Whole: varies	Whole: 4 days	Whole: 8 months
Purée: 1 day	Purée: 2 days	Raw purée: 1 month
		Cooked purée: 1–2 months

ARTICHOKES

NUTRITION. They have fair amounts of vitamins and good amounts of minerals, especially potassium.

INTRODUCE. Artichokes can be given around seven months. They are a good finger food when they are cooked until very soft.

BUY. Pick compact, tightly closed heads that are heavy, with green, fresh leaves. Do not buy artichokes with spreading brownish leaves. Their peak season is March through May and they are easily grown in warm areas.

STORE. Keep in refrigerator for three to five days.

Cooked Artichokes

This is a vegetable the entire family should share. The leaves are pulled off and the ends dipped in lemon and butter and then eaten. When the leaves are all eaten, lift out the light-colored cone of leaves and the fuzzy center. Now it's the baby's turn. Just mash the remaining heart with milk or the lemon-butter sauce, adding liquid as necessary.

- 1 **artichoke per person, washed and trimmed**
- 1 **tablespoon oil**
- 1 **tablespoon fresh lemon juice**

1. Steam, tightly covered in 2 inches water with oil and lemon juice, for 45 minutes or until tender.

- **MICROWAVE METHOD**

Sprinkle each artichoke with 1 tablespoon water and cover tightly. Artichokes may be wrapped separately in plastic wrap, or placed in a covered dish. Cook on high 6 minutes for 1 artichoke. Add 2–3 minutes for each additional artichoke. Let stand 3 minutes. Continue as directed.

ASPARAGUS

NUTRITION. Asparagus is a fair source of vitamins A and C. Babies love its mild taste and smooth texture.

INTRODUCE. Cooked asparagus can be introduced at seven months.

BUY. Asparagus is very expensive unless it is in season—April through June. Buy rich green spears with closed, compact tips. *Do not buy* spears that are ribbed with up-and-down ridges or tips that are open, spread out, or decayed. These are all signs of aging, which means toughness and poor flavor. Very thin or thick stalks also indicate toughness. Avoid very sandy asparagus, since the sand can lodge in the tips and is very difficult to remove. Frozen and canned asparagus are available; the latter may have stannous chloride added as a color preservative.

STORE. Asparagus should be kept in a plastic bag, in the coldest part of the refrigerator, for up to two days.

FINGER FOOD. A steamed stalk of asparagus is tender and easy to handle.

Cooked Asparagus

1 **pound asparagus**

1. Prepare asparagus by breaking off each stalk as far down as the green. Remove scales with a knife and scrub in water to remove the sand.
2. Steam for 12–18 minutes over boiling water. Or bake in covered medium-size dish or wrapped in aluminum foil, at 325°F for 20 minutes.
3. You will make the smoothest purée by removing the fibers with a strainer or food mill. A blender or food processor gives a slightly coarser consistency. The purée should not require thinning or thickening.

STORAGE: Refrigerate up to 2 days or freeze up to 2 months.

YIELD: 1½ cups purée or 8 food cubes.

• **MICROWAVE METHOD**
Arrange prepared spears so the ends are to the outside edge of the plate. Add ¼ cup water. Cover tightly and cook on high for 7–8 minutes. Continue as directed.

BEANS, GREEN AND WAX

NUTRITION. Both varieties are equally high in vitamin A and calcium.

INTRODUCE. Cooked beans can be given at six months.

BUY. Choose young, tender beans with firm and crisp pods. Avoid wilted, flabby pods, serious blemishes, decay, or thick pods, which indicate overmaturity.

STORE. Cover beans and keep in refrigerator for three to five days.

FINGER FOOD. A whole steamed bean is tender and easy to handle.

Cooked Green / Wax Beans

1 pound beans

1. Wash beans and remove ends and strings, if any.
2. Steam 20–30 minutes over boiling water. Or bake in covered medium-size dish or wrapped in aluminum foil for 30 minutes at 325°F.
3. Purée with any equipment. Beans should require little or no thinning.

STORAGE: Refrigerate up to 2 days; freeze up to 2 months.

YIELD: 1½ cups purée or 8 food cubes.

- **MICROWAVE METHOD**

Place prepared beans in medium-size dish. Add ¼ cup water. Cover tightly and cook on high 7–8 minutes. Let stand for 3 minutes. Continue as directed.

BEANS, LIMA

NUTRITION. Incomplete proteins, B vitamins, carbohydrates.

INTRODUCE. Cooked limas can be given at eight months.

BUY. The pods should be well filled, clean, shiny, and dark green. Hard or discolored skin indicates overmaturity. Canned baby limas of grades A and B are the most tender and least starchy.

STORE. Keep in pods in refrigerator for one to two days.

Cooked Lima Beans

---

    1   **pound lima beans**
   ½   **cup liquid, such as milk or juice**

1. Snap open pods and remove beans. Or cut off a strip from the inner edge of the pod and push out the beans.
2. Boil lima beans, not pods, and liquid in medium-size saucepan for 20–30 minutes. Or steam beans over boiling water for 25–35 minutes.
3. Purée with strainer or food mill to remove skin for the smoothest purée. A blender or food processor will result in a coarser texture. Thin with about ½ cup of the cooking liquid, juice, or milk.

YIELD: 1½ cups purée or 12 food cubes.

- **MICROWAVE METHOD**
Place prepared beans and ¼ cup liquid in dish. Cover tightly and cook on high 10–12 minutes. Let stand for 3 minutes. Continue as directed.

BEETS

NUTRITION. Fair amounts of most vitamins and minerals, good carbohydrates in sugar. The green tops are highly nutritious (see "Greens").

    INTRODUCE. Cooked beets can be given at eight months; raw, at nine months. Beets will cause bowel movements and urine to have a red color; this is harmless.

    BUY. Choose beets that are firm and round, with a rich red color and fairly smooth surface. Badly wilted or decayed tops may indicate long storage, but the roots are still usable if they are firm. *Do not buy* long or large beets with round, scaly areas around the top; these are signs of toughness, fibers, and a strong flavor. Wilted and flabby beets have been too long in storage and are not fresh. Canned and frozen beets are also available. They are called Harvard beets when they are packed in a thick, sweet vinegar sauce, and these should not be used.

STORE. Keep beets, after removing root tips and most of the green tops, in the refrigerator, covered, for one to two weeks.

Cooked Beets

The older and larger the beet, the longer the cooking time.

1 pound (4–6) beets

1. Wash beets but do not peel. Leave 1 inch of stem.
2. Place beets in large-size saucepan and cover with water. Boil 35–60 minutes. Or steam over boiling water for 40–65 minutes. Or place beets in covered dish or wrap in aluminum foil and bake for 40–60 minutes at 325°F.
3. Rub off the skins and remove the stems from the beets. Purée with any equipment.

STORAGE: In refrigerator up to 2 days; or freeze 1–2 months.

YIELD: 1¾ cups purée or 8 food cubes.

• **MICROWAVE METHOD**
Prick whole beets and place in medium-size dish. Add ¼ cup water. Cover tightly and cook on high 16–18 minutes. Let stand for 3 minutes. Continue as directed.

<u>VARIATION</u>

Purée equal amounts of beets and pineapple.

Raw Beets

2 medium beets
½ teaspoon vegetable oil (corn, safflower)
1 teaspoon fresh lemon or orange juice

1. Wash beets and peel skin.
2. Grate or purée in a blender or food processor, adding juice and oil to improve the consistency.

STORAGE: In refrigerator 1 day; freeze 1 month.

YIELD: ½ cup or 3 food cubes.

BROCCOLI

NUTRITION. Excellent source of vitamins A and C. Good source of calcium and potassium. The leaves contain the highest amounts of nutrients and should be cooked with the broccoli or saved and used as greens. It is one of the most valuable vegetables, and may help stimulate the production of anticancer enzymes in the body.

INTRODUCE. Serve broccoli cooked only at eight months. Some babies may react with gas to broccoli. If so, postpone it for another month and try again in small amounts. If your baby has this reaction to broccoli, also postpone the introduction of the leafy green vegetables.

BUY. Choose broccoli that has a firm, compact cluster of the small dark green flower buds. None should have opened enough to show the yellow flower. The stems should be thin and free of decay. *Do not buy* broccoli with spread bud clusters, yellowish green color, or wilted. These are all signs of overmaturity and too-long storage. Avoid thick stems since these will be tough. Soft, water-soaked spots on the bud clusters are signs of decay. Frozen broccoli is available in several styles. The chopped variety is nutritious and more economical for use in baby food.

STORE. Broccoli should be covered and kept in the coldest part of the refrigerator for up to two days.

FINGER FOOD. The small bud clusters of cooked broccoli are tender and easy to handle.

Cooked Broccoli

1 **pound fresh broccoli**
⅓ **cup liquid (evaporated milk is good)**

1. Cut off lower end of stalk. Do not remove leaves. Wash well. Slit the stalks in half if they are thick.

2. Steam broccoli over boiling water for 10 minutes—remove cover for first few minutes for a milder flavor. Or bake in covered medium-size dish or wrapped in aluminum foil for 20 minutes at 325°F.

3. Purée with strainer or food mill for the smoothest texture. Add liquid. A good blender or food processor will also produce a smooth purée. Add liquid while blending.

STORAGE: In refrigerator 2 days; freeze 2 months.

YIELD: 1½ cups or 8 food cubes.

• **MICROWAVE METHOD**
Arrange broccoli on plate so ends (stalks) are on the outside. Add ¼ cup water. Cover tightly and cook on high 7–8 minutes. Let stand for 3 minutes. Continue as directed.

BRUSSELS SPROUTS

NUTRITION. Brussels sprouts have a fair amount of vitamin C and potassium.

INTRODUCE. Use cooked only and give at nine months. This vegetable is part of the cabbage family (they look like very small cabbages) and may cause gas.

BUY. They are in good supply from October through December. Look for a bright green color with tight outer leaves. *Do not buy* sprouts with yellow or yellowish green leaves, or those that are loose, soft, or wilted. These are signs of overmaturity and too-long storage. Small holes or ragged leaves indicate worm injury.

STORE. Keep brussels sprouts covered in the coldest part of the refrigerator for two days.

FINGER FOOD. Cut sprouts into small pieces to prevent choking.

Cooked Brussels Sprouts

---

1   **pound fresh Brussels sprouts**
¼   **cup liquid (evaporated milk is good; it dilutes the strong taste)**

1. Wash sprouts and remove any damaged leaves.
2. Steam over boiling water for 10–12 minutes. Or bake in covered medium-size dish or wrapped in aluminum foil for 15 minutes at 325°F.
3. Cool and purée with any equipment, adding liquid.

STORAGE: In refrigerator 2 days; freeze 2 months.

YIELD: 2 cups or 10 food cubes.

• **MICROWAVE METHOD**
Place prepared sprouts in medium-size dish and add ¼ cup water. Cover tightly and cook on high for 7–8 minutes. Let stand for 3 minutes. Continue as directed.

CABBAGE

NUTRITION. Cabbage, both red and green varieties, is a fair source of vitamin C, and is high in vitamin K.

INTRODUCE. Serve cooked only at nine months. Cabbage contains a high amount of roughage and may produce gas. If your baby has had reactions to broccoli or green leafy vegetables, he may also have a reaction to cabbage.

BUY. Choose firm, hard heads of cabbage that are heavy for their size. The outer leaves should be a good red or green and without serious blemishes. *Do not buy* cabbage with wilted or decayed or yellow outer leaves. Worm-eaten outer leaves often indicate that the worm injury extends into the rest of the cabbage. If the leaves on cabbage are discolored, dried, or decayed, or the stems of the leaves are separated from the base, the cabbage is overaged. Canned cabbage is usually pickled and not suitable for a baby.

STORE. Keep cabbage covered, in the refrigerator, for up to two weeks.

Cooked Cabbage

1 **pound cabbage**

1. Remove any wilted leaves, wash, and cut in quarters.
2. Steam cabbage over boiling water for 15 minutes. Remove cover for first few minutes for a milder flavor.
3. Purée with any equipment.

STORAGE: In refrigerator 2 days; freeze 2 months.

YIELD: 2 cups or 10 food cubes.

• MICROWAVE METHOD
Place prepared cabbage in medium-size dish. Add ¼ cup water. Cover tightly and cook on high 7–8 minutes. Continue as directed.

VARIATION

Lemon Cabbage. Sprinkle with 1 tablespoon fresh lemon juice.

Carrot / Cabbage Purée

The flavor of carrots sweetens the cabbage taste.

½ **pound carrots, unpeeled and scrubbed**
½ **pound cabbage, cut in chunks**
2 **tablespoons evaporated milk (undiluted) or water**

1. Steam whole carrots over boiling water for 15 minutes. Add cabbage and steam another 15 minutes.
2. Purée, adding milk.

STORAGE: In refrigerator 2 days; freeze 2 months.

YIELD: 2 cups or 10 food cubes.

• MICROWAVE METHOD
Cut carrots into large pieces and place in medium-size dish. Add cabbage and ¼ cup water. Cover tightly and cook on

high 8–10 minutes. Let stand for 3 minutes. Continue as directed.

CARROTS

NUTRITION. Carrots are a highly nutritious vegetable, high in vitamin A, carbohydrates, and potassium. They are a fair source of vitamin C.

INTRODUCE. Cooked can be given at seven months; raw, at ten months. Cooked carrots actually supply more carotene, which the body turns into vitamin A. They are easily digestible and babies love the flavor. Carrot purée may be useful in the treatment of diarrhea.

BUY. Pick carrots that are smooth, well colored, and crisp. The smaller the carrot, the more tender and the milder the flavor. However, the deeper the color, the more vitamin A. Canned baby carrots are especially tender. *Do not buy* carrots with large green areas at the top, since the trimming will be wasteful. Also avoid carrots that are flabby or wilted or show spots of decay. These have been in storage too long and have lost much of their nutritional value.

STORE. Carrots kept covered in the refrigerator will last for one week. Remove root tips and tops before storing.

Cooked Carrots

  1   **pound (4–5) carrots, unpeeled and scrubbed**
  ¼   **cup liquid (milk, orange juice, or cooking water)**

1. Steam whole carrots over boiling water for 20–30 minutes (you can shorten the time by slicing the carrots). Or bake in covered dish or wrapped in aluminum foil for 35 minutes at 325°F.
2. Cool and rub off skin if preparing for a young baby or when first introducing. Otherwise the skin can be puréed with a blender or processor.

3. Purée with any equipment, adding liquid. A strainer or food mill will also remove the skin.

STORAGE: In refrigerator 2 days; freeze 2 months.

YIELD: 1½ cups or 8 food cubes.

• **MICROWAVE METHOD**
If carrots are large, cut into chunks. Place prepared carrots in medium-size dish and add ¼ cup water. Cover tightly and cook on high for 9–11 minutes. Let stand for 3 minutes. Continue as directed.

Raw Carrots

Introduce grated raw carrot in small amounts by mixing it with a fruit (see Raw Apple/Carrot Purée, page 136).

CAULIFLOWER

NUTRITION. Cauliflower is a good source of vitamin K.

INTRODUCE. Serve cooked only at nine months. It may cause gas. If so, wait a month or two, then offer again.

BUY. Cauliflower heads should be white and compact, with clean tops or curd. It is in season from September through January. Frozen Grade B cauliflower may look slightly gray or brown, but it is usable. *Do not buy* heads where the curd is spread, shows severe wilting or discolored spots. These are signs of aging or overmaturity. Also avoid curd with a smudgy or speckled appearance, which are signs of insect injury, mold growth, or decay.

STORE. Cauliflower can be kept covered in the refrigerator for three to five days.

FINGER FOOD. Small cooked flowerets are easy to handle.

Cooked Cauliflower

---

1 **pound fresh cauliflower**
⅓ **cup liquid (milk or cooking water)**

1. Remove any spots on head, base or stem. Wash thoroughly and cut in chunks.
2. Steam over boiling water for 10–18 minutes. Remove cover for first few minutes for a milder flavor. Or bake in covered dish or wrapped in aluminum foil for 20 minutes at 325°F.
3. Purée, adding liquid, in strainer, food mill, food processor, or blender.

STORAGE: In refrigerator 2 days; freeze 2 months.

YIELD: 1½ cups or 8–10 food cubes.

• **MICROWAVE METHOD**

Place prepared cauliflower in medium-size dish. Add ¼ cup water. Cover tightly and cook on high for 7–8 minutes. Let stand for 3 minutes. Continue as directed.

<u>VARIATION</u>

A small amount of grated cheese will add a good flavor.

CELERY

NUTRITION. Celery is a good source of sodium and cellulose. It contains a large amount of liquid and is a good vegetable to mix with a more solid one such as carrots or peas.

INTRODUCE. Cooked celery can be given at seven months; raw, at ten months.

BUY. Celery should be fresh and crisp. The surface should be shiny with light or medium green color. Good celery is available year-round. *Do not buy* wilted celery with flabby upper branches or leaf stems. These are signs of overlong storage, toughness, and lower nutritional value. Also avoid celery with hollow or discolored centers in the branches. A sign of this internal discoloration is gray or brown on the inside surface of the larger branches. In general, the larger the stalks, the less tender.

STORE. Celery can be kept covered in the refrigerator for three to five days.

Cooked Celery

1 pound celery

1. Remove any leaves and trim the roots. Separate the stalks and wash well. Scrape off any discolorations. If a blender or food processor will be used, remove the strings from the large outer stalks or cut in short pieces; otherwise the strings may tangle in the blades. (If you cut celery on a diagnal, you won't get any strings.)
2. Steam over boiling water for 30–35 minutes. Or bake in covered dish or wrapped in aluminum foil for 35 minutes at 325°F.
3. Purée with food mill or strainer for the smoothest purée, because the strings will be removed. A blender or food processor can also be used.

STORAGE: In refrigerator 2 days; freeze 2 months.

YIELD: 2 cups purée or 10 food cubes.

• MICROWAVE METHOD
Place prepared celery in medium-size dish. Do not add water. Cover tightly and cook on high for 10–12 minutes. Continue as directed.

VARIATIONS

Celery/Carrots. Use ½ pound celery and ½ pound carrots. Cut up carrots and cook with the celery. Continue as directed.

Celery/Peas. Use ¾ pound celery and ⅓ cup peas. Cook peas along with the celery. Continue as directed.

CORN

NUTRITION. Corn is a good source of carbohydrates and phosphorus. Yellow corn is better than white corn.

INTRODUCE. Offer cooked only, at seven months.

BUY. Choose fresh corn in season during May through September. Look for fresh husks with good green color, silk ends without decay or worm injury, and stem ends that are not too discolored or dried. The small kernels are usually the most tender and juicy. *Do not buy* corn with husks that are yellowed, wilted, or dried, or with stems that are discolored or dried out. These are signs of too-long storage. Corn with very large kernels or of dark yellow color is overmature and will be starchy and tough.

Frozen whole corn and kernels are available and are useful for baby food if good fresh corn is out of season.

Canned corn is available in several styles. The creamed corn is packed in a thick, creamy sauce made from corn, salt, sugar, water, and often starch. Here you are paying for preparation and ingredients that are not necessary or desirable in baby food. Only use this style when nothing else is available. Corn is also canned in a clear liquid or in a vacuum pack with little or no liquid. The latter is usually the more tender. Only Grade A canned corn should be used in puréeing, since it is the sweetest, most tender, and juicy. Canned corn does not require cooking, but if you are puréeing the hulls, it will be more tender if you simmer it for a while. Use a food mill to prepare a smooth purée and remove hulls.

STORE. Fresh corn in the husks can be kept, uncovered, in the refrigerator for one to two days.

FINGER FOOD. Cook corn; then, with a sharp knife, cut off only the tops or slice down the middle of each row of the kernels. Your baby will love holding the cob and sucking the corn from the kernels.

Cooked Corn

Frozen corn kernels may also be cooked, according to package directions, then puréed.

4 ears fresh or frozen corn
3 tablespoons milk

1. Remove husk, all silk, and any bad spots.
2. Steam corn over boiling water for 10 minutes. Or boil in water to cover for 7–10 minutes.
3. Cool and, with a sharp knife, cut the kernels off as close as possible to the cob.
4. You will prepare the smoothest purée by using a strainer or food mill to remove the hulls of the kernels. A high-speed blender or food processor will also prepare a purée that most babies can digest.

STORAGE: In refrigerator 2 days; freeze 2 months.

YIELD: 1½ cups or 8 food cubes.

• **MICROWAVE METHOD**
The easiest way to microwave corn is right in the husk. Just place in the oven and cook on high. Allow 2 minutes for each ear. Cool, then remove husks and silk. Continue as directed.

CUCUMBERS

NUTRITION. Cucumbers contain only fair amounts of vitamins and minerals. However, they have a high liquid content and can be puréed with other vegetables as a thinner.

INTRODUCE. Give raw only at nine months.

BUY. Choose firm cucumbers with good green color and fairly thin. *Do not buy* cucumbers that are overgrown, large in diameter, with dull color, or turning yellowish. Other signs of toughness and bitter flavor are withered or shriveled ends.

STORE. Washed cucumbers, covered or stored in the crisper, can be kept in the refrigerator for three to five days.

Cucumber Purée

¼ medium cucumber

1. Peel. Cut in half lengthwise and scoop out the seeds with a spoon. Purée only in a blender.

STORAGE: Cucumber does not store or freeze well. It is best combined with another vegetable for a single serving.

YIELD: ¼ cup or 1 food cube.

EGGPLANT

NUTRITION. Eggplant has only fair amounts of nutrients.

INTRODUCE. Offer cooked only at nine months.

BUY. Look for firm, heavy eggplants with smooth, dark purple skin. *Do not buy* those that are poorly colored, soft, shriveled, or show decay with soft, dark brown spots.

STORE. Keep at cool room temperature (60° to 70°F) for two to three weeks. At warmer room temperature, only one week. Do not store in refrigerator.

Cooked Eggplant

---

1 pound (1 medium) eggplant

1. Wash, do not peel.
2. Steam over boiling water for 10–15 minutes. Or bake for 15–25 minutes at 325°F.
3. Remove skin and purée with any equipment.

STORAGE: In refrigerator 2 days; freeze 2 months.

YIELD: 2 cups or 10 food cubes.

• **MICROWAVE METHOD**

This is the best way to cook eggplant. Leave whole and prick skin in several places. Cook uncovered on high for about 12 minutes. You'll know it's done when it looks like a collapsed balloon. Then the skin can be easily removed. Continue as directed.

GREENS

NUTRITION. The various leafy green vegetables are some of the best sources of all the vitamins and minerals, especially iron. They are also very inexpensive and easy to prepare as baby food. The various greens include

Spinach—potassium, vitamin A, magnesium

Kale—vitamins A and C, magnesium

Collards—vitamins A and C, riboflavin, niacin

Turnip greens—vitamins A, C, and B-complex, iron

Beet greens—vitamin A, iron, magnesium

Chard—iron, magnesium, potassium, sodium, vitamin A

Mustard greens—high iron, potassium, vitamins A and B-complex

Broccoli leaves—vitamins A and C, potassium

Dandelion greens—high iron, potassium, vitamins A and B-complex

Parsley—vitamins A and C

Watercress—vitamins A and C

INTRODUCE. Cooked greens can be given at eight months; raw, at nine months. If your baby has reactions of gas or rashes to any of these greens, postpone them a month. It is important to keep trying, because they are so nutritious. Parsley, watercress, and dandelion greens have a strong flavor, so introduce them in very small quantities, mixed with eggs, white sauce, or a favorite vegetable.

When your baby reaches the trying stage of eating paper, give him some large pieces of raw leafy greens, such as spinach or lettuce, to chew on. He may not actually eat any, but at least they are better than paper.

BUY. Choose greens that are fresh, young, tender, free

from blemishes, with a good green color. Beet greens and some chard will have a reddish green color. The spring months are the best time to buy young greens. Frozen greens are also available and can save preparation and cleaning time. Use the grade A for the most tender greens. *Do not buy* leaves with coarse, fibrous stems, yellow-green color, softness, or wilting. If greens show signs of insect damage, the insects may be hidden in the leaves and are very difficult to wash away.

STORE. Keep unwashed greens in plastic bags in the refrigerator for one to two days.

Cooked Leafy Greens

A 10-ounce package of frozen greens will yield 1¼ cups purée; use only 2 tablespoons liquid.

1 **pound fresh greens**
1 **tablespoon butter, margarine, or yogurt (optional)**
3 **tablespoons milk or fruit juice**

1. Wash the leaves thoroughly. Cut off any blemished areas. If the leaves have large or tough center stems, you may discard them without losing nutritional value. These stems will produce a coarser purée.
2. Steam most greens over boiling water for 5–15 minutes, depending on the thickness of the leaves. You may leave the cover off for the first few minutes for a milder flavor. Boil strongly flavored greens, such as dandelion, for 20 minutes in an uncovered pot.
3. Purée in a blender for the smoothest texture, adding the butter and milk. *Do not use cooking water.* In a food processor, purée the greens without adding liquid.

STORAGE: In refrigerator 2 days; freeze 2 months.

YIELD: 1¾ cups or 9 food cubes.

• **MICROWAVE METHOD**
Greens are better cooked uncovered because the flavor is

milder. Place in glass pie plate or shallow casserole. Do not add water. Cook 1 pound on high for 5½ minutes; ½ pound for 4 minutes. Continue as directed.

VARIATION

If your baby objects to cooked greens, try introducing them in small amounts in Microwave Meal-in-One Vegetable Soufflé (page 213) or one of the vegetable custard recipes (pages 214–216) (see also "Eggs," in Chapter 10).

Scrambled Raw Greens

When your baby is eating eggs, you can use them as a way of introducing raw greens. The main problem is the texture of the greens, since they tend to stick to the mouth and are difficult to swallow. Mixed with eggs, they go down quite easily. This can be a protein/vegetable serving.

> ¼   **cup raw greens (cooked can also be used)**
> 1   **egg**
> 1   **tablespoon milk**

1. Wash and prepare raw greens as for Cooked Leafy Greens.
2. Put egg, milk, and greens in food processor or blender (a small jar is perfect) and purée. The mixture will be bright green.
3. Scramble the egg mixture to a soft consistency.

STORAGE: In refrigerator 2 days; freeze 2 months.

YIELD: 2 servings or ½ cup.

VARIATION

Raw chopped greens may also be added to cereal, or mixed with cooked egg yolk. Chop the greens in a blender or food processor with a small amount of water. Mix in the greens and use a little liquid to thin the cereal or egg yolk. See also Jellied Vegetables (page 216), Vegetable Custard (page 214), and Vegetable/Egg Yolk Custard (page 215).

KOHLRABI

NUTRITION. Good source of vitamin C and potassium. This is a little-used vegetable that is part of the cabbage family, although the edible portion looks like a turnip. The tops may also be used as greens.

INTRODUCE. Cooked kohlrabi can be offered at nine months.

BUY. Choose small or medium-size roots with smooth surfaces and fresh tops. *Do not buy* large vegetables, because they will be more fibrous and tough or those with blemishes or cracks.

STORE. Kohlrabi should be kept, covered, in the refrigerator for up to one week.

Cooked Kohlrabi

1 **pound kohlrabi**
3 **tablespoons liquid (evaporated milk is good)**

1. Wash, remove skin, and cut into large pieces.
2. Steam over boiling water for 30–40 minutes. Or bake in covered medium-size dish or wrapped in aluminum foil for 1 hour at 325°F.
3. Purée with any equipment, adding liquid.

STORAGE: Refrigerate 2 days; freeze 2 months.

YIELD: 1½ cups or 8 food cubes.

• **MICROWAVE METHOD**
Place prepared kohlrabi in medium-size dish. Add ¼ cup water. Cover tightly and cook on high for 8–10 minutes. Let stand 3 minutes. Continue as directed.

LEGUMES: DRIED PEAS, BEANS, LENTILS

NUTRITION. The legumes (dried peas, beans, and lentils) are very economical sources of protein (incomplete), and contain high amounts of iron, phosphorus, calcium, magnesium, potassium, and the B-complex vitamins. They are also low in fat. Soybeans are a source of complete protein and are included in the "Protein Foods" chapter.

The various legumes include peas (green, split, black-eyed, cow, and yellow), beans (navy, kidney, pinto, lima), and lentils.

They are similar in nutrition and can be substituted for a serving of cereal grains. Cooked peas and beans are very thick and are good to combine with juicy fruits and vegetables. They can also be thinned with milk, to supplement their incomplete protein, or combined with a small amount of complementary or complete protein foods and served as a low-cost meat substitute. See "Inexpensive Protein," in Chapter 10 for specific recipes and combinations. Another means of supplementing their protein is to soak the dried legumes in skim milk instead of water, then cook them slowly in the milk. As you can see, they are a very good buy in terms of their nutritional cost.

INTRODUCE. Cooked legumes can be introduced at eight months. They can be served as a finger food if cooked until very soft.

BUY. Dried peas, beans, and lentils keep well and can be bought in large quantities. Canned cooked beans are also available in different varieties—baked beans, limas, or kidney beans—often with sauces. This is the most convenient way of using these beans because they require little, if any, cooking but they are much more expensive than preparing your own. For an older baby, they can be mashed directly from the can. Remember to read the labels—if they are packed in a salt brine, *drain the beans and do not use the liquid*. U.S. Grade B canned beans are adequate and economical.

STORE. Dried peas, beans, and lentils can be kept in tightly covered cans or plastic bags at cool room temperature for up to two years. Cooked purées will keep in the refrigerator for three days and can be frozen for one month.

COOKING. You may feel that dried peas, beans, and lentils require lengthy cooking time. They do, but little of your time and effort is involved. A time-saver is to cook a large quantity, then freeze them. If you have a good blender or food processor, you can also shorten the cooking time in half by first grating the dried legumes.

The packaged soup mixes of dried peas, beans, noodles, and vegetables are convenient and require a shorter cooking time. Remember to omit the seasoning packet and reduce the amount of cooking water to about half of that stated on the package; you are not preparing soup.

• STOVE-TOP METHOD

Soaking:
Rinse legumes briefly. Soak in water in stockpot overnight (about 3 cups water to 1 cup legumes). Or bring legumes to a boil, boil 2 minutes, remove from heat, and cover. Let legumes sit for 2 hours. Presoaking is unnecessary if you will be using a pressure cooker.

Cooking Times:
  Split peas, lentils, black-eyed peas or beans: 30 minutes

  Whole peas, lima beans: 1 hour

  Navy pea beans, Great Northern beans, garbonzo beans (chick-peas): 1½ hours

  Black beans, cranberry beans, kidney beans, pinto beans: 2 hours

• MICROWAVE METHOD

A microwave will cut the cooking time for legumes in half, which means you don't need to plan so far ahead. However, it still pays to presoak all legumes except lentils.

Soaking:
Place 1 cup of legumes in medium-size casserole with 2 cups of water. Cover tightly and cook on high for 15 minutes. Let stand for 5 minutes. Add 2 cups of very hot water, re-cover, and let stand for 1 hour.

To Cook 1 Cup:

Large presoaked beans: Add 3 cups of water to beans in medium-size dish. Cover tightly and cook on high for 35 minutes. Let stand for 20 minutes.

Small presoaked beans: Add 4 cups of water to beans in medium-size dish. Cover tightly and cook on high for 40 minutes. Let stand for 30 minutes.

Presoaked garbonzo beans (chick-peas): Add 4 cups of water to beans in medium-size dish. Cover tightly and cook on high for 35 minutes. Let stand for 30 minutes.

Lentils (do not need to be presoaked): Add 4 cups water to lentils in medium-size dish. Cover tightly and cook on high for 35 minutes.

Pea / Bean / Lentil Purée

If you are cooking beans or peas for the rest of your family, do not add salt until the last few minutes of cooking. If it is added at the start of cooking, the beans will take much longer to soften. For the same reason, do not add acid foods, such as tomatoes, until the end of cooking.

1 cup any legume (uncooked)
3 cups water or skim milk
1 tablespoon butter, margarine, or oil
¼ cup milk

1. Presoak legumes in stockpot in water, following one the methods described above.
2. Add butter to pot (to prevent foaming over). Simmer partly covered (also to prevent foaming over) until legumes are done, following the guidelines listed above. Skim off any skins that float to top of pot for the smoothest purée.
3. Purée with any equipment, adding milk.

STORAGE: In refrigerator 2–3 days; freeze 2 months.

YIELD: 2½ cups or 12 food cubes.

LETTUCE

NUTRITION. Romaine lettuce has fair amounts of vitamin A and iron. The iceberg variety has very little nutritional value.

INTRODUCE. Served cooked lettuce at seven months; raw, at nine months. As with the other green leafy vegetables, lettuce can be used as a substitute when your baby shows a desire for chewing paper.

BUY. Choose romaine or leaf lettuce that is dark green and crisp. *Do not buy* lettuce with considerable discoloration or decay of the outer leaves. Avoid wilted lettuce, which is a sign of overlong storage and lower nutritional value.

STORE. Lettuce will keep in a plastic bag in the refrigerator for two to three days.

USE. Lettuce can be used raw or cooked as a green leafy vegetable (see "Greens," in this chapter).

MUSHROOMS

NUTRITION. Mushrooms are very high in niacin and have fair amounts of other vitamins and minerals. They have a high liquid content and are good in combinations with other vegetables or meats.

INTRODUCE. Offer cooked only at nine months.

BUY. Pick young mushrooms that are small to medium. The caps should be either closed around the stem or slightly open with pink or light tan gills. The surface of the cap should be white, creamy, or light brown depending on the variety. Canned mushrooms are available; the "stems-and-pieces" style is less expensive. *Do not buy* mushrooms with wide-open caps, dark gills, or pitted and discolored caps. These are all signs of overripeness and decay.

STORE. Keep in plastic bag in the refrigerator for one to two days. They are very perishable, often expensive, but freeze well. So if you come across a sale, prepare a purée and freeze at once.

FINGER FOOD. This is one of the few vegetables that

are *not* a good finger food. The small pieces tend to be tough but slippery. So a baby may swallow the pieces whole and choke.

Cooked Mushrooms

1   **pound fresh mushrooms**
1   **tablespoon butter, margarine, or oil (optional)**
2   **tablespoons wheat germ, rice, or instant cereal**

1. Prepare mushrooms by washing thoroughly. Leave the stems, but cut off tough ends.
2. Steam the caps and stems in the top of a double boiler over boiling water for 5–10 minutes (do not use a steamer or you will lose the juice). Or sauté in a medium-size frying pan with the butter for 5–10 minutes. Or bake in covered dish or wrapped in aluminum foil for 15 minutes at 325°F.
3. Purée mushrooms and their juice with blender or food processor for the smoothest texture. Add wheat germ. A food mill may also be used. Add the liquid and thickener after putting mushrooms through the food mill.

STORAGE: In refrigerator 2 days; freeze 2 months.

YIELD: 2½ cups or 12 food cubes.

- **MICROWAVE METHOD**
Place prepared mushrooms in medium-size dish. Add 2 tablespoons water and cover tightly. Cook on high for 4 minutes. Let stand 3 minutes. Continue as directed.

OKRA

NUTRITION. Okra has only fair amounts of vitamins and minerals.

INTRODUCE. Serve cooked only at eight months.

BUY. Fresh okra is the immature seedpod of the okra

plant and should be small, no more than 4 inches long. On tender pods, the tips will bend with a slight pressure. They should have a bright color and be free from blemishes. Frozen okra can also be used. Canned okra is usually pickled and salted and is not suitable for a baby. *Do not buy* fibrous pods with stiff tips, hard bodies, or pale, faded green color.

STORE. Fresh okra should be kept covered in the refrigerator for three to five days.

Cooked Okra

1 pound okra

1. Wash and scrub the pods thoroughly. Cut off the stem end. If the pods are large, cut them in half. Do not peel.
2. Steam okra over boiling water for 15–20 minutes or just until tender (when okra is overcooked, it will become gummy). Or bake in covered dish or wrapped in aluminum foil for 30 minutes at 325°F.
3. Purée with any equipment.

STORAGE: In refrigerator 2 days; freeze 2 months.

YIELD: 1½ cups or 8 food cubes.

• **MICROWAVE METHOD**
Place prepared okra in medium-size dish with 2 tablespoon of water. Cover tightly and cook on high for 6–7 minutes. Let stand 3 minutes. Continue as directed.

VARIATION

Okra produces a thin purée, so it is good combined with other vegetables such as carrots or in stews.

ONIONS, LEEKS

NUTRITION. Onions and leeks contain fair amounts of many nutrients. They have a high liquid content and are good to combine with less juicy vegetables or stews.

INTRODUCE. Offer cooked only at nine months. If you want to purée a family dish that contains a small amount of onions for flavoring and the other ingredients have been introduced, you can try it as early as seven or eight months.

BUY. Choose onions that are firm and dry. They should be fairly free of green sunburn spots or blemishes. Bermuda and Spanish onions are the sweetest and mildest flavored. Leeks should have crisp green tops. Canned onions are usually packed in a salt brine and should not be used. *Do not buy* vegetables that are wet, with soft spots or necks. These are either immature or decayed inside. Also avoid onions with thick, hollow, woody centers in the neck, or with fresh sprouts.

STORE. Onions can be kept at cool room temperature for two to three months. They should either be spread out or piled in open mesh containers. Moisture or high temperature will cause sprouting or decay.

Cooked Onions / Leeks

Hold onions under running water when preparing them to prevent your eyes from watering.

> **1 pound onions/leeks**
> **2 tablespoons wheat germ, cooked rice, or instant cereal**

1. Wash and remove outer peel and any blemishes.
2. Steam whole onions over boiling water for 30–40 minutes; sliced, for 10 minutes. Or bake at 325° in covered dish or wrapped in aluminum foil, whole for 30 minutes; sliced, for 10 minutes. (Overcooking will produce a strong flavor.)
3. Purée with any equipment. Add wheat germ.

STORAGE: In refrigerator 2 days; freeze 2 months.

YIELD: 2 cups or 10 food cubes.

• **MICROWAVE METHOD**
Cut onions into quarters if large. Do not add water. Place in

medium-size dish and cover tightly. Cook on high 5–6 minutes. Let stand 5 minutes. Continue as directed.

PARSNIPS

NUTRITION. Good source of carbohydrates and potassium, fair amounts of other minerals and B vitamins. This often-neglected vegetable has a mild, sweet flavor.

INTRODUCE. Cooked parsnips can be given at eight months.

BUY. Choose parsnips that are small to medium size, well formed, smooth, firm, and free from major blemishes. They look like white carrots and are sweetest during late winter. *Do not buy* large parsnips, which will have tough, woody centers, or badly wilted or flabby ones, which will be tough and fibrous.

STORE. Parsnips can be kept covered in the refrigerator for up to one week.

Parsnip Purée

1 **pound (4 medium) parsnips, well scrubbed**
¼ **cup liquid (evaporated milk or apple juice is good)**

1. Boil whole parsnips in medium-size saucepan in water to cover for 10–20 minutes. Or bake in covered medium-size dish or wrapped in aluminum foil at 325°F for 45 minutes.
2. Plunge in cold water and rub off skins.
3. Purée with any equipment, adding liquid.

STORAGE: Refrigerate 2 days; freeze 2 months.

YIELD: 2 cups or 10 food cubes.

- **MICROWAVE METHOD**

Cut parsnips into quarters. Place in medium-size dish and add ¼ cup water. Cover tightly. Cook on high 8–9 minutes. Let stand 5 minutes. Continue as directed.

VARIATION

Baked Apple/Parsnips. Cut up ½ pound pared parsnips; combine with 1 cup chopped raw apples or applesauce in medium-size dish. Cover tightly. Cook in microwave on high 4–5 minutes. Let stand 5 minutes. Purée and thin with liquid (water, milk, juice) as necessary. Continue as directed.

PEANUTS AND NUTS

NUTRITION. Peanuts and nuts are excellent sources of protein (incomplete), fat, linoleic acid (essential fatty acid), magnesium, phosphorus, niacin, folacin, and vitamin E. They also have fair amounts of other minerals and the other B vitamins. As with legumes, the protein of nuts is improved when it is combined at the same meal with an animal protein. Milk is the most practical source and can be used as a thinner in preparing the nut butter.

INTRODUCE. Offer at eight to nine months. Peanut butter is a nutritious staple for many toddlers; you might think twice about giving it to your baby, but properly thinned, he will love it! *Never give any child peanut butter on a spoon. A thick glob can cause choking.*

BUY. There are many commercial peanut butters on the market, so read the labels carefully to find one with no additives, and low in sugar and salt. It is amazing what can be added to such a simple food—monoglycerides and diglycerides, hydrogenated vegetable oil, dextrose, sugar, and salt. Avoid the peanut "spreads," which contain a lower amount of peanuts. All the commercial peanut butters will require thinning with milk or they will never get past the roof of your baby's mouth. The consistency is probably the major reason we never think of feeding peanut butter to babies.

If you live near a health food store, you will be able to buy raw unsalted nut butters that require little, if any, thinning; however, they are quite expensive. You will find it most nutritious and economical to make your own peanut butter with raw or roasted peanuts. You must use a good blender, and a small jar is ideal. A food processor is even easier and faster. You can make a family-size amount with a very smooth texture. Your baby will prefer both the consistency and the taste of homemade peanut butter. *Do not buy* nuts that are preserved with BHT, or are dry roasted.

STORE. Keep unopened commercial peanut butter for nine months at cool room temperature; opened peanut butter for up to 6 months in the refrigerator. Homemade peanut butters do not have preservatives and will not keep as long. These may be kept for two months in the refrigerator. If you thin with milk, only store for one to two weeks. Whole peanuts should be kept in a tightly covered can in the refrigerator for up to four months. These butters may also be frozen for four to six months.

Note: Nuts can be frozen virtually forever, and can be used without thawing.

Peanut / Nut Butter

> 1   **cup peanuts or nuts (raw or roasted)**
> 2–3 **tablespoons milk or safflower, corn, or olive oil**

1. If you must use roasted salted peanuts, rinse them to remove the salt.
2. Purée the nuts with the milk in the blender at a medium speed. If you do not use a small jar, you must stop and push the mixture down as it blends. In a food processor, finely chop the nuts, then add liquid as necessary.

STORAGE: See "Peanuts and Nuts," (page 199).

YIELD: ¾ cup.

VARIATIONS

Try Peanut Butter Custard (page 264) and Peanut Butter Cookies (page 295).

PEAS

NUTRITION. Peas supply good amounts of iron, B vitamins, especially niacin, and carbohydrates.

INTRODUCE. Serve cooked peas at six months.

BUY. Choose pea pods that are crisp, green, and unspotted, with a velvety surface and well filled with peas. *Do not buy* pods that are swollen, light in color, or spotted with gray. These will contain tough and poorly flavored peas. Immature peas will have dark green, or wilted flat pods. Wilting or flabbiness is also a sign of overlong storage. Canned and frozen peas are available in several sizes and grades. Grade A or fancy peas will have the tenderest skins and sweetest taste. These will produce the smoothest purée. Grade B or extra standard peas will be more mealy, but have a good flavor. Grace C should not be used for baby food. Canned peas that have been graded for size will be more expensive, but the smaller the peas, the more tender they will be. Tenderness is important since peas are one of the first vegetables introduced.

STORE. Keep fresh pea pods, covered, in refrigerator for one to two days. Like corn, peas will lose sweetness and tenderness as they are stored. Remove from pods just before using.

Pea Purée

> 2 **pounds peas (in pods)—about 2½ cups shelled**
> 3–4 **tablespoons liquid (milk or cooking water)**

1. Just before cooking, shell peas and place in steamer basket. Steam over boiling water for 10–12 minutes.
2. For the smoothest purée, use food mill or strainer, which will also remove the skins. Add liquid. A blender or food processor will prepare a coarser purée.

STORAGE: In refrigerator 2 days; freeze 2 months.

YIELD: 2 cups or 10 food cubes.

- **MICROWAVE METHOD**

Place shelled peas in medium-size bowl and add ¼ cup water. Cover tightly and cook on high for 9–10 minutes. Let stand 5 minutes. Continue as directed.

PEPPERS

NUTRITION. Green peppers are very high vitamin C and are fair in other vitamins and minerals. Sweet red peppers are high in vitamin A. They have a high liquid content and are good combined with a thicker vegetable or in stews.

INTRODUCE. Cooked peppers can be given at eight months; raw, at ten months. Do not give a baby hot peppers.

BUY. Pick either green or red sweet peppers that are shiny, have a heavyweight, and have firm walls or sides. *Do not buy* those that have thin walls, are lightweight, and are wilted or flabby. (The vitamin C will have been reduced due to overlong or improper storage.) Also avoid peppers with soft watery spots which are signs of decay.

STORE. Washed and covered peppers can be kept in the refrigerator for three to five days.

Cooked Peppers

Peppers have a high juice content and are good combined with thick vegetables such as potatoes or in stew. Allow about 10 minutes of cooking when stewing or baking with other foods.

- **MICROWAVE METHOD**

Place peppers in dish and cover tightly. Do not add water. For 1 pound, cook on high for 6–8 minutes. Let stand 3 minutes. Remove stem and seeds.

Raw Pepper

Since the main value of peppers is vitamin C, and this vitamin is destroyed by heat, peppers are best used raw.

1. Prepare by removing stem, seeds, and membranes.
2. Purée in blender or food processor in equal amounts with other raw, hard vegetables such as carrots.

POTATOES, WHITE

NUTRITION. High carbohydrates and potassium, good source of vitamin C if cooked in skins.

INTRODUCE. Cooked potatoes can be offered at seven months.

BUY. Choose a variety of potatoes, depending on your cooking method. The new potatoes are good for boiling and should not be baked. They are available in late winter and early spring. They should be well shaped, firm, and without green sunburn discoloration. Some amount of skinned surface is normal. General-purpose potatoes are better for boiling but can be baked. Baking potatoes are used for baking in the skin. These types of potato are available year-round and should be firm, well shaped, and free from blemishes, sunburn, and decay spots. *Do not buy* potatoes with large cuts or bruises that must be cut away or those with green sunburn spots. Sprouted and shriveled potatoes have been kept too long in storage and they are lower in nutritional value.

Canned and frozen potatoes are available in many styles. Avoid those canned styles that are packed in a salt brine. Dehydrated or "instant" potatoes can be used as an instant food, but they have large amounts of additives and should not be served often. Potatoes are a very thick, bland vegetable and are good in combination with leafy greens.

STORE. Unwashed potatoes, kept in a dark dry place with good ventilation and a temperature of 45° to 50°F will last for two months. Exposure to light will cause greening or lower eating quality. High temperatures will speed sprouting and shriveling. Potatoes stored at room temperature should be used within one to two weeks.

Refrigeration can stretch storage life, but will change the starch to sugar. Leave potato at room temperature for a day or two, and the sugar will reconvert to starch. (Also, don't store potatoes and onions next to each other; they'll both rot faster!)

Mashed Potatoes

1   **pound (2 large) potatoes**
½   **cup liquid (milk is good)**
1   **tablespoon butter or margarine**

1. Wash well and scrub with brush. Remove eyes and blemishes. Do not peel.
2. Place potatoes in medium-size saucepan and cover with water. Cover pot, bring to boil, and boil for 20–40 minutes. Or steam over boiling water for 30–45 minutes. Or bake in the skin or wrapped in aluminum foil for 40–60 minutes at 400°F.
3. Rub off skin (boiled) or scoop out flesh (baked). Purée with a potato masher, fork, strainer, food mill, or mixer. Add liquid and butter. *Do not* mash in blender. In a food processor, use the shredding disk, then the metal blade (if necessary) for a smoother purée. *Do not overprocess.*

STORAGE: In refrigerator 3–4 days; freeze 2 months.

YIELD: 2 cups or 10 food cubes.

• MICROWAVE METHOD
This is really a time-saver. For 1 potato: Pierce prepared potato and wrap in plastic wrap. Or place pierced potato on plate and cover with plastic wrap. Do not add water. Cook on high for 6–8 minutes. Turn over halfway through. Let stand 5 minutes. (Increase cooking time by 2 minutes for each additional 8-ounce potato.) Continue as directed.

VARIATION

Add a little grated cheese for flavoring.

Stewed Apples and Potatoes

1½ **pounds (6 medium) potatoes, peeled**
1 **cup milk**
2 **medium cooking apples, cored, peeled, diced**

1. Prepare potatoes as for Mashed Potatoes. Cut potatoes into thin slices or chop.
2. Place potatoes and milk in medium-size saucepan. Bring to a boil, cover, and simmer for 20 minutes.
3. Add apples, re-cover pot, and cook for another 15 minutes. Add more milk if the mixture is very thick.
4. Purée with any equipment. It should be soft enough for even a fork or spoon.
5. To serve as a family dish, just add a little salt and pepper.

STORAGE: In refrigerator 3–4 days; freeze 2 months.

YIELD: 4 cups or 20 food cubes.

• **MICROWAVE METHOD**
Prepare potatoes and put in medium-size dish. Add ¼ cup water and cover tightly. Cook on high for 8–10 minutes. Add apples and milk. Re-cover and cook on medium for 8–10 minutes. Let stand 5 minutes. Continue as directed.

SUMMER SQUASH

NUTRITION. High in potassium, good amounts of vitamins A and C, and niacin.

INTRODUCE. Offer cooked only at seven months. This is a juice vegetable, so it is good combined with more solid vegetables or in stews.

BUY. Pick any of the varieties—yellow are crookneck, straightneck, greenish-white patty pan, or green zucchini, Italian marrow. A new variety is mirliton, or chayote, which has an applelike flavor. Look for squashes that are well developed, firm, with glossy skin. *Do not buy* overmature or aged squashes, which have dull skins and a hard surface. These will have enlarged seeds and dry, stringy flesh.

Canned and frozen summer squash is available and useful.

STORE. Keep summer squash covered in the refrigerator for three to five days.

Cooked Summer Squash

1 **pound summer squash**
2 **tablespoons wheat germ (optional)**
2 **teaspoons butter, margarine, or oil (optional)**

1. Wash well, remove a slice from both ends. For the smoothest purée, cut squash in half lengthwise and remove seeds.
2. Steam over boiling water 15–20 minutes. Or bake in covered dish or wrapped in aluminum foil for 25–30 minutes at 325°F.
3. Purée with any equipment. A strainer or food mill will also remove the seeds and skin. Wheat germ may be added as a fortifier or thickener. Butter may be added for flavor, if your doctor approves.

STORAGE: In refrigerator 2 days; freeze 2 months.

YIELD: 1½ cups purée or 8 food cubes.

• **MICROWAVE METHOD**
Place prepared squash in medium-size bowl. Add 2 tablespoons water. Cover tightly and cook on high for 6–7 minutes. Let stand 3 minutes. Continue as directed.

SQUASH, WINTER

NUTRITION. The winter squashes are high in carbohydrates, potassium, and vitamin A. They also contain some iron, magnesium, and riboflavin.

INTRODUCE. Serve cooked only at six months.

BUY. Choose any variety that is in season. Acorn is green and available all year. Other varieties are butternut, Hubbard, delicious, and banana, which are in season from early fall to late winter. Buy squashes that have hard, tough rinds and are heavy for their size. Variations in skin color do not affect the flavor. *Do not buy* squashes with cuts, sunken spots, or mold on the rind; these are signs of decay. A tender or soft rind indicates immaturity and poor eating quality.

STORE. Winter squashes can be kept at cool room temperature (60° or 70°F) for several months. Keep them at warmer room temperature for only one to two weeks. Do not store them in the refrigerator.

INSTANT USE. Canned and frozen squash is already cooked and mashed. The only preparation might be the addition of a little milk.

Cooked Winter Squash

To shorten the baking time, cut squash in half and place cut side down on baking sheet or on aluminum foil. Or cut up squash and bake in covered dish or wrapped in aluminum foil.

> 1 **pound (1 medium) squash**
> 1 **tablespoon milk (optional)**
> 1 **tablespoon butter or margarine (optional)**
> 2 **teaspoons brown sugar (optional)**

1. Wash well. Cut acorn squash in half; other varieties, cut in large pieces. Remove seeds and stringy centers. Do not remove skin.
2. Steam over boiling water for 25–30 minutes. Or bake in moderate (325°F) oven for 45–55 minutes.
3. Scoop the flesh out of the skin and purée with any equipment. Add milk for a thinner purée. Add butter or brown sugar for a family dish.

STORAGE: Refrigerate 2 days; freeze 2 months.

YIELD: 1 cup purée or 5 food cubes.

• MICROWAVE METHOD
Place prepared squash in medium-size dish and add ¼ cup water. Cover tightly and cook on high for 8–9 minutes. Let stand 3 minutes. Continue as directed.

SWEET POTATOES, YAMS

NUTRITION. Sweet potatoes and yams are high in carbohydrates and vitamin A. They contain fair amounts of other vitamins and minerals.

INTRODUCE. Offer cooked only at seven months.

BUY. Choose well-shaped, firm sweet potatoes with smooth, bright orange skins that are free from signs of decay. Yams have white to reddish skins and are more moist when cooked. However, they are a tropical vegetable and are difficult to find fresh. Frozen yams and sweet potatoes are available in several styles, including cooked and mashed. Canned sweet potatoes should be bought in a vacuum pack without any syrup. The canned solid pack may have a small amount of liquid. *Do not buy* sweet potatoes with worm holes, cuts, or any injury that penetrates the skin. These defects will increase the spoilage. Even if you cut away the decayed spot, the rest of the flesh will have a bad taste. Sweet potatoes decay easily, so look for such signs as wet, soft spots; discolored or shriveled ends; or sunken, discolored spots on the sides.

STORE. Sweet potatoes can be kept at cool room temperature (60° to 70°F) for a month or two. Keep them for only one week at warmer room temperature. Never store them in the refrigerator.

INSTANT USE. Some styles of canned and frozen sweet potatoes are already cooked and mashed. It is only necessary to thin with milk.

Cooked Sweet Potatoes / Yams

1	**pound (2 large) sweet potatoes/yams**
⅓–½	**cup liquid (milk, orange juice, or apple juice is good)**
1	**tablespoon butter or margarine (optional)**

1. Scrub and wash potatoes. Trim roots and any bad spots. Do not peel.
2. Cut in pieces and steam over boiling water for 30–35

minutes. Or pierce skin and bake whole for 40 minutes at 400°F or for 60 minutes at 350°F.

3. Scoop potato flesh out of skins and mash with food mill, mixer, or strainer, adding liquid, then butter. *Do not use* blender. In a food processor, use the shredding disk and then the metal blade for a smoother purée if necessary. *Do not overmix.*

STORAGE: In refrigerator 3–4 days; freeze 2 months.

YIELD: 1½ cups purée or 8 food cubes.

• MICROWAVE METHOD
Pierce each potato and wrap in plastic wrap. Or place potatoes on plate and cover tightly. Do not add water. Cook on high for 6–8 minutes. Turn potatoes over halfway through the cooking time. Let stand 5 minutes. Continue as directed.

Baked Sweet Potatoes and Apples

This is a good family dish.

    1   cup cooked sweet potatoes
    ½   pound apples or 1 cup applesauce
    ¼   cup liquid (milk or fruit juice)

1. Preheat oven to 350°F.
2. Remove skin and slice sweet potatoes. Pare and core apples and then slice.
3. Mix sweet potatoes and apples in buttered medium-size baking dish and pour liquid over. Bake, covered, for 30 minutes.
4. To purée, mash with fork.

STORAGE: In refrigerator 3–4 days; freeze 2 months.

YIELD: 2 cups or 10 food cubes.

• MICROWAVE METHOD
Place potato and apple mixture in medium-size dish. Cover

tightly and cook on high for 4–5 minutes. Let stand 5 minutes. Continue as directed.

TURNIPS, RUTABAGAS

NUTRITION. Fair amounts of carbohydrates, vitamins, and minerals.

INTRODUCE. Offer cooked only at eight months.

BUY. Turnips (white flesh) and rutabagas (yellow flesh) are available year round. Look for small or medium-size firm vegetables that are heavy for their size. If the tops are attached on turnips, they should be green and fresh. These greens are high in nutritional value and should be used. (See "Greens," in this chapter). *Do not buy* large vegetables, which tend to be fibrous and tough, or those with skin punctures or signs of decay. Frozen turnips and rutabagas are available and convenient.

STORE. Turnips can be kept at cool room temperature (60° to 70°F) for up to five months. Keep them only one week at warmer room temperature.

Cooked Turnips / Rutabagas

1 **pound (2–3 medium) turnips/rutabagas**
2 **tablespoons evaporated milk**
1 **tablespoon butter or margarine (optional)**

1. Wash and remove skin. Cut into large pieces.
2. Steam over boiling water for 20–30 minutes. Or bake for 35–45 minutes at 350°F.
3. Purée with any equipment, adding milk. Butter may be added for flavor.

YIELD: 2 cups purée or 10 food cubes.

• **MICROWAVE METHOD**

Place prepared vegetable in medium-size dish. Add ¼ cup water. Cover tightly. Cook on high for 8–10 minutes. Let stand 3 minutes. Continue as directed.

TOMATOES

NUTRITION. Tomatoes contain good amounts of vitamins A and K. They contain about half as much vitamin C as oranges and can be used as a substitute, if your baby is allergic to orange juice. Remember to double the serving. Their high juice content makes tomatoes a good vegetable to combine with other foods as a thinner. (Tomatoes are actually a fruit, though we use them as a vegetable.)

INTRODUCE. Cooked tomatoes can be offered at six months; raw, at nine months.

BUY. Tomatoes are either picked unripe or ripe; the latter will have better flavor and more nutrition. They are most plentiful from July to October. Look for tomatoes that are smooth, well formed, and reasonably free from blemishes. Marks around the top of a ripe tomato are harmless and sometimes indicate excellent flavor. Fully ripe tomatoes should yield to slight pressure and should have a rich red color. Underripe tomatoes will be hard and have a pink to light red color. *Do not buy* overripe and bruised tomatoes, those with green or yellow areas, or those with deep growth cracks near the stem scar. Also avoid decayed tomatoes with soft, water-soaked spots, depressed areas, or surface mold.

STORE. Ripe tomatoes will keep in the refrigerator for several days. Ripen tomatoes at room temperature for three to five days. Do not place them in the sun. Greenish or very hard tomatoes can be kept for several weeks at around 50°F.

INSTANT USE. Both canned and raw tomatoes are good instant foods. With raw tomatoes, cut them in half, remove the seeds, and scrape out the flesh. Buy canned tomatoes that are packed without added salt or preservatives *Do not give canned tomato purée or paste to a baby, as these are concentrates.*

FINGER FOOD. Small pieces of raw, peeled, and seeded tomato are juicy and nutritious.

Cooked Tomatoes

An easy way to peel tomatoes is to dip them briefly in boiling water and then plunge them in cold water. The skins should then slip off.

> 1 **pound (4–5 medium or 2 large) tomatoes**
> 3 **tablespoons wheat germ or instant cereal or 2 tablespoons whole wheat flour or cooked rice or cereal**

1. Wash tomatoes. If a blender or fork will be used, remove the seeds and skins. However, a strainer or food mill will remove the skins and seeds. This seems the easier preparation.
2. Steam over boiling water for 5 minutes in a pot with a tightly fitting lid or in the top of a double boiler. Or bake in a covered dish or wrapped in aluminum foil for 8 minutes at 325°F. (Do not use a steamer/blancher or you will lose the juice.)
3. Purée with fork, strainer, food mill, food processor, or blender, depending on your preparation and whether you want to remove skins. Add thickener. (If flour is used, heat until thickened. If rice is added, purée with the tomatoes.)

STORAGE: In refrigerator 3 days; or freeze up to 1 year.

YIELD: 1½ cups or 8 food cubes.

- **MICROWAVE METHOD**

Core tomatoes, prick skin, and place in medium-size dish. Do not add water. Cover tightly and cook on high for 3–4 minutes. When cool, the skins should be easy to remove. Continue as directed.

Raw Tomatoes

This is very economical in season and very nutritious, because all the vitamin C is preserved.

> 1 **pound (4–5) ripe tomatoes**
> 3 **tablespoons wheat germ or 2 tablespoons rice or cereal**

1. Prepare as directed in Cooked Tomatoes.
2. Purée tomatoes as directed in Cooked Tomatoes. Add thickener (do not use flour). You can also freeze the purée without thickening, then use the individual food cubes as a thinner for meats, etc.

STORAGE: In refrigerator for up to 2 days. Or freeze in food cubes for up to 1 year.

YIELD: 1½ cups or 8 food cubes.

GENERAL VEGETABLE RECIPES

The easiest way to prepare vegetables is to serve them plain or in combinations. For variety, with strong-tasting vegetables or those with consistency problems, such as greens, you may do a little extra work and use one of the following recipes for variation. Where an egg or cereal is used, remember to increase the serving so that it counts as an all-in-one meal of vegetable, protein, and/or cereal. These recipes can be prepared for the rest of the family and used as a vegetable dish.

Good vegetables to prepare this way are asparagus, broccoli, carrots, cauliflower, and leafy greens.

Microwave Meal-in-One
Vegetable Soufflé

1½	pounds fresh (or 2 10-ounce packages frozen) mixed vegetables
¼	cup butter or margarine
2	cups cooked rice
2	cups shredded cheese
⅔	cup milk
4	large eggs, beaten
1	teaspoon salt
½	teaspoon nutmeg

1. Prepare and cook each vegetable according to individual recipe. Drain and chop if necessary. Place warm vegetables in medium-size glass casserole.

2. Stir in butter until melted. Add rice and cheese.
3. Combine milk and eggs in medium-size bowl, blend in seasonings. Stir into vegetable mixture until well blended. Cover tightly.
4. Microwave on medium for 25 minutes or until knife inserted near center comes out clean. Let stand, covered, 5 minutes.
5. Serve at once for best texture. For baby, purée if necessary.

STORAGE: In refrigerator for 1–2 days. The texture may not be the same, but your baby won't know the difference. Do not freeze.

YIELD: 6–8 adult servings.

Vegetable Custard

The Medium White Sauce can be substituted for step 2.

1 **teaspoon butter or margarine**	**or**
1 **teaspoon whole wheat**	**⅓ cup**
or enriched flour	**Medium**
¼ **cup hot milk**	**White**
1 **tablespoon nonfat dry milk**	**Sauce**
1 **large egg, beaten**	
½ **cup cooked, mashed vegetables**	

1. Preheat oven to 350°F. Grease 2 custard cups.
2. Melt butter in medium-size saucepan over medium heat. Gradually add hot milk and nonfat dry milk. Cook and stir until thickened.
3. Stir a small amount of hot sauce into egg in small-size bowl, then mix egg into rest of sauce. Add mashed vegetables.
4. Pour mixture into custard cups. Place the cups in a pan of hot water that comes up to level of mixture. Bake 30 minutes or until a knife inserted in the center comes out clean.

STORAGE: Covered in the refrigerator for up to 3 days. Do not freeze.

YIELD: 2–3 baby servings.

• **MICROWAVE METHOD**
See Microwave Custard (page 216).

<u>**VARIATION**</u>

Easy Vegetable Custard. Substitute for the white sauce any of the following: ¼ cup milk, ¼ cup cooking or canning liquid plus 2 tablespoons nonfat dry milk, or ¼ cup fruit juice. Skip step 2. Continue as directed.

Vegetable / Egg Yolk Custard

This is a good supper dish that counts as a serving of vegetables and egg yolk, if you double the amount given. You can make this as soon as your baby had been introduced to egg yolk, and it is also very useful if he shows an allergy to egg whites.

> ¼ **cup cooked vegetable purée (asparagus, broccoli, carrots, leafy greens, peas, and sweet potatoes are good)**
>   1 **large egg yolk, beaten**
> ¼ **cup whole milk**
> ½ **teaspoon brown sugar**

1. Preheat oven to 350°F. Grease 2 custard cups.
2. Blend together in medium-size bowl vegetable purée, egg yolk, milk, and brown sugar.
3. Pour into custard cups. Place the cups in a pan of hot water that comes up to level of mixture. Bake for 30 minutes or until a knife inserted in center comes out clean. (The cups may also be placed in a saucepan with 1 inch of simmering water for 10 minutes.

STORAGE: In refrigerator for up to 3 days. Do not freeze.

YIELD: 2 servings.

• **MICROWAVE METHOD**
See Microwave Custard (page 216).

Microwave Custard

This is very fast and convenient because there's no need for a hot water bath.

1. Beat all ingredients for either Vegetable Custard or Vegetable/Egg Yolk Custard together in a medium-size bowl.
2. Cook on high, uncovered, for 30 seconds or until hot.
3. Stir well. Pour into 2 greased custard cups.
4. Cook on medium, uncovered, for 5–6 minutes. (Center may still jiggle, but will set on standing.)
5. Let stand 20 minutes.

Jellied Vegetables / Fruit

You can combine almost any food or raw grated vegetable or fruit with gelatin to improve the "swallowability" or to add variety. It is an especially good way to serve leafy green vegetables, raw carrots, and raw beets, and is very easy to make with a blender.

½ **envelope plain gelatin (the dessert gelatins can also be used, but they contain sugar and preservatives)**
½ **cup boiling water or vegetable cooking water**
⅓ **cup vegetable or fruit juice, or cold water**
1 **cup cubed vegetables or fruit or ¾ cup purée vegetables or fruit**

1. Dissolve gelatin in boiling water in medium-size bowl.
2. In blender or food processor, combine fruit juice with the vegetables until they are finely puréed. Or finely grate raw vegetables.
3. Drain the vegetables and add ⅓ cup of the liquid to the gelatin mixture. If completely puréed, add purée at this point. Chill until the mixture is very thick (about ½ hour).
4. Fold in the vegetables. Pour into 2–3 cup mold and chill until firm.

STORAGE: Covered in refrigerator for up to 5 days. Do not freeze.

YIELD: 1½–1¾ cups, or 8–9 servings.

Medium White Sauce

This sauce can be used to improve the texture of leafy green vegetables or in custards and soufflés.

> 1½   **tablespoons butter, margarine, or vegetable oil**
>   2   **tablespoons whole wheat or enriched flour°**
>   1   **cup hot milk**
>   ⅓   **cup nonfat dry milk (optional)**

1. Heat butter in small-size saucepan over medium heat.
2. Blend in flour until smooth. Gradually add hot milk and stir until blended and thickened. Add dry milk if desired.

STORAGE: In refrigerator for up to 3 days.

YIELD: 1 cup.

°*Note:* Instant white sauce can be made by substituting 4 tablespoons dry infant cereal for the flour. You can mix it with oil without heating.

10

Protein Foods

At least two servings of a good source of complete protein should be included in your baby's daily diet. These proteins also supply some vitamins and minerals, especially iron, that are lacking in milk. Included in this group are meats (beef, lamb, veal, pork), organ meats (liver, kidney, brains, sweetbreads), poultry, fish, and eggs. Soybeans are also a good source of high-quality protein. Some of these protein foods are less expensive than others and some are easier to prepare as baby food. However, as long as you balance your selection, you can count any of these foods as an equal serving of a protein food.

MEATS: BEEF, LAMB, VEAL, PORK

NUTRITION. Meat is one of the essentials in your baby's diet. Veal is meat from young cattle. It is grayish pink with very little fat. Beef comes from mature cattle, lamb from young sheep, and pork from young hogs. The different meats, or cuts of meat, contain nearly the same high amount of complete protein. Meat is especially valuable as a source of iron, with beef and veal supplying the highest amounts.

INTRODUCE. When your baby is seven to eight months old you can introduce lean meat purées of veal, beef, and lamb. Pork and ham are usually given a month later. After meat is introduced, your baby should be eating several servings weekly.

BUY. Because meat is probably the most expensive but necessary food that you will feed your baby, it is important to know how to get the best value for your money. According to law, all meats and meat products that are shipped between states must be inspected for wholesomeness and proper labeling and to make certain the meat has not been adulterated or contaminated. Each state must supply the same inspection service for meat sold only within that state. The inspection seal is a circle with the words *U.S. Inspected and Passed by Department of Agriculture* inside. Only buy meat that carries the seal (see "U.S. Grades," in Chapter 2).

The government has also published a handy table (see page 220) so that you can easily compare the serving cost of different meats and cuts of meat at various prices. Inflation keeps raising the price per pound, but you can easily adjust this table. For example, if you are considering paying $2.29 a pound for round steak, you can find out the cost per serving by adding $0.40 (at $1.39 a pound) to $0.25 (at $0.89 a pound). The cost per serving is now $0.65.

Cost per Serving of Red Meat and Poultry

RETAIL CUT		PRICE PER POUND (IN DOLLARS)			
		0.69	0.79	0.89	0.99
	SERVINGS PER POUND	COST PER SERVING (IN CENTS)			
BEEF					
Sirloin steak	2½	28	32	36	40
Porterhouse, T-bone, rib steak	2	35	40	45	50
Round steak	3½	20	23	25	28
Chuck roast, bone-in	2	35	40	45	50
Rib roast					
boneless	2½	28	32	36	40
bone-in	2	35	40	45	50
Rump, sirloin roast	3	23	26	30	33
Ground beef	4	17	20	22	25
Short ribs	2	35	40	45	50
Heart, liver, kidney	5	14	16	18	20
Frankfurters	4	17	20	22	25
Stew meat, boneless	5	14	16	18	20
LAMB					
Loin, rib, shoulder, chops	3	23	26	30	33
Breast, shank	2	35	40	45	50
Shoulder roast	2½	28	32	36	40
Leg of lamb	3	23	26	30	33
PORK—FRESH					
Center cut or rib chops	4	17	20	22	25
Loin or rib roast	2½	28	32	36	40
Boston butt—bone-in	3	23	26	30	33
Blade steak	3	23	26	30	33
Spare ribs	1⅓	52	59	67	74
PORK—CURED					
Picnic—bone-in	2	35	40	45	50
Ham—fully cooked					
bone-in	3½	20	23	25	28
boneless and canned	5	14	16	18	20
shankless	4¼	16	19	21	23
center slice	5	14	16	18	20
POULTRY					
Broiler, ready to cook	1⅓	52	59	67	74
legs, thighs	3	23	26	30	33
breasts	4	17	20	22	25
Turkey, ready to cook					
under 12 lb.	1	69	79	89	99
12 lb. and over	1⅓	52	69	67	74

Cost per Serving of Red Meat and Poultry

| \multicolumn{10}{c}{PRICE PER POUND (IN DOLLARS)} |
1.09	1.19	1.29	1.39	1.49	1.59	1.69	1.79	1.89	1.99
\multicolumn{10}{c}{COST PER SERVING (IN CENTS)}
44	48	52	56	60	64	68	72	76	80
55	60	65	70	75	80	85	90	95	100
31	34	37	40	42	45	48	51	53	57
55	60	65	70	75	80	85	90	95	100
44	48	52	56	60	64	68	72	76	80
55	60	65	70	75	80	85	90	95	100
36	40	43	46	49	53	56	59	62	66
27	30	32	35	37	40	42	45	47	49
55	60	65	70	75	80	85	90	95	100
22	24	26	28	30	32	34	36	38	40
27	30	32	35	37	40	42	45	47	49
22	24	26	28	30	32	34	36	38	40
36	40	43	46	49	53	56	59	62	66
55	60	65	70	75	80	85	90	95	100
44	48	52	56	60	64	68	72	76	80
36	40	43	46	49	53	56	59	62	66
27	30	32	35	37	40	42	45	47	49
44	48	52	56	60	64	68	72	76	80
36	40	43	46	49	53	56	59	62	66
36	40	43	46	49	53	56	59	62	66
82	89	97	104	111	118	126	133	141	149
55	60	65	70	75	80	85	90	95	100
31	34	37	40	42	45	48	51	53	57
22	24	26	28	30	32	34	36	38	40
26	28	30	33	35	37	39	42	44	46
22	24	26	28	30	32	34	36	38	40
82	89	97	104	111	118	126	133	141	149
36	40	43	46	49	53	56	59	62	66
27	30	32	35	37	40	42	45	47	49
109	119	129	139	148	158	168	178	187	198
82	89	97	104	111	118	126	133	141	149

The government also supplies a voluntary grading service, which is widely used for beef. The grade shield is marked on the wholesale cut and may appear on the meat you buy or on the label. If you are not sure of the grade, ask the butcher. The main basis for the grade is the tenderness, which results from liberal marbling, or fat, in the meat. *There is no difference in wholesomeness or nutrition among the grades.* You can use the less-expensive grades for a considerable saving of money in buying meat for purées.

The most expensive grades are USDA prime and USDA choice; the latter is the grade sold by most supermarkets. The next grades are USDA good, which has even less fat, and USDA standard with the least amount of fat. These two lower grades will cost less and contain more lean meat. What an opportunity for a bargain! After the meat is braised and puréed your baby will never know how tender the original piece of meat was.

You can also save money in your choice of the cut of meat that you use. The boneless chuck roasts, the various round roasts, and stewing meat are easy to prepare and are very tender when braised. You should look for the cuts with the least amount of fat and take advantage of sales. Remember that stewing chuck meat has at least the same amount of protein, possibly even more, than prime sirloin steak.

Ground meat, if you do not have a food processor or blender, is easy to purée with a food mill. Select a lean piece of boneless meat—beef, veal, or lamb—and ask the butcher to grind it. Even if the whole cut is more expensive than the packaged preground meat, you will still get more value for your money, because ground meat can legally contain as much as 30 percent fat. If you must buy preground meat, make sure it is bright red and is as lean as possible. Dark red or brownish red meat may not be fresh.

Another type of meat that is easy to purée without a blender is the precooked meat that is sold sliced in many delicatessens. Roast beef and baked or boiled ham are usually available. These meats are quite expensive, but they can be puréed with a grater or food mill—quite handy when you are short of time or are traveling. They also make good finger foods because the thin slices are very tender. The ham, if preserved with nitrate, should not be served too frequently.

Do not give your baby precooked luncheon meats. They contain salt, additives, and fillers and are also expensive in terms of nutritional cost. (Frankfurters will be discussed in Chapter 14).

Bacon, a salted meat that contains a high percentage of saturated fat, is very expensive for a small amount of protein and should not be counted as a serving of protein.

STORE. Because meat is expensive, you should store it properly. Uncooked meat should be stored in the coldest part of the refrigerator. Meat can be kept in the store wrapper for one to two days; just put a couple of holes in it for the air to circulate. If the surface of the meat is dry, the bacteria will grow less quickly. Large cuts of meat can be wrapped loosely and stored up to five days. However, ground meat spoils quickly and should be used within one to two days. Cured or smoked meats can be kept for one week. Uncooked meat can easily be frozen if it is wrapped properly. Remove any excess fat and wrap the meat tightly in plastic or aluminum foil freezer wrap. Label and date the packages if you plan to freeze them for a long period. Freeze the meat quickly, at 0°F or lower. Here are suggested keeping times for different meats and cuts.

Lamb, beef (roasts and steaks): 12 months

Veal, pork (roasts): 8 months

Veal, lamb, pork (chops or cutlets): 4 months

Cured or smoked meats (such as ham): 2 months

Ground and stew meat of any kind: 3 months

Meat should be thawed in its wrappings, in the refrigerator, before cooking. Meat may also be cooked frozen; allow twice as much cooking time.

Cooked meats should be covered, refrigerated promptly, and can be kept in the refrigerator for two to three days. Cooked purées can be frozen up to four months without losing quality (see Chapter 5).

Cooking Meat You can use any meat that you have cooked for your family for your baby's purée or you can cook a month's supply of meat, three to four pounds, only for use as baby food. (Each pound of meat will yield about 1½ cups of purée or eight to ten food cubes, depending on the cut of meat you use.) Always cook meat at low to moderate temperature for as short a time as possible. If you overcook meat or use a high heat, the meat will shrink and become tough and tasteless. When meat is done properly, it will be tender and easy to purée. Pork must be thoroughly cooked until well done. If you are using the less tender cuts or lean grades you should always microwave, braise, or stew the meat. See page 228 for information about puréeing cooked meat.

MICROWAVING. Microwave cooking of meats, especially the less-tender cuts, must be done carefully to avoid ending up with meat that is dry and tough. In general follow these steps.

1. Trim away as much fat as possible.
2. Place large cuts of meat, fat side down, on a microwave roasting rack in a glass baking dish. Do not cover. Smaller pieces of meat like chops, cutlets, and cubes are more tender when microwaved, tightly covered, in a dish or on a plate. Rearranging the pieces during cooking will ensure more even cooking.
3. Tender roasts, such as sirloin tip and rib should be cooked on high during the first half of the cooking time. Turn over, then continue on medium to finish cooking. (See "Timetable for Microwaving Meats," page 225).
4. Microwave less-tender cuts, such as rump roast, on medium for the first half of the cooking time. Turn over, then continue on medium-low to finish cooking. The lower cooking temperatures, and longer times, allow the meat to tenderize.
5. Roasts that weigh more than 7 pounds should be turned three times to allow for even cooking.
6. At end of the cooking time, if not already covered, cover the meat and allow to stand for 10 minutes.

The following table gives times for microwaving meat in a full-power oven (650 to 700 watts).

Timetable for Microwaving Meats

CUT	FIRST SETTING	SECOND SETTING	TOTAL TIME (MINUTES/POUND)
BEEF			
Sirloin tip	High	Medium	10–11
Rump roast	High	Medium-low	13–14
Brisket, flank	Medium-low	Medium-low	25–30
Strips, cubes	High	High	4–5
Veal roast	Medium	Medium-low	20–21
PORK			
Loin roast	High	Medium	10–11
Shoulder (add ¼ cup water)	High	Medium-low	15–16
Chops	Medium	Medium	10–12
Ham	Medium	Medium	11–12
LAMB			
Roast	Medium	Medium	9–10
Steaks	Medium	Medium	8–9

BRAISING. Braising is cooking the meat with steam and a small amount of liquid or in the meat's own juices. Here's the general method for braising.

1. Preheat oven to 350°F.
2. Trim away as much fat as possible.
3. Brown the meat evenly in a heavy saucepan or Dutch oven over medium-high heat. If the meat is very lean, use a little oil. Flouring the meat will cause it to brown better, but it is not necessary. The browning seals in the meat juices and helps prevent shrinkage. (You can also wrap any meat tightly in aluminum foil and braise it in the oven. It will cook in its own juice.)
4. Place meat and pan juices in roasting pan. Add a small amount of liquid (½ cup for a roast). Cover the pan tightly and cook in the oven (see "Timetable for

Braising Meats," below). Meat can also be simmered, covered, on top of the stove over medium-low heat following the cooking times below.

5. Add more water if the liquid cooks away before the meat is done.

Timetable for Braising Meats

CUT	SIZE	TIME
BEEF		
Roasts	3–5 pounds	3–4 hours
Steak	1–1½ inches	2–2½ hours
Short ribs	2–2½ pounds	2–2½ hours
VEAL		
Shoulder	3–5 pounds	2–2½ hours
Chops	½–¾ inch	45 minutes
LAMB		
Chops	½–¾ inch	30–45 minutes
Shanks	1 pound each	1½–2 hours
Shoulder	3–5 pounds	2–2½ hours
PORK		
Chops	½–1 inch	45–60 minutes
Roast	3–5 pounds	3–4 hours

Note: Near the end of the cooking time, you can poke the meat to test for tenderness. If it looks stringy, the meat is getting overcooked. You can easily braise a small amount of cut-up meat or chops. Just remove the fat, wrap the meat in aluminum foil, and place in a 350°F oven for 45–60 minutes. This is practical if your oven is already in use.

STEWING. Stewing is similar to braising. However, more liquid is used and the meat is cut into pieces or cubes. Here is a recipe for a basic stew in which you may use pieces of veal, beef, or lamb. Stews are a good all-in-one meal; just serve two to three food cubes each feeding and omit other vegetables.

Basic Meat Stew

         2   **tablespoons fat or oil**
        1½   **pounds boneless stew meat, cut in 1-inch**
              cubes
        ⅓   **cup flour**
         3   **cups liquid (water, vegetable or fruit juice)**
         4   **medium potatoes, scrubbed and cut up**
         5   **medium carrots, scrubbed and cut up**
         1   **package (10-ounce) frozen peas (or any**
              other green vegetable)

1. Heat fat in a large-size heavy saucepan over medium-high heat.
2. Coat the meat in the flour and brown in the fat. Add the liquid and cover tightly. Simmer over medium heat for 1½ hours.
3. Add potatoes and carrots. Cover and simmer 15 minutes.
4. Add frozen peas, cover and simmer for 5 minutes.
5. Purée stew (see "Puréeing Meat," page 228).

STORAGE: In refrigerator up to 2 days; freeze 2–3 months.

YIELD: 4–5 cups of purée or 20–25 food cubes.

VARIATION

Any vegetable can be substituted and ½ cup of uncooked rice may be substituted for the potatoes. See Chapter 9 for cooking times of other vegetables.

Cooking Ground Meat You can also cook ground meat of any type to use in meat purées. It has the advantage of faster cooking and it can be puréed easily in a food mill or strainer, if you do not have a blender. Ground meat can also be used in Microwave Meat Loaf (page 304). Here are general instructions for preparing ground meat.

1. Place ground meat in a heated saucepan.
2. Stir over low heat to break up the meat.

3. Cook ground meat until it is thoroughly cooked, but not browned. If it is crunchy, it will not make a smooth purée. Be sure to cook pork thoroughly.
4. Drain off fat.

To microwave, place meat in medium-size bowl and cover tightly. Cook on medium for 10–12 minutes per pound. Let stand covered 5 minutes. Drain off fat.

Puréeing Meat Cooking meat for use in baby food is very easy. The difficulty comes in puréeing the meat to a smooth consistency, so that a young baby can swallow it. If you have a high-speed blender or food processor, you can easily purée any cut or grade of meat, whether it is roasted, broiled, stewed, microwaved, or braised.

Other alternatives are a food mill or grater. You can use a food mill to purée meat that has been braised until very tender. The purée will have a fairly coarse mixture, and it is a time-consuming process. Ground meat can be puréed to a smooth texture with a food mill. You can grate small amounts of chilled meat in a hand grater, such as the Mouli. This will make a very smooth purée and is an economical way to use leftovers such as steak.

Here are some general tips for puréeing cooked meat.

- Thin the meat purée with the meat cooking juices and the juice that runs out when cutting the meat. If stewing or braising, cook the liquid down. You can remove excess fat from the cooking liquid by chilling it quickly in the refrigerator or freezer, then skimming off the fat that has solidified on the top.
- You can also use vegetable juice as a thinner or add a juicy vegetable or fruit to the meat while it is cooking.
- For a purée with a smooth consistency, 1 cup of cooked meat requires about ¼ cup of liquid. A little butter or mayonnaise can be added for a smoother consistency.
- When using a food processor, purée meat with little or no liquid, then thin. The purée may be slightly coarse.

A food processor will not purée gristle. It is easier to remove it before processing the meat; otherwise you can pick it out of the purée.

- Cool the purée quickly and freeze into food cubes immediately. Store frozen up to four months. Or store in refrigerator for up to two days.

ORGAN MEATS: LIVER AND KIDNEY

NUTRITION: Organ meats are some of the most nutritious and *economical* meats that you can easily prepare. Your baby will probably love the taste, even if you do not. So serve with a smile! Liver (calves, beef, lamb, pork, and chicken) and kidneys are some of the highest sources of iron, phosphorus, sodium, vitamin A, thiamine, riboflavin, and niacin. They contain the same amount of high-quality protein as meat.

INTRODUCE. Offer organ meats at eight to nine months.

BUY. Choose fresh meats and plan to cook them the same day.

STORE. Keep uncooked meat, loosely covered, in the coldest part of the refrigerator for one day. Uncooked meats can be frozen for two to three months. The cooked purées can be frozen for one month, or refrigerated for two days.

Liver Purée

Liver is one of the easiest protein foods that you can prepare for your baby, and you do not need a blender to make a smooth purée. Beef or lamb liver costs quite a bit less than calves' liver and is fine for baby food. You should always keep a supply of frozen cubes on hand and you can serve it two or three times a week. It is especially valuable for its high iron content.

A warning: Steamed or braised liver has a very strong odor, so make it on a day when you aren't having company and can open a window!

2   pounds liver (beef, lamb, or chicken)
1   cup liquid (milk or vegetable juice, or cooking liquid)

1. Rinse the liver under cold water. If you are using a blender or food processor to purée, remove the outer skin and any large veins.
2. Steam liver over boiling water for 10 minutes, covered. Or simmer in a pot with a little water. Or broil for 3–4 minutes on each side.
3. Purée, adding the liquid to thin. A food mill, food processor, or blender will give the smoothest purée. Cooked liver is also one of the few meats that can be scraped with a spoon or dull knife to prepare a purée. Chicken livers can be mashed with a fork.

STORAGE: In refrigerator up to 2 days; freeze up to 4 months.

YIELD: 3 cups or 15 food cubes.

• MICROWAVE METHOD

Organ meat, especially liver, needs low gentle cooking to remain tender and avoid "popping." Place prepared meat in medium-size bowl and cover tightly. Cook on medium-low. Allow 10–12 minutes per pound. Let stand 5 minutes. Continue as directed.

VARIATION

Liver Stew. Combine equal amounts of liver, carrots, and green beans or broccoli to make a complete dinner dish.

You can steam them all together; just follow the individual cooking times.

Kidney / Carrot Stew

Kidneys are more difficult to prepare than liver, and they also give off a very strong odor when cooking. But babies like them. They are inexpensive and highly nutritious, so take an hour one day and make enough for a month.

> 1 **pound kidneys**
> 4 **medium carrots, scrubbed and cut up**
> ½ **cup liquid (milk, juice, or cooking liquid)**

1. Preparing the kidney is the most work. Remove the outer membrane, split the kidney lengthwise through the center, and remove the inner fat and tubes. Soak them in cold water for 1 hour, drain.
2. Place kidneys in a medium-size saucepan, cover with cold water, and simmer for 1 hour over medium-low heat.
3. Drain the water. Add enough new water to cover. Add the carrots and simmer for another 15–30 minutes until tender.
4. Purée, adding liquid to thin. A blender, food processor, or food mill will produce a smooth purée, but the food mill takes a longer time. A hand grater will produce a coarser texture.

STORAGE: In refrigerator up to 2 days; freeze up to 4 months.

• MICROWAVE METHOD
Place prepared and soaked kidneys, carrots, and the liquid in a medium-size casserole. Cover tightly and cook on medium-low for 20–25 minutes. Let stand 5 minutes. Continue as directed.

VARIATION

The kidneys can be prepared without any vegetable, or you can add any other vegetable; tomatoes are good.

POULTRY

NUTRITION. Poultry, either chicken or turkey, offers the same amount of high-quality protein as meat and can be substituted often. It is also an excellent source of niacin, with good amounts of thiamine, riboflavin, and linoleic acid. Turkey supplies the most iron. Some types of poultry, which are very adequate for use in baby food, can be considerably less expensive than meat.

INTRODUCE. Chicken and turkey can be introduced at seven months.

BUY. Any poultry that carries the U.S. Department of Agriculture inspection seal is fine. Federal inspection of poultry is compulsory, and it is your guarantee of wholesomeness, both while the bird was alive and during processing. The grading is voluntary. However, most of the poultry sold carries the U.S. Grade A. The lower grades are not usually available to the consumer and are used in processed foods where the appearance is not important. If you can buy the lower grade, you will be able to save money, and the cooked poultry will be fine for baby food purées. Any poultry product, frozen or canned, must also carry the U.S. Inspected for Wholesomeness seal on the label.

You can use any type of poultry—roasters, fryers, or broilers—that you usually buy for your family meals. However, you can save money by using the lower-priced mature chickens or turkeys that may be labeled "mature," "old," or "stewing." These terms refer to the age of the bird when killed and not the freshness when sold. These older birds are not tender enough to be broiled, fried, or roasted, but they are perfect for stewing or braising.

If you want to save time, buy the frozen boned chicken and rolled-turkey roasts. However, you are paying a premium for the preparation, as they are more expensive. Look for sales on these. Also, dark meat is as nutritious as white meat and may be less expensive.

As a rule, whole chickens are more economical than cut-up parts. Breast sections should not be priced more than 40 percent higher than the whole chicken. Leg and thigh sections should not cost more than 30 percent higher.

For example, if the whole chicken is $0.79 per pound, the breast sections should be about $1.10 per pound, and the leg and thigh sections only about $1.03 per pound. If they are priced higher, you will save money by buying the whole chicken, and it is just as easy to use in preparing baby food. Large turkeys are usually more economical than smaller ones. The self-basting variety is very costly for the little time you save and up to 6 percent of the weight can be injected vegetable oil used in the basting.

STORE. Keep uncooked poultry in the coldest part of the refrigerator and use within one to two days. Do not store in butcher paper, but rewrap it in waxed paper or plastic, first removing the giblets.

Frozen uncooked poultry, tightly wrapped, can be kept at 0°F for as long as twelve months for chicken and turkey, and three months for livers and giblets.

Cooked purées can be stored, tightly covered, in the coldest part of the refrigerator for two days. You may also freeze it in food cubes or store for one to two months.

To thaw frozen poultry, either raw or cooked, place it unwrapped in the refrigerator or in cold water. *Do not thaw it at room temperature.* If you allow additional cooking time, you can cook poultry still partially frozen. Frozen food cubes should be heated while frozen, just before a feeding. Thawed poultry spoils quickly, so do not save leftovers.

Note: Chicken and turkey may be contaminated with salmonella bacteria, which can cause a serious intestinal illness. It is important to handle raw poultry very carefully. Always wash, with hot water and soap, any surfaces and utensils—and that includes your hands—used in preparing raw poultry. For example, don't cut up chicken and use the unwashed knife to cut up lettuce for salad. The good news is that this bacteria is destroyed by thorough cooking.

Cooking Chicken and Turkey The easiest way to cook poultry for baby food, either whole or in parts, is to braise, stew, or microwave. Always cook the poultry completely; that is, do not partially cook it one day and finish it the next day. As a rule, you will obtain 1 cup of cooked poultry (without the bone) from each 1½ pounds of a whole chicken or turkey. For each pound of a boneless turkey roast, you will obtain 1 cup of cooked turkey. (Since there is some indication that the chemical steroids used in poultry food tend to accumulate in the skin, you should remove most of the skin before cooking.)

BRAISING. To braise poultry, you will cook it in a small amount of liquid in a tightly covered pot. Here are the general directions:

1. For oven braising, preheat the oven to 325°F.
2. Put the poultry in a heavy, covered roasting pan. You may need to add additional liquid during cooking. Place in the oven or simmer on the stovetop over medium heat.
3. Allow 45 minutes per pound for whole birds up to four pounds. For larger birds, cook about ½ hour per pound.

Some additional tips to follow.

* You can also braise small parts such as drumsticks or breasts in the oven by tightly wrapping the pieces in aluminum foil. They will cook in 30 to 45 minutes.
* If you have a large steamer, you can use it to braise small birds or parts. Braising is really the same method as steaming. Depending on the size of the poultry, the cooking time should be 30 to 60 minutes.
* You can test for doneness by piercing a fleshy part and noting the color of the juice that runs out. If it is at all pink, the poultry is not done. You may also be able to tell by pressing the flesh and moving the drumstick. However, these are rather subjectives tests with which I have never been too successful. Just be sure the juice and the flesh show no sign of pinkness. The flesh should also be separating from the bones.

STEWING. This is a good way of tenderizing the more mature poultry. You can leave the chicken whole or cut it into parts—be sure to remove the skin. Here is the technique:

1. Place poultry in a deep stock pot. Add enough water to half-cover the whole bird or, if cut up, to completely cover the parts.
2. Cover the pot tightly and simmer 2 to 3 hours for a three to four pound stewing chicken, ½ hour per pound for a larger chicken or turkey, and 45 to 60 minutes for a broiler fryer.
3. Check for doneness. The meat should be well separated from the bones, thus saving you time and effort.

Note: When you have stewed the poultry, you will have a considerable amount of cooking liquid with a mild flavor and some nutrients. Cool, skim off the fat, and freeze it as food cubes. You can then use it as thinner, or serve it to your baby as soup if he is sick or unable to eat solids.

MICROWAVING. Poultry should be completely thawed before cooking. Thoroughly cook the poultry until there is no trace of pink. For whole birds follow these steps.

1. Whole poultry can be cooked uncovered on a microwave roasting rack.
2. Birds weighing 10 pounds or less, should be turned twice during cooking; over 10 pounds, turn three times.
3. One setting may be used for the first half, another for the second half of cooking time (see "Timetable for Microwaving Whole Birds," page 236).
4. Standing time is essential for tender doneness. Let birds below 10 pounds stand, covered with aluminum foil, for 5 to 10 minutes after cooking. Birds over 10 pounds should stand for 10 to 15 minutes, covered with aluminum foil.

Timetable for Microwaving
Whole Birds (Full-Power Oven)

TYPE AND WEIGHT	FIRST SETTING	SECOND SETTING	TIME (MINUTES/ POUND)
CHICKEN			
Fryer, 2–3 pounds	High	High	9
Roaster, 3–4 pounds	High	Medium	10
TURKEY			
8–10 pounds	High	Medium	9
10–14 pounds	High	Medium	10

To microwave poultry parts follow these steps.

1. Remove the skin; the parts won't dry out.
2. Place in one layer in baking dish, with the thicker parts on the outside.
3. Add ¼ cup liquid and cover tightly. Cook according to "Timetable for Microwaving Poultry Parts," below.
4. Let stand 5 minutes after cooking.

Timetable for Microwaving
Poultry Parts (Full-Power Oven)

PART	SETTING	TIME (MINUTES/POUND)
CHICKEN		
Breasts	High	9
Legs and thighs	High	11
TURKEY		
Breast	Medium	11
Legs and thighs	Medium	15

Meal-in-One Poultry Stew

Cooked poultry can be combined with vegetables, cereals, rice, etc., or you can save pots and time by adding vegetables or rice to the poultry while it is stewing. Just check the cooking time for the individual vegetable. You can also thin the cooked poultry with a juicy vegetable such as tomatoes, raw or cooked. If you use equal amounts of poultry, a yellow vegetable, and a green vegetable, you will have a balanced stew to use as a complete all-in-one meal. For example:

1½	**pounds poultry parts**
½	**cup uncooked rice**
3–4	**medium carrots, scrubbed and cut up**
1	**package (10-ounces) frozen greens**

1. Remove skin from poultry and place in stockpot with water to cover. Cover pot, bring to simmer, and cook for 15 minutes.
2. Add rice, cover, and cook for 15 minutes.
3. Add carrots, cover, and cook for 15 minutes.
4. Add greens, cover, and cook for 15 minutes, or until poultry is done.
5. Purée stew (see "Puréeing Poultry," below).

STORAGE: In refrigerator 2 days; freeze up to 3 months.

YIELD: About 4 cups of purée or 20 food cubes.

Puréeing Poultry If you have braised, stewed, or microwaved the poultry, the meat should be falling away from the bones. Just pull it off, making sure you remove all the small bones.

- Purée each cup cooked poultry with about ⅓ cup liquid. Use the cooking juices or vegetable juice.
- You can use a food mill, food processor, or blender for a very smooth purée.
- To prepare small amounts with a coarser texture, you can chill the poultry and use a hand grater.
- You can add a small amount of butter, or oil, to im-

prove the texture—about 2 teaspoons for 1 cup purée if your doctor approves.

FISH

NUTRITION. Fish is one of the most valuable foods and is also easy to prepare and to purée. It can be an excellent source of high-quality protein, containing the same amount as the highest quality meats. Saltwater fish is also one of the few good sources of iodine. Other nutrients that are found in good amounts in fish are vitamins A and D (higher in fatty fish), thiamine, riboflavin, niacin, calcium, phosphorus, and iron (although a smaller amount than in meat).

INTRODUCE. Offer lean fish at eight months; fatty fish, at nine to ten months; and shellfish (a high allergy food), after your baby is one year old. Although fish is not commonly served as a baby food in America, it is widely used in Europe and other areas. Most babies love the soft texture and the mild flavor of fish, so try to feed your baby fish at least twice a week as a protein dish.

Fish, especially shellfish, may cause an allergic reaction in some babies, usually in the form of a rash. Introduce fish in a very small amount, about a teaspoon, and wait four days to make sure there is no reaction. If there is, wait a month and try it again.

LEAN FISH

Bass, black	Kingfish	Sheepshead
Carp°	Perch	Smelts
Catfish°	Pickerel	Snapper
Cod	Pike	Sole
Flounder	Pollack	Spot
Fluke	Redfish	Suckers
Grouper	Red Snapper	Sunfish
Haddock	Robolo (snook)	Walleyed pike or perch
Hake	Rockfish	Weakfish (sea trout)
Herring, lake	Rosefish	Whiting (silver hake)

FATTY FISH

Alewife	Mullet	Striped Bass°
Bluefish°	Pompano	Sturgeon
Bonito	Porgies	Swordfish°
Butterfish	Salmon	Tuna
Eels	Sablefish	Whitefish
Halibut	Sardines	Yellowtail
Herring, sea	Sea Bass	
Mackerel	Shad	

SHELLFISH

Crab	Scallops
Crayfish	Shrimp
Lobster	

BUY. Choose fish either whole, as steaks, or in fillets; fresh or frozen. If your family eats fish, you can use whatever type of fish that you usually cook. If you are buying fish only to prepare as baby food, the steaks and fillets will be the easiest type to use. In recent years, there has been concern about levels of chemicals and bacteria in fish. The government tests the waters and our best protection is to buy from reputable stores that sell only fish caught in legal waters. If you do your own fishing, check with your local health department.

Whole fresh fish should have clear, bright eyes; reddish gills, shiny scales, firm flesh that is not separated from the bones; and a fresh, mild odor. If you notice a distinct fishy smell in any type of fresh fish, do not buy it. Steaks and fillets should be moist, white, and free from brown, yellow, or dried spots. If you plan to freeze the uncooked fish, make sure that it was not already frozen and defrosted. You should not refreeze thawed fish. You can test by placing the fish in water; if fresh it will float, if thawed the fish will sink.

Frozen fish is available whole, in steaks, and fillets. Look for the U.S. Grade A or B on the package. The "U.S."

°These fish are likely to have high levels of contaminants and should not be fed to infants.

means that the fish was processed and packed under continuous in-plant inspection by the U.S. Department of the Interior. This inspection and grading is done on a voluntary basis, and many products may be packed without this control, which is your guarantee of a wholesome product.

If, when you open or thaw the frozen fish, it has a cottony look, darkened or yellow areas, a fishy smell, or an excess of liquid, do not use the fish, but return it to the store. The signs indicate that the fish has been thawed and refrozen.

Frozen fish products such as sticks, portions, etc., should not be used as food for your baby, since they usually contain various additives and fillers.

STORE. Fish should be stored carefully, because it does spoil easily. The faster you use fresh fish, the better the taste and texture. Fresh fish should be stored, tightly wrapped in plastic or aluminum foil, in the coldest part of the refrigerator for one to two days. Do not store in butcher wrap or newspaper. Frozen uncooked fish should be tightly wrapped in freezer wrap and kept frozen at 0°F for four to six months. Cooked fish should be tightly covered and stored in the refrigerator for no longer than two days. Cooked frozen fish purées can be kept for up to one month.

THAW. Frozen fish should be thawed in the refrigerator or under cool running water. You can always cook fish frozen or partially thawed.

Cooking Fish There are dangers in eating raw fish, and there is no reason for a baby or toddler to acquire a taste for sushi or sashimi. So always cook fish thoroughly. Fish is one of the easiest foods to prepare. The main thing to remember is not to overcook fish since it will become tough. Fish is done when the color changes from translucent, or watery, to white, and the flesh flakes easily and separates from the bones. Here are some general tips for cooking fish. See page 242 for information about puréeing cooked fish.

- Prepare the fish as baby food as soon as possible after cooking, and freeze the purée at once.
- The best way to cook fish for baby food is to bake, microwave, poach, or steam it. If your family eats fish

prepared by these methods, just make some extra for the baby. (Do not give a young baby fried fish.)

- One pound of fish fillet yields about 1½ cups purée or 8 food cubes. Prepare and freeze a month's supply at one time.

BAKING. Here is the general method for baking fish.

1. Preheat oven to 350°F.
2. Place the fish on a buttered pan or aluminum foil. Dot with butter. You can also wrap the fish in aluminum foil, but this is actually steaming it.
3. Bake dressed whole fish (about 3 pounds) for 30 to 45 minutes and fillets or steaks (about 2 pounds), for 20 to 25 minutes. It is not necessary to turn the fish.

MICROWAVING. This is the easiest and best way to cook fish. Frozen fish should be defrosted before cooking. Here's how to microwave fish.

1. Place fish in shallow dish or on plate. The trick in even cooking is in the arrangement. The thicker and larger parts should be on the outside edge. The thin, narrow end of fillets can be folded under to create an even thickness.
2. Cover tightly and cook on high: For fillets or steaks, allow 4 to 5 minutes per pound, for whole fish up to 3 pounds, allow 5 to 6 minutes per pound, and for whole fish over 3 pounds, allow 3 minutes per pound.
3. Let fish stand for 5 minutes to complete cooking.

POACHING. This method is good for thin fillets, steaks, and small whole fish. It is quick, easy, and the cooked fish is very digestible. If you have a steamer, it is perfect for poaching. Or use a shallow pan.

1. In the steamer or pan place enough court bouillon, water with a little lemon juice, or milk to cover the fish. Do not add fish yet. Bring the liquid to a boil and reduce heat to a simmer.

2. Lower the fish into the steaming basket (or place in the pan of cooking liquid). Cover and simmer for 5 to 15 minutes, depending on the thickness of the fish. You can boil the liquid down and use it as a thinner.
3. To steam the fish, use only enough water to cover the bottom of the steamer and keep it boiling for 10 to 15 minutes.
4. Test for flakiness—the fish is done when it flakes easily.

STEWING. Fish can be combined with most vegetables to make an all-in-one stew. If you are steaming vegetables, just add the fish during the last 10 to 15 minutes. Cooked fish can also be used in custards and soufflés, but you needn't bother just for the baby.

Puréeing Fish Although fish is easily and quickly cooked, you must be especially careful to remove all bones before you prepare it as a purée. Even fillets, which are considered boneless, should be checked.

• When the fish has been thoroughly flaked and the bones removed, you can purée it with a blender, food processor, or food mill for the smoothest purée; or simply mash it with a fork for coarser texture. Fish is an easy food to chew, so it is a good way to start introducing coarser texture. Larger flakes can be used as one of the first finger foods.
• Purée each cup of fish with about ¼ cup liquid—either milk, cooking juice, or vegetable juice.

SOYBEANS

NUTRITION. Although soybeans are a vegetable, they supply almost the same amount of high-quality complete protein as meat or poultry, and can be counted as a serving of protein food. They are also high in linoleic acid, iron, potassium, thiamine, and fat. As you can see, soybeans are quite a nutritional bargain at around $0.40 to $0.50 a pound—and that is the *dry* weight. Although we do not usually consider them as desirable a food as sirloin steak, your baby will never know the difference.

INTRODUCE. Offer at eight to nine months.

BUY. If you cannot find soybeans in your local supermarket, try the nearest health-food store. Buy them in quantity, since they keep well.

STORE. Dry soybeans can be kept in tightly covered cans or plastic bags, at cool room temperature for up to two years. Cooked purées will keep in the refrigerator for up to three days and can be frozen for two months.

Soybean Purée

Presoaking or precooking (step 1) is not necessary if you are using a pressure cooker.

    1   cup dry soybeans
    3   cups water
    1   tablespoon butter, margarine, or oil
    ¾   cup liquid (milk or tomato juice is good)

1. Rinse the soybeans, then soak them in the water overnight. You can also bring them to a boil for 2 minutes, cover, and allow them to sit for 2 hours.
2. Add the butter (to help prevent the beans from foaming while cooking). Do not add salt. Return the pot to medium heat and simmer about 2 hours. Leave the cover ajar to prevent foaming and spilling.
3. When the skins float to the top, you can skim them off to prepare the smoothest purée.
4. Purée with any equipment, adding the liquid to thin.

YIELD: 2½ cups or 12 food cubes.

• **MICROWAVE METHOD**
See "Legumes," in Chapter 9.

VARIATION

If you do not thin the mashed soybeans, you can use the purée as a nutritious thickener for juicy fruits and vegetables.

EGGS

NUTRITION. Eggs should be one of the staples of your baby's diet. They are nutritious, inexpensive, and easy to cook and purée. Eggs contain a good amount of complete protein, iron, riboflavin, vitamins B_6, B_{12}, and A and are one of the few foods that contain natural vitamin D. The yolk has most of the fat, iron, and vitamins A and D in the egg. The yolk also contains cholesterol, an important part of your baby's diet. (see Chapter 1). The white contains half the riboflavin and protein of the whole egg. So if you want to use only the egg yolk, you can double the amount and come out ahead nutritionally. At $1.09 a dozen for large eggs, the cost comes to about $0.73 per pound. Very economical for a high-protein food!

INTRODUCE. The cooked egg yolk can be introduced in small amounts at seven months. The cooked egg white is a possible source of allergy and should not be introduced until your baby is nine to ten months old.

Note: In some areas, eggs have been found to carry salmonella bacteria. To be safe, do not give your baby raw or undercooked eggs.

BUY. The grade, size, and color of an egg do not affect its nutritional value. The nutritional value of brown and white eggs is exactly the same. The important thing to look for in buying eggs is freshness. In some areas, the last date of sale must be stamped on the carton. Another guarantee of freshness is the Grade AA or fresh fancy, which shows that the eggs have been produced under the U.S. Department of Agriculture's Quality-Control Program. This grade must be dated with the last day of sale, which is ten days after the eggs were inspected. The main difference in the grades is the appearance of the eggs. Grade AA or A eggs have a better appearance and are good for frying or poaching. Since your baby won't be concerned with the appearance and will be eating his eggs well cooked and mixed, you can save money by buying the Grade B eggs. Just be sure they are fresh!

The size on the egg carton refers to the minimum weight for the dozen eggs and ranges from 30 ounces for jumbo eggs to 18 ounces for small eggs. If you are buying eggs specifically to feed your baby, the medium-size egg should be adequate for one feeding without wasteful left-overs. You can easily figure out which size is the most economical by the $0.07 rule: If the difference in price between two sizes of eggs is less than $0.07, buy the larger size.

Besides freshness, the important sign to look for in buying eggs is a clean, uncracked shell. If the shell is cracked or dirty, the egg might contain salmonella bacteria.

STORE: Whole eggs in the refrigerator, in the original carton, with the large end up. Each day at room temperature can reduce freshness by one week. Do not wash them or you will remove the natural protective coating. They should be used within four weeks, or else they may develop off-flavors and lose some of their thickening ability.

Whole hard-cooked eggs keep in the shell for up to two weeks. Peeled, one week. Cooked yolks and/or whites should be covered and can be saved for two to three days.

Cooked egg yolks may be frozen in food cubes for up to one month. Other cooked egg dishes should not be frozen.

Raw yolks should be covered with water in a tightly covered container and stored for one to two days. Raw whites should be tightly covered and stored for one to two days. If your baby is eating only yolks, you can use these whites in cakes, meringues, soufflés, and whipped in many desserts. You can also beat an egg white and use it as an inexpensive facial mask! Frozen raw eggs (whole, yolk, or whites) may be stored for six months. If you are freezing the whole egg, first mix the white and yolk together. Do not freeze raw or cooked eggs in the shell.

Using Eggs You can prepare eggs in many ways and this is one area in which you can really use your ingenuity.

Both the egg yolk and the white are useful as a way of smoothly binding together many nutritious foods that would be difficult for your baby to swallow, such as leafy green vegetables, wheat germ, etc. Almost any food can be combined with eggs.

As a binder you can cook eggs in the form of custards, soufflés, or just plain scrambled—the easiest.

If you are using only the egg yolk, remember to substitute two yolks for each whole egg that a recipe calls for. Yolks can be substituted for whole eggs in any custard recipe and in most baked goods. The main exception is a soufflé, which depends on the beaten egg white for its lightness. Here are some tips.

- Eggs will separate easily if they warm to room temperature.
- When you are cooking any dish with eggs as the main ingredient, use a low to medium heat, to prevent the egg from becoming tough or hard.
- You will also find hard-boiled egg yolks useful as a highly nutritious thickener for juicy fruits and vegetables, or when you have overthinned a purée.
- Finally, you can combine a small amount of eggs, with their complete protein, with many inexpensive foods that contain incomplete proteins, such as dried peas, beans, lentils, cereals, noodles, and rice.

The following recipes cover the basic and easiest ways to prepare eggs that your baby will enjoy eating.

Egg Yolk Purée

This is the easiest food to cook and mash. There is no reason for you to buy the commercially prepared baby food egg yolks; you can save considerable money by preparing them yourself. The yolks of two large eggs, thinned to the same consistency, make the same amount of purée (3⅓ ounces) as in a jar of commercial egg yolks. The cost of the eggs, at $1.09 a dozen, is $0.20 (and you will still have the whites to use), as compared with an average cost of $0.57 for a jar of egg yolks. Now, see how easy it is to prepare your own! You can use the hard-cooked egg whites in sandwiches, salads, and casseroles. Or serve it to an older child.

> **4   large eggs**
> **¼–⅓ cup liquid (milk, fruit, or vegetable juice)**

1. Place eggs in a saucepan and cover with cold water. Bring water to a simmer and cook for 15–20 minutes. Do not let the water boil.
2. Plunge the eggs, in the shell, immediately into cold water. This allows the shell to peel off easily.
3. Cut the eggs in half and remove the yolks. With a spoon or fork, mash the yolks with the liquid. If you are using the yolk as a thickener, store or freeze it without thinning. Use a blender or food processor for larger amounts.

STORAGE: In the refrigerator for up to 3 days. Or freeze in food cubes for up to 1 month.

YIELD: 1 cup purée or 5 food cubes.

- **MICROWAVE METHOD**

Do not microwave eggs in the shell—they will explode. Break eggs into a medium-size buttered bowl. Cover tightly and cook on medium for 40 seconds for 1 egg, 1 minute for 2 eggs, and 2 minutes for 4 eggs. Let stand 1 minute. Continue as directed. Soak bowl immediately.

VARIATION

Egg Yolk/Wheat Germ Purée. Mix 1 tablespoon wheat germ with 2 tablespoons milk or fruit juice, and allow to soften for 10 minutes. Mix together with the cooked egg yolks and rest of liquid. (For a single egg yolk, use about 1 teaspoon wheat germ and 2 teaspoons liquid.)

Scrambled Eggs

You may scramble the whole egg or only the yolk. The size of the egg to use for 1 serving depends on your baby's appetite.

- ½ **tablespoon butter, margarine, or oil**
- 1 **medium egg (or 2 egg yolks)**
- 1 **tablespoon milk (vegetable or fruit juice)**

1. Melt butter in a small frying pan.
2. Beat the egg and milk in a small-size bowl. (If you want to save a dish, you can do it quickly in the pan.) Pour the mixture into the frying pan.
3. Cook the egg slowly over medium heat, stirring until it is loosely cooked. (If the egg is cooked too long, it will be dry and difficult to swallow.)
4. Serve at once. It should not be necessary to thin the eggs.

STORAGE: Leftover scrambled eggs become hard and should not be saved. Do not freeze.

- **MICROWAVE METHOD**

Beat eggs and milk in small-size bowl. Cover tightly and cook on medium. Allow 1 minute for 1 egg, 2–2½ minutes for 2 eggs, and 4½–5 minutes for 4 eggs. Continue as directed. Soak bowl immediately.

VARIATION

Meal-in-One Eggs. You can add up to ¼ cup of almost any purée to a medium egg while you are beating it, or you can purée a food with the egg. Try fruit, vegetable, or meat purées, grated cheese, cottage cheese, leftover cooked cereal or rice, etc.

This is also a good way to feed your baby highly nutritious wheat germ. Soften 1 teaspoon wheat germ in 2 teaspoons milk for a few minutes before beating it with the egg and milk. For a balanced meal, combine a cereal grain and a fruit/vegetable with the eggs.

Smooth Eggs

This is an easy way of preparing an egg dish with the consistency of custard.

2   **eggs (or 4 yolks)**
½   **cup milk**
2   **teaspoons butter, margarine, or oil**

1. Mix the eggs and milk together in a medium-size bowl.
2. Melt the butter in the top of a double boiler. Add the egg mixture. Cover the pot and cook for 10–15 minutes without stirring. Cool.

STORAGE: In the refrigerator for up to 3 days.

YIELD: 3 servings.

Basic Baked Custard

Custard takes more effort to make, and because the main ingredient is milk, it should not be counted as a serving of eggs. You may wish to make a custard for a family dessert, and the baby will also enjoy it as a good supper dish. You may find that custard is useful as a way of feeding your baby some valuable foods such as green leafy vegetables, wheat germ, etc.

2½   **cups milk (whole, skim, or evaporated)**
4   **eggs (or 8 egg yolks)**
1   **teaspoon vanilla extract**
⅓   **cup brown sugar or 2 tablespoons molasses**

1. Preheat oven to 350°F.
2. Bring milk to boiling point in medium-size saucepan and remove from heat.
3. Beat the eggs, adding vanilla and brown sugar in

medium-size bowl. Pour a little hot milk into the eggs, and mix. Pour the egg mixture into the rest of the milk, stirring until it is mixed.

4. Pour the custard into cups or casserole and place in a pan of hot water that reaches to the level of the custard. The water will cook the custard evenly.

5. Bake for about 40 minutes or until a knife inserted in the center comes out clean. If you overcook the custard, it will pull away from the sides of the cup, leaving liquid around it, and the custard will have a harder texture. Cool.

STORAGE: Covered in the refrigerator for up to 3 days.

YIELD: 4–6 servings.

VARIATIONS

Stirred Custard. Prepare custard as directed except pour the mixture into the top of a double boiler and cook over simmering water for about 5 minutes or until the spoon is well coated. Stir constantly. The custard will have a smooth, creamy texture.

Wheat Germ Custard. Add 1 tablespoon wheat germ to the milk before heating it. Continue as directed.

Anything Custard. You can add ¼–½ cup of almost any purée—vegetable, fruit, cereal, meat, fish, etc.—for each whole egg used in a custard. Mix the purée (or chopped food) with the eggs before mixing with the milk or liquid. Continue as directed. See also Vegetable Custard (page 214), Easy Vegetable Custard (page 214), Vegetable/ Egg Yolk Custard (page 215), and Fruit Custard (page 264).

Soufflés. A soufflé is a very light custard that often uses a white sauce (page 217). The lightness is obtained by beating the egg whites separately and folding them carefully into the egg yolk mixture. A soufflé takes even more time and dishes than a custard, and it must be eaten immediately. Most likely, the only time that your baby will eat a soufflé is when you have made one for the rest of the family. As with custard, you can add almost anything to a soufflé (see Microwave Meal-in-One Vegetable Soufflé, page 213).

Microwave Custard

This is the easiest way to make custard.

1¾   **cups milk**
¼   **cup sugar**
¼   **teaspoon salt**
½   **teaspoon vanilla extract**
3   **eggs**

1. Mix all ingredients thoroughly in medium-size bowl.
2. Pour equal amounts into four glass custard cups.
3. Cook on defrost for 15–16 minutes, or until a knife inserted in center comes out clean.
4. Let stand 5 minutes.

YOGURT

NUTRITION. Yogurt contains all the valuable nutrients in milk—complete protein, calcium, riboflavin, and others. If you make your yogurt with milk that has been fortified with vitamins A and D, they will also be present in the yogurt. Some brands of commercial yogurt are also fortified with vitamins A and D. In addition, the bacteria in yogurt stimulates the body to produce vitamin K, which is important in blood clotting and liver functions. Breast milk contains an adequate supply of vitamin K, but cow's milk contains less.

INTRODUCE. Offer plain yogurt as early as four to five months. It is easily digested and is easy to swallow. The fruited varieties can be used after the specific fruit has been introduced. When your baby is accustomed to the taste and consistency of yogurt, you can use it, mixed with meats and vegetables, as a way of introducing new tastes and textures.

BUY. Choose commercial yogurts without preservatives or fillers (see "Yogurt," in Chapter 13, for a full discussion of commercial yogurt). The purest yogurt will contain only fresh milk, nonfat dry milk, and real yogurt cultures.

STORE. Yogurt can be kept in the refrigerator for one week to ten days. It will develop a stronger flavor the longer it is kept. *Do not freeze.*

Homemade Yogurt

Yogurt is one of the easiest foods that you can make yourself. It will have a milder, less acid taste than the commercial yogurts. You can also save quite a bit of money! An 8-ounce container of plain yogurt costs around $0.59. You can make yogurt, using nonfat dry milk, that costs as little as $0.10 for the same 8 ounces. Now see how easy it is!

> 1 **quart milk (any kind)**
> ½ **cup nonfat dry milk**
> ¼ **cup plain yogurt (commercial or homemade)**

1. Mix the milk and dry milk together in a large-size saucepan.
2. Bring the milk to a boil and remove from heat at once. This will destroy any bacteria already in the milk. Be careful not to allow the milk to scorch the pan.
3. Cool the milk to about 105°–110°F. You can use the same wrist test that is used in warming a baby's bottle. A few drops of milk on the inside of your wrist should feel warm.
4. Mix a spoonful of milk into the yogurt, then stir the yogurt into the milk, blending well.
5. Now you must find a warm place for the yogurt to sit for about 5 hours. There are several choices, but the main principle is to keep the yogurt at a temperature of around 105°–110°F so that the yogurt bacteria will grow. Too hot or too cold a temperature will kill the bacteria and you will have only sour milk. But if you are off by a few degrees, it will just take longer for the yogurt to set. So you needn't be too worried about thermometers and exact degrees.

   • If you can easily replace the light bulb in your oven with a 100-watt bulb and can leave the light on with the door closed, you will have a good temperature.
   • I have had good results by simply warming the oven at 150°F for 5 minutes then turning it off. After

2–3 hours you may check to see whether it needs another minute or so of warming. The oven should feel warm, but not hot when you open the door. You can always use a thermometer, of course.

• Probably the simplest and oldest way of making yogurt is to mix it in a heavy warmed casserole, cover, and wrap it in a blanket for 12 hours or until set. A wide-mouthed thermos can also be used for a small amount.

• There are commercial yogurt makers that you can buy for about $12, but they really are not necessary.

6. Using the oven method, the yogurt should set in about 5 hours. The longer you allow it to set, the more sour the yogurt will be. Do not stir.

7. Chill the yogurt before dividing into smaller containers or transferring.

VARIATIONS

Easy Yogurt. Here is an even easier method that can save cleaning a pot. Bring 1 quart of water to a boil. Pour the water into a medium-size container and add 1¾ cups nonfat dry milk. Proceed with step 3. (Since nonfat milk is already sterile, you do not need to boil it.)

Flavored Yogurt. There are many ways that you can add flavor and variety to your homemade yogurt.

• Before heating the milk, add ¼ cup brown sugar or 2 tablespoons molasses.

• After heating the milk and cooling, add ⅓ cup of any cooked fruit (prunes, apricots, peaches), puréed or chopped, or even some vegetable purée such as squash. You can also add ½ cup of fresh chopped or puréed fruit.

• Before serving, you can stir in any flavoring you happen to have around.

Yogurt Cheese. You can make a tasty cream cheese by hanging yogurt in cheesecloth and allowing it to drain several hours.

You can feed the yogurt cold or slightly warmed to your baby. Another way you can use yogurt is to mix it with foods that are difficult to swallow, such as green leafy vegetables, wheat germ, etc. When you are first introducing meat, you can mix it with a little yogurt as you are feeding your baby. The meat purée will be easier to swallow.

CHEESE

NUTRITION. Cheese contains the same nutrients as milk and is a valuable food. It does lack the iron that is in other protein foods. For example, a 1-inch cube of Cheddar cheese has the same calcium as ½ cup milk; and ½ cup cottage cheese equals ⅓ cup milk.

As for protein, 1 ounce of hard cheese (Cheddar, Swiss, or American) or ¼ cup cottage cheese equals the protein of 1 ounce lean meat, fish, or poultry.

If your baby is drinking milk, there is no need to add large amounts of cheese to his diet. You will find small amounts of cheese useful as an easy way of improving the quality of protein in such low-cost foods as noodles, cereal, rice, dried peas, beans, and lentils.

INTRODUCE. All types of cheeses can be introduced around seven to eight months.

BUY. Firm cheese—Swiss, American, Cheddar, etc.— should not be diluted with various additives and fillers (see "How to Read Labels," in Chapter 2). In general, you should not buy any cheese that is labeled with the words *imitation*, *spread*, or *food*. Cottage cheese varies as to the types of additives, so read labels to buy the brand with the least amount. Sorbic acid is usually added as a preservative. Also, try to buy a brand that carries a government or state grade or inspection seal. In some areas the containers will be dated with the last day of sale, so look for it.

STORE. Keep firm cheeses tightly wrapped in the refrigerator for 2 to 3 weeks. Any mold spots can be cut away. Hard cheese may also be frozen for several months. Cottage cheese should be kept in the refrigerator for up to one week. It should not be frozen.

Using Cheese

- Grated hard cheese can be used as a protein supplement and as flavoring in many purées. It is especially good in rice and vegetable dishes.
- To grate, cut hard cheese into small cubes and grate in a food processor, blender, or with a hand grater. Softer cheese will grate better if it is well chilled or placed in a freezer for 20 to 30 minutes. (One-half pound cheese makes 1 cup grated cheese.)
- Always cook cheese at low to medium temperatures and add near the end of cooking.
- For one way to use cottage cheese, see Noodle and Cheese Pudding (page 122).
- Creamed cottage cheese may be mashed with a fork or puréed in a food processor or blender, and fed directly to your baby. It is a good instant food that is readily available.

NONFAT DRY MILK

NUTRITION. Nonfat dry milk powder is an excellent source of complete protein and contains all the vitamins and minerals of fresh milk. Only the fat and water have been removed. At a cost as low as $0.40 for the equivalent of a quart of milk, it is a very low cost and convenient way to serve protein to your baby, especially as a supplement with the economical cereal grains and legumes.

BUY. The U.S. extra grade mark on the label indicates that the dry milk meets the government's standards of composition and wholesomeness. The label will also tell you whether vitamins A and D have been added as supplements.

STORE. The unopened powder can be kept at cool room temperature for several months. The opened packages of powder should be kept dry and used within two weeks.

Using Dry Milk

- You can add dry milk as a fortifier in any recipe that contains liquid. It is especially good in any fruit or vegetable purées that are naturally thin or have strong tastes.
- Added to baked goods, it supplements the incomplete protein in the flour. Use 2 to 4 tablespoons powder for each cup of liquid.
- Remember that ⅓ cup powder supplies the same nutrients as 1 cup skim milk.
- You can also increase the amount of nonfat dry milk powder, when it is specified in a recipe, by up to 50 percent.

PROTEIN ECONOMY

Protein is an essential part of everyone's diet and is especially important for a baby's growth. Yet prices of what we commonly think of as protein sources—beef, lamb, pork, veal, and fish—have risen astronomically. Fortunately, poultry, eggs, soybeans, and milk are still economical in terms of their "nutritional cost." The following lists give an idea of the protein values of various foods. Keeping in mind the different "completeness" of the proteins, these amounts of food will supply the same quantity of protein:

COMPLETE PROTEIN

Cheese (Cheddar, American, or Swiss: 1 ounce

Eggs: 1 whole or 2 yolks

Lean meat, fish, or poultry: 1 ounce

Milk (whole or skim): 1 cup

Soybeans (cooked): ⅓ cup

INCOMPLETE PROTEIN

Legumes (cooked peas, beans, or lentils): ½ cup

Peanut butter: 2 tablespoons

Wheat germ: 2 tablespoons

SUPPLEMENTING PROTEIN. All the incomplete protein foods are inexpensive sources of protein. These include rice, pastas, legumes (peas, beans), and seeds (peanuts, sesame). You probably prepare many family dishes that stretch the more expensive meats by combining them with inexpensive rice, beans, or pastas. Turkey is an excellent complement, because using turkey as only one-fifth of a dish makes the protein value of the dish the same as if it were all beef. If you combine the incomplete protein foods in dishes with the inexpensive milk, eggs, cheese, or soybeans you have an even more economical source of complete protein. Most of these family dishes can be puréed for a baby if they are not highly seasoned. Some recipes included in this book are

Macaroni and Cheese
(page 123)
Noodle and Cheese
Pudding (page 122)
Pea/Bean/Lentil Purée
(page 193)
Peanut Butter Custard
(page 264)
Rice and Wheat Germ
Purée (page 127)

Rice Cheese (page 127)
Rice Pudding (page 128)
Sautéed Rice (page 130)
Soybean/Rice Purée (page
127)

COMPLEMENTING PROTEINS. Incomplete protein foods each lack some of the essential amino acids that make up protein; however, the amino acids that are lacking in one food (such as legumes) are present in another food (rice). *You can obtain very inexpensive high-quality complete protein by combining complementary foods in the right amounts—either in the same dish or at the same meal!* It is even easier to combine these foods in purées; a baby has no built-in bias against sesame seeds with rice. For some interesting family dishes using complementary proteins, see the Bibliography and look into some vegetarian-oriented cookbooks. The baby's portion can be removed before seasoning is added, but most recipes are not highly seasoned.

You should combine these foods in the following proportions, although you have some leeway, especially when you thin the purées with milk. The amounts given are for uncooked rice and legumes. In general, 1 cup dry legumes = 2 to 2½ cups cooked; and 1 cup rice = 3½ cups cooked rice. Sunflower seeds can be substituted for sesame seeds. Thin with milk, fruit, or vegetable juice until desired consistency.

COMPLEMENTARY PROTEIN PROPORTIONS

Cornmeal (1 cup)	+	Legumes (¼ cup)
Legumes (⅓ cup)	+	Sesame seeds (½ cup)°
Milk (2 cups) or Cheese (⅔ cup)	+	Legumes (1 cup)
Milk (1½ cups)	+	Peanuts (1½ cups)
Milk (1 cup) or Cheese (¼ cup)	+	Rice (¾ cup)
Rice (1⅓ cups)	+	Legumes (½ cup)
Rice (1 cup)	+	Sesame seeds (⅓ cup)
Rice (2½ cups)	+	Soybeans (¼ cup)
Sesame seeds (1 cup)	+	Peanuts (¾ cup) or Peanut butter (½ cup)

°Use fewer sesame seeds and purée with milk.

Hummus

In this recipe for hummus—a Middle Eastern food—garbanzo beans (chick-peas) are combined with sesame seeds. It is a high-protein purée that can also be seasoned with garlic, lemon juice, salt, and pepper to be used as a vegetable dip.

   1 **cup dried garbanzos (chick-peas)**
   3 **cups water**
   ½ **cup sesame seeds**
   1 **cup milk, or ½ cup milk plus ½ cup yogurt**
   ½ **cup cooking liquid from beans**
   ¼ **cup oil**

1. Cook garbanzos in 3 cups simmering water for 1½–2 hours (2 cups canned beans may be substituted; do not cook).
2. If using a food processor, blend garbanzos and sesame seeds until finely puréed, then add liquids. In a blender, add the liquid first.

STORAGE. In refrigerator 3–4 days; frozen for up to 4 months.

YIELD: About 2 cups.

Peanut Butter Pancakes

These pancakes have only a slight taste of peanuts; however, the combination of milk, eggs, flour, and peanuts provides a high *8 grams* of complete protein in just *1* pancake. They can be served as a finger food or puréed (1 tablespoon milk for each pancake).

2 **eggs, beaten**
¼ **cup honey**
½ **teaspoon vanilla extract**
½ **cup peanut butter**
¾ **cup milk**
1 **cup whole wheat flour**
¼ **cup dry milk**
½ **teaspoon salt**
2 **teaspoons baking powder**

1. Beat eggs, honey, vanilla, and peanut butter together in medium-size bowl. Add milk and mix.
2. Combine flour, dry milk, salt, and baking powder in medium-size bowl. Add to egg and milk mixture and stir until smooth.
3. Fry on lightly oiled griddle.

STORAGE. In refrigerator 3–4 days; freeze up to 2 months.

YIELD: 8 pancakes.

11

Desserts

Desserts are not a necessity in your baby's diet. The highly sweetened or starchy ones, such as puddings, add "empty" calories. However, I have included some basic recipes for nutritious desserts that your family will enjoy and that you can also feed your baby as fruit, cereal, protein, or dairy servings.

Fruit Milk Sherbet

This is a different way to serve fruit. There are egg whites, a possible allergen, in this dessert, so be sure that you have already introduced your baby to whole eggs. Any fruit that has been introduced can be used; bananas, peaches, apricots, pears, plums, berries, are especially good.

        1   teaspoon plain gelatin powder
        1   tablespoon water
     1½   cups fruit purée
        1   tablespoon sugar (optional, depending on
               tartness of fruit)
       ¾   cup milk (whole or skim)
        1   egg white

1. Soften the gelatin in the water in a small-size bowl. Blend into the fruit purée in a medium-size bowl.
2. Add sugar, if used. Add milk and blend thoroughly.
3. Pour into a shallow baking dish. Cover and freeze until it is frozen around the edges.

4. While the mixture is freezing, beat the egg white until stiff.
5. Pour the frozen mixture into a large-size bowl or blender and blend slowly until it is smooth. Fold in the egg white.
6. Return to the baking dish and freeze until it is solid.

YIELD: 2½ cups.

Note: All the steps may be done in a blender except for dissolving the gelatin and beating the egg white. A food processor is not recommended. Excess liquid may rise over the drive shaft and leak out.

Citrus Fruit Sherbet

Once citrus juices have been introduced, this dessert is a good way of feeding your baby the entire fruit, which contains additional nutrients. This recipe requires a high-speed blender to purée the pulp finely.

1   tablespoon sugar (omit if a sweet orange is used)
1   cup fruit juice
1   teaspoon plain gelatin powder
1   lemon or orange or ½ medium grapefruit, peeled

1. Dissolve the sugar in the fruit juice in a small bowl. Add the gelatin and dissolve.
2. In a blender, liquefy the fruit. Add the juice mixture and blend.
3. Pour into a shallow baking dish.
4. Cover and freeze until fairly firm—about 1 hour.
5. Pour back into blender, and blend at a slow speed until smooth.
6. Return to the baking dish and freeze until firm.

YIELD: 1½ cups.

Fruit / Egg Yolk Custard

This is a dessert that counts as a serving of fruit and egg yolk. It makes a good supper dish and can be given as soon as your baby has been introduced to egg yolk. You will find it especially useful if your baby shows an allergy to egg whites.

>   1   **piece fruit (banana, pear, or peach is good)**
>   **or ¼ cup fruit purée**
>   1   **egg yolk, beaten**
>   ¼   **cup milk (whole or skim)**

1. Preheat oven to 350°F. Grease 2 custard cups.
2. Blend together the fruit, egg yolk, and milk in medium-size bowl.
3. Pour into custard cups and place in pan of hot water that reaches to the level of the custard.
4. Bake for 30 minutes or until a knife inserted in the center comes out clean. The cups may also be placed in a pot of simmering water for 10 minutes if you do not have an oven available.

STORAGE: In the refrigerator for up to 3 days.

YIELD: 2 servings.

• MICROWAVE METHOD
Pour custard in custard cups and cook on defrost for 5 minutes or until knife inserted in center comes out clean. Let stand 5 minutes. Note: There is no need to place cups in water, when microwaving any custard.

Fruit Custard

This is a highly nutritious dessert for the entire family. It contains eggs, so wait until you have introduced the whole egg to your baby's diet.

> 2 **cups milk (whole or skim) plus ½ cup nonfat dry milk (optional)**
> 3 **beaten eggs**
> ½ **cup fruit purée, raw or cooked (banana, peaches, plums, or apricots are good)**

1. Preheat oven to 350°F. Grease 8 custard cups.
2. If you have a blender, the milk, eggs, and fruit can be slowly blended at the same time. Do not use a high speed because you will have too much foam. This may be too much liquid for a food processor. If so, purée fruit, then add to liquid in a separate bowl.
3. Pour the mixture into custard cups. Place in pan of hot water that comes to the level of the custard.
4. Bake for 30 minutes or until a knife inserted in center comes out clean.

STORAGE: Refrigerate, covered, for up to 3 days.

YIELD: 8 servings.

- **MICROWAVE METHOD**

Pour prepared custard into cups. Cook on defrost for 18–20 minutes or until knife inserted in center comes out clean. Let stand 5 minutes.

Peanut Butter Custard

> 1⅓ **cups milk (whole or skim)**
> ⅓ **cup smooth peanut butter**
> 2 **eggs, beaten**
> 1 **tablespoon sugar (optional)**

1. Preheat oven to 325°F. Grease small-size baking dish or 4 custard cups.

2. Add the milk gradually to the peanut butter in a medium-size bowl, stirring until smooth.
3. Blend in the eggs and sugar.
4. Pour into a small baking dish or custard cups. Place in pan of hot water that comes to the level of the custard.
5. Bake for 30 minutes or until knife inserted in center comes out clean.

STORAGE: Refrigerate, covered, for up to 3 days.

YIELD: 4 servings.

• **MICROWAVE METHOD**
Pour custard into dish or cups. Cook on defrost for about 15 minutes or until knife inserted in center comes out clean. Let stand 5 minutes.

Fruit Crunch

This is an easy family dessert that your baby can eat as a serving of fruit and cereal. Some good fruits to use are apples, peaches, plums, nectarines, blueberries, and rhubarb (2 cups, or 12 ounces, frozen, with 1 cup of any other fruit).

    3   cups sliced fruit
    ⅔   cup brown sugar (or less, depending on
          tartness of fruit)
    ½   cup quick-cooking rolled oats
    3   tablespoons flour (whole wheat, unbleached,
          or enriched)
    3   tablespoons melted butter or margarine or
          safflower oil

1. Preheat oven to 350°F.
2. Peel fruit if your baby does not eat skins and you are puréeing in a blender or food processor.
3. Place fruit in an 8-inch-square baking pan. Sprinkle with the sugar.
4. Combine the dry ingredients in a small-size bowl. Mix in the butter until crumbly. Sprinkle over the fruit.

5. Bake 1 hour.
6. Purée baby's portion in blender or food processor for smoothest texture.

STORAGE: In refrigerator up to 3 days; freeze up to 4 months.

Apricot Whip

This dessert is high in iron and contains some protein. It is also a way to use leftover egg whites.

  1   **pound dried apricots**
  2   **teaspoons fresh orange or lemon juice**
  ¼ **cup brown sugar, light or dark**
  3   **egg whites**

1. Prepare the apricot purée as in Stewed Dried Apricots (page 140).
2. Return the purée to the saucepan and add the juice and sugar. Heat until the sugar is dissolved. Cool.
3. Beat the egg whites until stiff. Fold the apricot mixture into the egg whites.

STORAGE: In the refrigerator, covered, for up to 3 days.

YIELD: 6 servings (adult); 12 servings (baby).

VARIATION

You can also use other stewed dried fruits such as prunes or peaches.

Gelatin Desserts

Gelatin contains no vitamins or minerals, but it does supply a fair amount of protein. It also gives a thicker consistency to some thin or difficult-to-swallow foods. You can use it to give some variety to your baby's meals, either plain or combined with almost any puréed food. The gelatin dessert powders contain mainly sugar and a variety of preservatives, flavorings, and colors. Instead, buy the envelopes of plain dry gelatin, which are less expensive and just as easy to prepare. Here is a basic recipe.

½	**cup cool water**
1	**envelope plain gelatin**
1½	**cups fruit or vegetable juice**
1	**cup puréed fruit, vegetables (optional)**

1. Place water in a small saucepan. Sprinkle in gelatin and stir to dissolve.
2. Add juice and heat over medium heat for a minute or so, stirring well.
3. Pour into 4 small cups and cool in refrigerator. If you are adding a purée, stir it in after the gelatin has begun to thicken, after about ½ hour.

STORAGE: In refrigerator for up to 4 days.

YIELD: 4 servings.

12

Beverages

Beverages are essential in your baby's daily diet. Milk is the most important, but fruit and vegetable juices also supply vitamins and minerals. Because there is a wide variety of milks and juices for you to choose from, I feel it is important for you to be aware of the differences. I have also included basic information on buying, storing, and using milk and juices.

MILK FOR YOUR BABY

The American Academy of Pediatrics recommends breast milk as the preferred source of milk for the first twelve months. However, many mothers stop breast-feeding well before that time. The question is When is it acceptable to switch to regular cow's milk?

Until six months of age, commercial infant formula is recommended as the only adequate alternative to breast milk, and formula can be continued to one year or older. After six months, the academy advises, "If breast-feeding has been completely discontinued and infants are consuming one third of their calories as supplemental foods consisting of a balanced mixture of cereal, vegetables, fruits, and other foods (thereby assuring adequate sources of both iron and vitamin C), whole cow's milk may be introduced."

Of course, each baby has individual needs and it's best to consult your baby's doctor. It is important that a baby not drink more than 1 quart of whole milk daily. Reduced fat (1 or 2 percent) milk or skim milk is *not* advised (see "Fats," in Chapter 1).

Whole milk, whether it is pasteurized, homogenized, or evaporated, contains at least 3.25 percent butterfat if it is stamped U.S. Grade A. This grade also indicates that the milk was processed under sanitary conditions and is wholesome. The fresh milk was heated to kill harmful bacteria, but this pasteurizing also destroys the vitamin C. The butterfat in unhomogenized milk will rise to the top, and the bottle must be shaken, before pouring, to distribute the fat.

Homogenized milk is pasteurized fresh milk that has been processed to disperse the butterfat evenly through the milk. Read the label to make sure the particular brand has been fortified with vitamin D.

Evaporated milk is concentrated by removing half of the water. It is sterilized and sold in cans and is usually fortified with vitamin D. One advantage is that you can easily carry home a good supply and store the cans at cool room temperature for several months. It is also good to use when traveling, because it is readily available and of uniform composition throughout the world. It is also less expensive than fresh, whole milk.

You can easily prepare whole milk by mixing equal parts of evaporated milk and water. It is very convenient to mix it directly in your baby's bottle. Remember to wash the top of the can before opening. You can cover the opened can and store it in the refrigerator for up to five days. You can also use evaporated milk in concentrated form to thin purées, especially strong-flavored vegetables, and also in fruit and vegetable drinks to supply some extra nourishment.

Skim milk is whole milk that has had the butterfat removed. Since vitamin A is also removed with the fat, most skim milk is fortified with vitamin A. Skim milk should not be your baby's regular form of milk, because it is very low in fat and cholesterol.

Nonfat dry milk powder is skim milk from which almost all the water has been removed. You can buy it in any store, packed in boxes or in premeasured 1-quart envelopes. The U.S. Extra Grade on the label indicates that the milk meets the government's standards of composition and wholesomeness. The label also indicates whether vitamins A and D have been added.

This form of milk is very inexpensive as compared with a quart of fresh liquid milk.

You can store the unopened powder at cool room temperature (60° to 70°F) for several months. The opened package of powder should be kept dry and used within two weeks.

It is very convenient when you are traveling or visiting to carry a small amount of powder for an emergency bottle, if there's no fresh milk available. You can mix up a bottle wherever you find water—even a park or a gas station. To obtain liquid milk, you will usually mix 1⅓ parts nonfat dry milk powder to 4 parts water. For example:

1 cup (8 ounces)	= ⅓ cup powder	+ 1 cup water
1 bottle (8 ounces)	= 3 ounces powder	+ 8 ounces water
1 quart	= 1⅓ cups powder	+ 1 quart water

You can also use nonfat dry milk as a fortifier, to add nutrients in any recipe. Try adding 2 to 4 tablespoons powder for each cup liquid in a recipe.

Raw cow's milk or certified raw milk is one instance where an unprocessed food should not be used. All the original nutrients are there, but so are all the bacteria, which can cause various illnesses and intestinal troubles. Because you must boil it to make it sterile, you have the same loss of vitamin C as in pasteurized milk, so it hardly seems worth the trouble and risk.

Condensed milk is sold in cans, usually on the same shelf as evaporated milk. Be careful not to confuse them. Since this milk is highly sweetened, it is not suitable for your baby.

Filled and modified skim milk are milk products that were developed for diet-conscious people who do not like the taste of skim milk. If the name confuses you, read the list of ingredients on the label. The different brands vary in composition but are usually some mixture of skim milk, nonfat dry milk, water, and vegetable fat.

While there is nothing harmful in these ingredients, the government has not set standards to ensure that these milks have the same nutritional composition as cow's milk. The protein content may be higher or lower, and the vegetable fat is often coconut oil, which is a saturated fat that lacks essential fatty acids. They are usually more expensive than plain whole milk.

If this type of milk is the only one available, your baby will not be harmed by an occasional bottle, but he should not drink this milk regularly.

Synthetic, nondairy, and imitation milk are also sold in dairy departments. These products have no relation to cow's milk. They are a combination of vegetable fat, sodium caseinate, soy solids, corn syrup, flavoring agents, emulsifiers, stabilizers, and water. Government standards have not been set for their nutritional value. Needless to say, do not give them to your baby.

Chocolate milk is also sold in dairy departments. It is sweetened and chocolate is a high-allergy food, so don't even try it in an emergency. Naturally flavored fruit milks are fine occasionally as long as the fruit has already been introduced. However some brands contain added sugar.

Instant breakfasts are a form of milk drink, packaged in cans or in powder form. They are really a combination of sugar, flavorings, and some vitamin supplements. In an emergency, if milk is just not available, you can give your baby the liquid *vanilla* flavor. The powder form depends on being mixed with milk for its nutritional value. So don't just mix it with water and give it to your baby as milk.

Buttermilk is made from skim milk, and bacterial cultures have been added, which gives it a sour taste. The name sounds healthful, but it is not suitable for your baby.

Goat's milk and soybean-based milk may be given to babies who show an allergy to cow's milk. However, they do not have the same nutritional composition, so you should never use them without the advice of your doctor.

Diet drinks should never be given to a baby.

How to Store Milk Fresh milk, and evaporated or nonfat dry milk that has been reconstituted, should be carefully handled to retain nutrients and prevent spoilage. I've always felt so guilty when I've had to throw away a quart of spoiled milk.

- Always buy fresh milk that is as fresh as possible. In many states the cartons must be clearly stamped with the date of the last day that the milk can be sold. In areas that do not have this law, the cartons are usually stamped with a coded date, and you can ask the store manager to interpret it. If you are buying more milk than you will use immediately, select those cartons with the latest date. If you find milk in the case that is past the legal selling date, you should not buy it; instead, notify the manager to have it removed from the shelf.
- Cans of evaporated milk and packages of nonfat dry milk powder are often stamped with the packaging date. Buy the most recent date if you are buying large amounts. Store unopened evaporated and dry milk at cool room temperature.
- Keep liquid milk tightly covered and store it in the coldest part of the refrigerator. Remember that the door, which may have a shelf for milk, is usually the warmest area of the refrigerator, and milk should not be stored there.
- Plan to use milk within three to five days.
- Do not allow clear containers of milk to stand in the light, because light destroys the vitamin riboflavin. Opaque cardboard cartons are better than the clear plastic bottles. Since your baby's bottle may often be out for as long as an hour during a feeding, you can preserve the riboflavin by using opaque plastic bottles, or the disposable bottles that are used inside a solid holder.
- Do not pour unused milk back in the original container once it has been removed, or mix old milk in with fresh milk.
- You may freeze milk for up to a month, but it must be used soon after thawing.

Homemade Fortified Milk

If your baby becomes balky at eating solids, here are some fortifiers that you can add to one bottle daily. (You could also give an occasional bottle of formula.)

- 1 **cup milk**
- 2 **tablespoons nonfat dry milk powder**
- ¼ **teaspoon molasses (laxative, iron)**
- ½ **teaspoon powdered brewer's yeast (*not* baking yeast; B vitamins)**
- 2 **teaspoons vegetable oil (vitamin E, linoleic acid)**
- 2 **teaspoons plain yogurt (vitamin K)**

1. Blend the ingredients with an electric blender or egg beater.
2. Allow it to settle for a few minutes so that there are no air bubbles.
3. Use a nipple with an enlarged hole. You can enlarge the hole by piercing it with a hot needle (stick in a pencil eraser for easy handling).

STORAGE: In refrigerator 3–4 days if fresh.

YIELD: 1¼ cups.

JUICES: FRUIT AND VEGETABLE

Fruit and vegetable juices supply vitamins and minerals while satisfying your baby's thirst. The juices sold especially for infants are very expensive. Instead, you may serve your baby any of the canned and frozen juices on the market, or you can easily prepare juice from fresh fruits and vegetables.

NUTRITION. Juice is most valuable in your baby's diet as a source of vitamin C. This vitamin, although adequate in human milk, is destroyed in cow's milk by the pasteurization process. You can give your baby a vitamin supplement, but daily servings of certain juices will supply an adequate amount of vitamin C, together with other nutrients. Fruits and vegetables have different amounts of vitamin C.

- "An orange a day keeps the doctor away" should replace the old proverb about the apple. The citrus fruits—oranges, grapefruits, lemon—are your highest vitamin-C fruits. One 3-ounce serving each day of one of these juices, either fresh, dehydrated, or frozen, will give your baby enough vitamin C. When these juices are canned some of the vitamin is lost, so you should increase the serving to at least 4 ounces. The orange and grapefruit juices sold in bottles in the dairy section have been pasteurized and are the same as canned juices.
- Guava juice, available in cans, is as high as the citrus fruits in vitamin C.
- Canned tomato or papaya juice will supply an adequate amount of vitamin C, if you double the serving to 6 ounces daily.
- Never heat fruit juice before serving, because heat destroys vitamin C.
- Other fruits are low in vitamin C and should be considered only beverages.
- Apricot nectar, papaya, and mango juices are very high in vitamin A.

INTRODUCE. Orange juice, then other citrus juices, can be offered at nine months. Orange juice is a possible allergy food, so when you first introduce it, dilute the juice with an equal amount of water. Begin with 1 ounce daily, then gradually increase to 3 ounces. If your baby does show an allergic reaction to orange juice, you can try guava or tomato juice or give him a vitamin C supplement. Other juices can be given as beverages at around the same time you would introduce the fruit or vegetable.

Until your baby is drinking from a cup, many juices will have to be strained. You can try using a special nipple, or enlarging the hole with a hot thick needle.

Actually, the American Academy of Pediatrics recommends that babies be taught to drink juice from a cup as soon as possible. The reason? Bottles of juice are often given as pacifiers, and babies tend to drink them over extended periods. When the natural sugar in the juice is in prolonged contact with a baby's teeth, the result is cavities. Of course, you should *never* put a baby to bed with a bottle of juice, milk, or formula. Give only plain water.

BUY. The Food and Drug Administration has set standards of identity for the various forms of fresh, frozen, and canned orange juice that require a high content of juice. Unless you live in a tropical climate or buy oranges in season, the frozen orange juice concentrates are the most economical source of vitamin C. Since the juice content is set by the government, you can take advantage of the lower-priced store brands or private labels.

Standards have also been set for canned pineapple, tomato, and prune juice. Any sweeteners and preservatives must be stated on the label, so you can select the brands *without* additional sweeteners.

If you buy fruit juice, other than orange juice, that has been fortified with vitamin C, read the label carefully to check the amount of vitamin C in a serving that your baby is likely to drink. Remember that he should have 40 to 50 milligrams of vitamin C daily.

Please notice that I have been using the word *juice*. There are many beverages, both canned and frozen, that cannot be legally labeled "juice." These include the fruit *punches, cocktails, blends, nectars, drinks,* and *ades,* which are clearly labeled with these descriptive words. **The nutritional cost of these beverages is very high:** You are paying for and filling your baby up with mainly water and sugar. This is equally true of such citrus drinks as orangeade or lemonade. Many are more expensive than pure juice. Even if vitamin C is added (and advertised in large letters), you are still missing the other vitamins and minerals in the original fruit and paying more. You would come out ahead, in terms of nutritional cost, if you diluted frozen orange juice concentrate, instead of the usual three-to-one dilution, with the same amount of water as in these drinks—often as high as nine parts water to one part juice.

There are no government standards for these drinks, and the label does not have to state the percentage of real juice (except for orange juice drinks). Carefully read the ingredient list on any canned or frozen juices. Do not be misled by the word *natural* on the label: "100% natural juice" does not mean it is 100 percent juice.

Other beverages that your baby should not drink are the "instant breakfast drink powders" and the "imitation orange juices." Again, the label and list of ingredients are your warning. These drinks contain little or no real juice and instead are made up of a variety of fillers, artificial color, artificial flavor, vegetable oil, sugar, and preservatives. Some vitamin C is added, but they still lack the other nutrients found in orange juice. These imitation juices are usually sold in the same freezer section as frozen orange juice, so you must be careful not to confuse them. You can also buy dehydrated juice crystals that are real juice and should not be confused with the breakfast drink powders. If you are in doubt about a product, just read the list of ingredients.

STORE. Canned juices can be kept at cool room temperature (60° to 70°F) for several months. Before opening the can, shake it well and rinse the lid. The opened can can be covered and stored in the refrigerator for two to three days. The acid in citrus juices acts as a preservative and these juices keep the longest. Frozen juices can be kept solidly frozen for several months in a 0°F freezer. Do not refreeze thawed juices; use them within three to four days. Fresh citrus juices can be refrigerated for three to four days or frozen. Other fresh fruit and vegetable juices should be prepared just before serving and should not be saved.

Here are a few easy recipes for preparing fresh juices. For detailed buying and storing information, see Chapter 8 and Chapter 9.

Fresh Orange Juice

The best juice oranges are the Valencia, Hamlin, and Parson Brown. Select oranges that have smooth skins and are heavy for their size. Oranges with russet or greenish skin color are often less expensive, but just as nutritious as the oranges with a bright orange color. You'll save cleanup time if you make a large batch and freeze it in food cubes.

1   medium juice orange

1. Wash the orange. Cut it in half and squeeze the juice with either a hand or electric juicer. Or if you have a good blender, peel the orange, cut it in half, remove the seeds, and liquefy. This is a good method if you are making a large quantity and do not have an electric juicer.
2. Do not add any sweetener.

STORAGE: In refrigerator 3–4 days; however vitamin C will decrease.

YIELD: 3 ounces or 2 food cubes (1 serving).

VARIATIONS

Fresh Grapefruit Juice. Substitute ½ medium grapefruit for the orange.

Fresh Lemon Juice. Substitute 2 lemons for the orange. Add ½ teaspoon sugar and ½ cup water to dilute. This makes 8 ounces or 4 food cubes (2 servings).

All-Purpose Fruit Juice

You can prepare almost any fruit as a juice with a food processor or blender. Here is a general recipe with suggestions for some specific fruits. If you use a very juicy fruit such as berries, decrease the liquid to ½ cup. Do not combine milk with citrus fruits. And remember, don't add sugar—fruits contain natural sugar.

½ **cup chopped fruit**
¾ **cup liquid (water, fruit juice, or milk)**

1. Select ripe fruit. Take advantage of seasonal pieces or sales.
2. Wash the fruit. Peel and remove seeds.
3. Place fruit and liquid in blender and blend on highest speed until the fruit is liquefied. In food processor, purée fruit first, then add liquid. Serve at once, or freeze up to 1 year.

YIELD: 1 cup juice.

VARIATION

Combine thick fruits with juicy fruits such as banana and orange. Experiment with any fruit you may have on hand or left over from a family meal. This is a good way to use up a piece of very ripe fruit that you might otherwise throw away.

All-Purpose Raw Vegetable Juice

There are fewer vegetables that can be prepared and served as juices because of their generally stronger tastes; however, they do make highly nutritious drinks. Carrots are an excellent source of vitamin A; spinach and green leafy vegetables contain high amounts of vitamins and minerals; and beets are high in natural sugar; however, do not serve more than 8 ounces a day. See Chapter 9 for specific information on any vegetable you prepare as a juice. Here is a general recipe for use with a blender or food processor.

½ **cup chopped vegetable**
1 **cup liquid (water, milk, or fruit juice)**

1. Wash the vegetable. Peel if necessary.
2. Place vegetable and liquid in blender and liquefy on highest speed. In food processor, purée vegetable first, then add liquid. Serve at once or freeze up to 1 year.

YIELD: 1 cup.

Cooked Vegetable Juice

This is another way of preparing vegetable juice without a blender. You can also make a large amount and freeze it.

2 **cups chopped vegetable**
1 **quart water**

1. Wash and peel vegetable if necessary.
2. Place in medium-size saucepan. Cover tightly and simmer for 1 hour.
3. Cool and strain.

STORAGE: In refrigerator for up to 3 days. Or freeze in food cubes up to 2 months.

YIELD: 3½ cups.

VARIATION

You can combine many fruits and vegetables to make a variety of nutritious drinks. Here are some suggestions, but use your imagination and whatever you may happen to have on hand—either fresh, frozen, or canned.

Beet/pineapple	Carrot/pineapple
Carrot/apple	Orange/green leafy
Carrot/celery	Pear/green leafy
Carrot/orange	Tomato/green leafy

Fresh Carrot Juice

This is one of the first vegetable juices that you can serve your baby when he is seven to eight months old. You will need a blender or food processor to prepare this juice. Limit servings to 1 per day.

> 1 **medium carrot**
> ¾ **cup water (or skim milk)**
> 1 **tablespoon nonfat dry milk (optional)**

1. Wash carrot. Cut in half.
2. Place carrot and water in blender or food processor. Add dry milk, if desired. Blend on highest speed.
3. Strain and serve at once.

STORAGE: Do not store.

YIELD: 6 ounces juice.

Boiled Carrot Juice

This is really the same as raw carrot juice, but you will not need a blender and you can make enough for several servings. Unlike raw carrot juice, boiled can be refrigerated or frozen. Limit to 1 serving a day.

> 1 **pound (4–5 medium) carrots**
> 1 **quart water (or 2 cups water plus 2 cups skim milk)**
> ½ **cup nonfat dry milk (optional)**
> 1 **tablespoon brown rice (optional)**

1. Wash carrots and cut in small pieces or chop.
2. Place all ingredients in a medium-size saucepan. Cover tightly and bring to a boil. Reduce heat and simmer for 1 hour.
3. Cool and strain. Do not force the carrots through the sieve; you want a juice, not a purée. The cooked carrots can be puréed as a food.

STORAGE: Tightly covered in the refrigerator for up to 3 days. Or freeze in food cubes up to 2 months.

YIELD: 3½ cups or 16 food cubes.

13

"Instant" Baby Food

The foods that are described in this chapter form the basis of easy baby food preparation. In fact, they can all be used without any cooking or can be purchased already cooked in stores or restaurants. You can feed your baby some foods directly from the container. Other foods require only a fork or spoon to prepare the smoothest purée. A few foods may require the use of a blender, food mill, or strainer to prepare a smooth purée, but can still be mashed to a coarse texture with a fork or spoon. Because you are preparing your own baby food, you can quickly accustom your baby to eating coarser textures. You can always try a food; a hungry baby can become very adept at swallowing!

The small food mills that are sold specifically for processing baby food are very convenient to carry when traveling. Some prepare a finer purée than others, but they all process almost any food into at least a "junior" texture. Once your baby is eating most table food and coarser textures, you can prepare "instant" food from your regular family meals with this type of food mill. I tried a portion of a quiche that was very much enjoyed by a visiting baby!

Instant foods can be particularly valuable when you are traveling or visiting, since there is no need to carry or store specially prepared food for your baby. To make your life even easier, train your baby to eat any food cold. These foods may be found in any small store, restaurant, or home kitchen. You should also keep some of these foods on hand for quick use if you happen to run out of your supply of frozen food cubes or if you do not have adequate freezer space to take advantage of the food cube method.

You should keep a list of the more successful ones for use by baby-sitters and for your own quick reference. Use your imagination in finding new instant foods that I have missed; just keep in mind the basic good buying principles as described in Chapter 2. For more detailed information, look up any specific food in the preceding recipe chapters. The instant foods are also organized according to their basic food group (i.e., cereal grains, fruits, vegetables, and protein foods) so you can easily select a well-balanced menu.

CEREAL GRAINS

Dry infant cereals are easy to carry and prepare. They are usually mixed one part cereal to three to four parts cold milk or formula.

Hot cereals can usually be ordered in any restaurant. The smoothest ones will be the cream of wheat or rice. If your baby has been introduced to whole grain cereals, order oatmeal, Ralston, or Wheatena.

Graham crackers or other soft enriched or whole grain crackers can be soaked in milk and mashed to a soft purée. Bread can also be soaked. Avoid those that use BHT as a preservative.

Rice pudding is usually available in restaurants and can be mashed with a fork or spoon.

FRUITS

Fresh fruit is one of your most convenient instant foods. It is easy to carry and is available in any store or restaurant. As soon as possible, you should introduce raw fruit to your baby. Bananas can be served as early as four to five months, and other raw fruits at seven to eight months of age. You will be able to easily prepare a very smooth purée with only a spoon from any of the following fresh fruits. You will not even need a feeding dish.

Apples	Mangoes
Apricots	Nectarines
Avocados	Papayas
Bananas	Peaches
Cantaloupe	Pears
Guavas	Plums
Kiwis	

- Select ripe fruit.
- Wash the fruit. Do not peel; the skin will serve as the dish.
- Cut the fruit in half, or cut as large a slice as your baby will eat. Peel one side of a banana.
- Remove the pit or seeds.
- As you feed your baby, mash spoonfuls of fruit by scraping the cut side with the front or back edge of a spoon. This method is easy and will make a smoother purée than mashing with a fork.

Whole fruit keeps well, but when mashed, it turns brown quickly. So only mash as much as you will use in one feeding. The unpeeled part of the fruit can be wrapped and will keep at room temperature until the next feeding. You can also store it in the refrigerator for one to two days.

Canned or stewed fruits are also convenient as instant fruits. You can keep a supply on hand in your pantry. Buy the brands that are packed in water or in their own juice, not the sugared syrups. Always drain the fruit before puréeing, because it should not require any thinning, but use the juice (or water) as a beverage or thinner. Some good fruits are

Applesauce. Use the plain variety. The applesauce that is combined with other fruits often contains artificial color, flavor, or other additives, and is more expensive. You can serve applesauce to your baby without puréeing.

Baked Apples. Mash with a fork or spoon for a smooth purée.

Jellied Cranberry Sauce. This is high in sugar, but can

be served occasionally. Mash with a spoon for a smooth purée. Do not feed your baby the whole type, which contains skins.

Pears. Can be mashed with a fork for a smooth purée.

Peaches, Apricots, Fruit Salad, Prunes. Can be mashed with a fork for a coarser purée.

Pineapple. Requires a blender to prepare a purée.

VEGETABLES

There are many vegetables that you can keep on hand or order in a restaurant as instant food.

Mashed potatoes require thinning with a little milk. The "instant" or dehydrated potatoes should be used only as a last resort, because they may be lower in nutrients and usually are loaded with additives and fillers.

Canned yams or sweet potatoes are already cooked and can be mashed with a fork, adding a little milk. Buy the vacuum-pack, not the type that is packed in sugar syrup.

Beans, baked or kidney, and peas can be puréed to a coarse texture with a fork, and thinned with a little milk. Or use a blender for a smooth purée.

Peanut butter should be thinned with an equal amount of milk. If thick, it can cause choking.

Frozen winter squash (acorn, butternut, etc.) is cooked and mashed. It only requires thawing, because it is already puréed. You can usually order this squash in a restaurant.

Fresh ripe tomatoes should be cut in half. Remove the seeds, and scrape with a spoon.

Any canned vegetable can be used. Because they are already cooked, you only need to purée them in a blender or food mill (see Chapter 9). Most can be mashed with a fork to a coarse texture. Drain the canning liquid, then add a small amount for thinning if necessary. If the canning liquid is not salted, you can serve it as a nutritious beverage.

PROTEIN FOODS

Eggs One of the best and most convenient instant protein foods! They are included as an instant food because a boiled egg is so easy to make, stores well, and can be easily carried when traveling. You can always order an egg in any restaurant.

Here's how to use an egg yolk as an instant food. Keep the boiled egg in the shell until ready to use. It can be kept at room temperature for one day, or refrigerated for one week. Cut the egg in half and remove the yolk. Mash the yolk, adding about 1 tablespoon milk or juice to thin.

Scrambled eggs can also be thought of as instant food. The eggs should be soft, but thoroughly cooked. Mash them with a fork or spoon, adding a little milk.

Egg custard can be ordered in most restaurants and can be fed directly to your baby.

Liver Either chopped chicken liver or a pâté can be thinned to make a very smooth purée. It is available in most delicatessens and restaurants. Because these pâtés are rich and highly seasoned, use them only as a last resort to feed an older baby. You can also order sautéed or broiled chicken livers in many restaurants and mash them with a fork, adding a little milk. The beef and calf's liver is usually too tough to prepare with a fork, but you can scrape some off with a spoon or dull knife.

Prepared spreads such as deviled ham, chicken, and liver can be purchased in small cans. These can easily be thinned to make a smooth purée, but they are also highly seasoned and often contain additives.

Precooked Meat and Poultry Meals There are many canned and frozen prepared dishes that contain meat, poultry, cheese, vegetables, rice, pastas, beans. While they are more expensive than the same dishes that you can prepare yourself, they are easily stored and very convenient. They are also less expensive than the "toddler" type commercial baby foods. For a quick meal, just open the can (or defrost) and put the food through the blender.

Some dishes such as spaghetti or macaroni and cheese can also be mashed with a fork or food mill to a coarser purée. These dishes can often be ordered in a restaurant.

Read canned food labels carefully and buy brands that list protein foods first, as the major ingredient. Avoid those brands that contain many additives and fillers. Remember that these precooked foods should only be served occasionally when convenience is important.

Chicken and noodles

Chile con carne (for an older baby)

Macaroni and cheese

Spaghetti and meatballs

Stews (usually the highest in protein)

TV dinners (choose one with a plain meat and two vegetables)

Do not use the frozen chicken or meat pot pies, because they contain very small amounts of protein.

Leftovers can be stored in the refrigerator for two days. The canned foods can be frozen in food cubes for up to one month. *Do not* refreeze the frozen foods.

Dairy Foods These dairy foods can also be used as sources of protein, and they contain the same nutrients as milk. They are very convenient and readily available instant foods.

Yogurt can be one of your baby's earliest foods. There is a wide variety of brands and flavors.

- Buy the brands that do not contain fillers, additives, or artificial sweeteners. The simplest list of ingredients is fresh milk, nonfat dry milk, and yogurt cultures.
- You should introduce *plain* yogurt first.
- Older babies will enjoy the various fruit flavors. But keep in mind they usually contain sugar. The Swiss-style yogurts have small pieces of fresh fruit that are easily mashed.

- Do not feed your baby the *chocolate* or *coffee* flavors. Chocolate is a high-allergy food, and contains caffeine, as does coffee.
- You can feed your baby yogurt, at refrigerator temperature.
- Unused yogurt must be stored in the refrigerator and can be kept up to one week.
- See Chapter 10 for instructions on how you can easily make your own yogurt.

Cottage cheese is easy to prepare.

- Use the creamed variety or add a little milk. Mash with a spoon for a smooth purée. It is also good when mixed with a little fruit such as applesauce.
- "Diet" or low-fat cheese is fine for occasional use, but regular cottage cheese (4 percent fat) is best.
- Avoid those brands that contain fillers, preservatives, and added fruits that have not yet been introduced.
- Cottage cheese spoils easily, so buy by the date, or taste it yourself before feeding it to your baby.
- You can store it in the refrigerator for up to one week.

Puddings, if they are homemade, can be served occasionally as an instant food. The canned and frozen puddings are highly sweetened and contain a high percentage of fillers and additives, so don't bother feeding them to your baby.

14

Finger Foods

Sooner or later, often around eight months, your baby will decide that he wants to feed himself. He will not too subtly indicate this by grabbing for the spoon, hitting the spoon away, or simply refusing to eat. By this time you will probably be more than happy to give him the opportunity to feed himself. Unfortunately, this desire may come before he can handle a spoon well enough to consume an adequate meal. The result can be a hungry, cranky, frustrated baby, and a mess of splattered purées for you to clean up.

One way to handle this difficult stage is to serve your baby a well-balanced selection of finger foods that he can pick up, chew easily, and swallow without choking. Don't worry about discouraging his willingness to eat with a spoon. You can always give him a spoon and serve a thick purée (see "Self-Feeding," in Chapter 3). He is more likely to become discouraged if he becomes frustrated in trying to get enough to eat. He may then give up entirely and you will end up feeding him for much longer than is necessary. Instead, as your baby picks up his finger foods, he will be gaining valuable eye, hand, and muscular coordination and will also be eating the foods that are so necessary for his growth. This stage can be a happy and healthy one for both of you!

SOME GENERAL SUGGESTIONS

- For your own convenience, serve finger foods that fit in with the meals you are preparing for the rest of your family.
- Just as you planned to keep on hand a store of purées, plan to have a ready supply of finger foods, frozen, canned, or fresh.
- For specific nutritional, buying, storage, and preparation information, look up any food in the recipe chapters.
- The consistency of any finger food should be firm enough for your baby to pick up, yet tender enough for him to chew and swallow easily. A cooked food is the proper consistency if you are able to pierce it easily with a fork.
- Begin with small pieces of very tender food.
- Be careful if your baby is teething very young. Just because he has teeth doesn't mean he knows how to chew food. He is more likely to bite off a piece, try to swallow it whole, and start choking.
- *Do not give* small pieces of firm food such as meat, nuts, popcorn, or raw hard vegetables that may cause choking. The most dangerous foods are round, slippery ones like grapes and hot dogs. Always cut these into small pieces. Never leave your child alone when he is eating and don't allow him to walk around while eating.
- If your baby is swallowing food whole and it is not being digested, it will show up whole in his bowel movements. In that case, you should cut the food into smaller pieces and make sure it is very tender.
- There is one thing that you should buy that will save you considerable cleanup time. It is a plastic "catch-all" bib and it means just that. The bottom of the bib is folded up to form a pocket so that the pieces of food that do not make it to your baby's mouth, or that he decides to reject, drop into the pocket instead of on the floor.

    You can easily make this bib by folding up the bottom of any plastic or cloth bib about 2 inches, then sewing or stapling the edges. Or you can fasten the edges with paper clips, which can then be removed for easy cleaning. Remember, when you fasten the edges, you must allow the pocket to buckle out so that the food will be caught.

- One additional word of warning: Your baby may discover that it is fun to drop these finger foods from his high chair and watch them land on the floor. This may be educational, but it is also a nuisance for you to clean up. Since your baby will usually do this when he is no longer hungry, the simplest thing is to just take him out of his chair and declare the meal finished. It all depends on your tolerance for mess.

The following sections list some easy and nutritious finger foods according to their basic food group—cereal grains, fruit, vegetables, and protein foods.

CEREAL GRAINS

The cereal grain foods are economical sources of incomplete protein, carbohydrates, minerals, and the B vitamins.

DRY, READY-TO-EAT CEREALS. These are some of the easiest finger foods and, because you are faced with an overwhelming selection, here are some general rules:

- Do not buy the sugar-frosted, honey-coated, or chocolate-flavored cereals.
- Buy those cereals with a definite shape that your baby can easily pick up, but avoid solid round shapes that are large enough for your baby to choke on.
- There is controversy over the nutritional value of some of these ready-to-eat cereals. You should read the labels carefully and buy only those that are "enriched."
- When you first introduce these cereals, soften them with a little milk, a few at a time. They will be easier to swallow.

PASTA. You can now buy spaghetti and macaroni in many different shapes that your baby can easily pick up. Even if he swallows them whole, they will be well digested.

- Always buy brands that are "enriched."
- Some good shapes are shells, wheels, twists, and small elbow macaroni. The long, thin spaghetti and noodles are very difficult to manage.
- You can serve these pastas plain, or with a little butter, tomato sauce, or melted cheese as in Macaroni and Cheese (page 123).
- You can take advantage of the prepared spaghetti and macaroni dishes, either frozen or canned. Again, read the labels and buy the brand that is enriched and contains the fewest additives and fillers.

BAKED GOODS. The first breads your baby can eat are either very moist, soft breads, or very hard baked goods that he can teethe on. If a bread or a cracker has a medium, crumbly consistency, he may choke on it.

- Always buy crackers, cookies, and breads that are baked with enriched, unbleached, or whole grain flour (see "Cereal Grains," in Chapter 7).
- You can harden almost any bread by baking it in a very low (150°–200°F) oven for 15 to 20 minutes.
- Stale bagels are also an excellent teething food.

Here are some easy and nutritious recipes for both moist and hard breads. You will be able to serve them to your baby and the rest of your family.

Banana Bread Sticks

¼   **cup brown sugar, light or dark**
2   **eggs**
½   **cup vegetable oil (safflower or corn)**
1   **cup banana, mashed (add whole if using a processor)**
1¾ **cups flour (whole wheat or unbleached and enriched)**
2   **teaspoons baking powder**
½   **teaspoon baking soda**

1. Preheat oven to 350°F. Grease 9 × 5 loaf pan.
2. Beat sugar, eggs, and oil together in medium-size bowl. Stir in banana.
3. Mix together flour, baking powder, baking soda in medium-size bowl. Add to banana mixture, stirring only until smooth.
4. Pour into loaf pan. Bake for about 1 hour or until firmly set.
5. Cool bread, remove from pan. Cut into roughly 1-inch sticks.
6. Spread out on cookie sheet or aluminum foil and bake at 150°F until the sticks are hard and crunchy. Or serve as a moist bread.

STORAGE: In tightly covered container in a dry place, about 1 week.

YIELD: About 2 dozen, depending on size of sticks.

VARIATIONS

Date Bread Sticks. Add ½ cup of finely chopped or puréed dates (good for iron) with the bananas.

Nut Bread Sticks. Add ½ cup finely chopped nuts with the bananas.

Fruit Bread Sticks. Substitute other fruit purées such as apricot, peach, etc., for the banana.

Carrot Bread Sticks. Substitute ¾ cup finely grated raw carrots for the banana.

Date-Oatmeal Bread

This is a moist bread that is highly nutritious. If you have a blender or food processor you can easily mix all the wet ingredients and chop the dates.

1½	cups unbleached flour (or ¾ cup unbleached flour plus ¾ cup whole wheat flour)
½	teaspoon baking powder
1	teaspoon baking soda
¾	cup quick-cooking oatmeal
1	egg
1	cup sour cream
½	cup brown sugar, light or dark
½	cup dark molasses
⅔	cup chopped dates

1. Preheat oven to 350°F. Grease a 9 × 5 loaf pan.
2. Combine flour, baking powder, baking soda, and oatmeal in medium-size bowl.
3. Blend together the egg, sour cream, sugar, and molasses in medium-size bowl. (If you are using a blender, add dates while blender is on.)
4. Mix the chopped dates into the egg mixture.
5. Pour the wet mixture over the dry ingredients and mix well.
6. Turn into the loaf pan and bake for 45–55 minutes.

STORAGE: In refrigerator up to 1 week.

YIELD: 1 loaf.

Peanut Butter Cookies

This is a healthful cereal/protein snack.

> 1 **cup shortening (melted butter or margarine or vegetable oil)**
> 1 **cup peanut butter (preferably homemade), chunky or smooth**
> 1 **cup brown sugar, light or dark**
> 2 **eggs**
> 1 **teaspoon vanilla extract**
> ½ **cup nonfat dry milk**
> 2½ **cups flour (whole wheat or unbleached and enriched)**
> ¾ **teaspoon baking soda**
> ½ **teaspoon baking powder**

1. Preheat oven to 375°F.
2. Beat shortening and peanut butter in medium-size bowl until creamy. It will be easier if the peanut butter is at room temperature.
3. Gradually add the sugar, beating until mixed.
4. Beat in the eggs and vanilla.
5. Blend in the remaining ingredients.
6. Shape dough into balls about 1 inch in diameter and place about 2 inches apart on an ungreased baking sheet. Flatten each cookie with tines of a fork.
7. Bake for 10–15 minutes. Cool.

STORAGE: In a tightly covered container in a dry place, up to 1 week.

YIELD: 4 dozen cookies.

Oatmeal Cookies

These old favorites count as a healthful cereal serving; good for an easy snack.

1	cup flour (whole wheat or unbleached and enriched)
1¼	teaspoons baking powder
½	teaspoon baking soda
½	cup melted butter or margarine or vegetable oil
½	cup light or dark brown sugar, packed
½	teaspoon allspice (optional)
1	egg
¾	teaspoon vanilla extract
1½	cups quick-cooking rolled oats
¼	cup wheat germ (optional)

1. Preheat oven to 350°F.
2. Mix together flour, baking powder, and baking soda in a medium-size bowl.
3. Beat butter with sugar and spice until creamy in a large-size bowl. Beat in egg and vanilla.
4. Blend in flour mixture, oats, and wheat germ. (If using a food processor, mix in the oatmeal by hand.)
5. Cover dough and chill.
6. Shape dough into balls about 1 inch in diameter. Place 2 inches apart on an ungreased baking sheet.
7. Bake for 10–15 minutes. Allow cookies to cool.

STORAGE: In a tightly covered container in a dry place, up to 1 week.

YIELD: 3–4 dozen cookies.

Sesame Crackers

This is a simple recipe that combines complementary foods to obtain more complete protein.

> 1½ **cups whole wheat flour**
> ¼ **cup soy flour**
> ¼ **cup sesame seeds**
> ½ **teaspoon salt**
> ¼ **cup vegetable oil**
> ½ **cup water (approximate)**

1. Preheat oven to 350°F.
2. Stir flours, sesame seeds, and salt together in medium-size bowl. Add oil and blend well.
3. Add only enough water to make it easy to roll—the consistency of pie dough.
4. Roll dough to ⅛ inch thick and cut into shapes or sticks.
5. Bake on ungreased baking sheet until crisp.

STORAGE: In tightly covered container up to 1 week.

YIELD: 3–4 dozen crackers.

FRUITS

Fruits are some of the easiest and most nutritious finger foods that you can serve your baby. You can look up the specific fruit in Chapter 8 for detailed information; however, here are some general suggestions.

- Prepare fresh fruit just before serving, to conserve nutrients.
- To remove skins, dip fruit in boiling water, then rub off skin under cold water. Or use a paring knife.
- Remove seeds and cut into small pieces.
- Apples are an exception, since small pieces are hard enough for your baby to choke on.
- When your baby is about ten months old, you can serve, unpeeled, such fruits as pears, nectarines, and

plums. Remember that the skins contain nutrients and fiber.

- Frozen and canned fruits can also be served. Buy those brands that are packed in their own juice instead of sugar syrup. You should also buy the Grade A fruits for use as finger foods, because they will have better shape and are usually more tender.

- Dried fruits, such as pitted prunes, apricots, apples, peaches, and dates are excellent finger foods. Either buy the moist variety or soak them in water overnight to soften them. If they have been preserved with any form of sulfites, be alert for allergic reactions (see "Food Allergies," in Chapter 3). Stewed dried fruit that is sold in jars is heavily sweetened and should not be served too often.

The following fruits are convenient to serve as finger foods. Unless noted, they should be introduced peeled and cut into small pieces to prevent choking.

Apricots	Mangoes
Avocados	Nectarines
Bananas	Oranges, grapefruit (sections)
Berries°	Papayas
Cantaloupes	Peaches
Cherries°	Pears
Grapes°	Plums, prunes

Fruit Leather

You can buy this ready made, but it will contain unspecified amounts of sugar and water. It is very easy to make at home and is a nutritious, soft "chewing" food for your baby. It is also a good snack for older children and adults. Combine any of listed fruits or use them singly.

°Do not serve until your baby is able to digest the skins, at around one year.

Apricots—fresh, canned (drained), or dried
   (soak overnight in water)
Peaches—fresh, canned (drained), or dried
   (soak overnight in water)
Apples—fresh (uncooked, peeled or unpeeled)
Prunes—canned (drained) or dried (soak
   overnight in water)
Bananas—fresh
1   tablespoon fresh lemon or orange juice
     (optional)

1. Process fruit in blender or food processor into a thick purée. If using raw fruit, add a little lemon or orange juice to prevent browning.
2. Spread on a lightly oiled cookie sheet to about ⅛ inch thick.
3. Allow purée to dry until the consistency of leather. The length of time depends on the amount of heat. You can dry the fruit in an oven that was preheated to 200°F and then turned off or you can replace the oven light with a 100-watt light bulb (see Homemade Yogurt, page 252). A sunny spot in the house will take longer and the fruit may pick up some general dust. Don't leave the fruit outside to dry in the sun unless you can devise a foolproof way of keeping insects off—they're one source of protein your baby doesn't need!
4. When purée is dry, roll it up in waxed paper or plastic wrap. Cut into 1-inch strips. Store in refrigerator 2–3 weeks, tightly wrapped.

• MICROWAVE METHOD

Spread ¾ cup prepared purée on a 14 × 11-inch flat dish or tray lined with parchment paper. Cook, uncovered, on high for 11 minutes. Cook on medium for 11 minutes more. Check to make sure the edges aren't getting too brown. Let stand until cool. Continue as directed.

VEGETABLES

Vegetables are essential in you baby's diet and you can use many as convenient finger foods. For more detailed information, look up the specific vegetable in Chapter 9. Here are some general suggestions:

- You will have to cook most vegetables. Whenever possible, cook them in their skins and in large pieces or whole. You will conserve nutrients and it will be easier to peel and cut the vegetables after they are cooked.
- The best way to cook most vegetables is to steam or microwave them until they are tender and can be pierced with a fork.
- Tomatoes are the only raw vegetables that a young baby can eat as a finger food. Dip them in boiling water to remove the skins easily and spoon out the seeds.
- Raw vegetables are not suitable for finger food because most are quite hard. If your baby has even a few teeth, he might bite off a piece of the vegetable and choke on it.
- You might try giving your baby raw leafy greens or lettuce, when he is at the stage of chewing paper. He may even obtain some vitamins!
- Frozen vegetables can be treated like fresh vegetables. You will save money and time if you buy the large bags of cut vegetables and use only a few pieces for each meal. The Grade A will be the most tender.
- Canned vegetables are very convenient to use as finger foods, since they do not require cooking and can be served directly from the can. Grade A vegetables will be the most tender and juicy.

The following vegetables, cut in small pieces, are good to serve as finger foods:

Asparagus

Beans, baked

Beans, green or yellow

Broccoli (flowerets)

Carrots

Cauliflower (flowerets)

Corn (kernels for a baby over one year)

Corn on the cob (make a slice down the middle of each row of kernels, so your baby will not eat the skins)

Leafy greens

Lima beans

Peas (young, small ones with tender skins)

Soybeans (cook until they are very soft)

Summer squash

Tomatoes

PROTEIN FOODS

After one year, children need at least two daily servings of high-quality protein food for good growth and energy. Yet, many protein foods are difficult for a baby to chew and swallow. Your baby may reject, at first, even the tenderest pieces of meat or poultry. However, there are finger foods with which you can satisfy your baby's need for protein. Here are some suggestions for foods that are both nutritious and convenient to prepare. For specific buying and storing information, look up the food in Chapter 10.

Eggs Eggs are almost a complete food—high in iron, protein, vitamins, and fat. They are your best protein finger food, since they are inexpensive and you can prepare them easily and quickly. Even a toothless baby will be able to swallow them. Eggs can be served as often as once a day.

You can also combine them with other foods, that cannot easily be prepared as finger foods. Here is the basic recipe for preparing eggs, along with some variations.

Basic Omelet

½   **tablespoon vegetable oil, butter, or margarine**
1   **egg or 2 egg yolks (the size egg depends on how much your baby will eat)**
1   **tablespoon liquid (milk, fruit, or vegetable juice)**

1. Lightly coat a small-size frying pan with vegetable oil. Heat the pan over low heat.
2. Beat the egg and liquid together and pour into the pan. Allow it to sit for about a minute, or until the bottom has set.
3. Fold the omelet in half, then in half again. You want the pieces of omelet to be thick enough for your baby to easily pick up. Allow it to cook another minute or until it is firm. Do not overcook, because the omelet will become dry and hard.
4. Cut it into small pieces and serve.

STORAGE: Wrapped and stored in the refrigerator for 1 day. Do not freeze cooked omelets.

YIELD: 1–2 servings.

VARIATIONS

You can add almost any food to an omelet, either finely chopped or puréed. You can make all-in-one meals by combining a vegetable, rice or cereal, and the egg. As you can see, it is a good way to use leftovers from family meals. Whatever combination of food that you use in your omelet, you must add enough egg for a firm consistency. Usually 1 egg for each added ¼ cup of food will be enough. A blender or food processor is very convenient for blending these omelets.

    Wheat Germ Omelet. Beat 1 tablespoon wheat germ

with the egg and liquid. Allow it to sit for 5 minutes before cooking. This is a cereal/protein serving. (You can also use cooked cereal or rice.)

Meat, Poultry, Fish Omelet. Place 2 tablespoons cooked meat in blender with egg and liquid; purée. If you do not have a blender, use very finely chopped meats, poultry, or fish. This is really a double protein serving.

Fruit/Vegetable Omelet. Beat in ¼ cup of any fruit or vegetable purée with the egg. Or use a blender to purée everything together. This is especially good for serving your baby leafy greens.

Meats and Poultry These are the most difficult foods for your baby to chew and swallow, no matter how tender they are. The best way to initially feed your baby beef, veal, pork, lamb, chicken, or turkey is to first cook and finely chop the meat, then prepare it either in Basic Croquettes or as Meatballs. An older baby will enjoy spareribs or drumsticks.

Basic Croquettes

This is a good finger food that can be made from leftovers, and frozen for future use. It is most easily prepared in a food processor. You can also use your family's favorite croquette recipe—just make smaller pieces.

> 3 **cups cooked vegetables, fish, meat, rice, etc. (try to combine equal amounts)**
> 2 **tablespoons fresh lemon juice (optional)**
> 1 **cup white sauce (page 217) or 1 cup milk with a beaten egg**
> 2 **eggs, slightly beaten**
> 1 **cup wheat germ or whole wheat bread crumbs**

1. Chop all cooked ingredients to desired texture, or purée, adding lemon juice and white sauce. The mixture should have a stiff consistency.

2. Shape into small balls or sticks, using about 2 tablespoons for each. You should have about 20 pieces.
3. Dip the balls in the beaten egg and then roll in the wheat germ.
4. Sauté in medium-size frying pan until brown. You can also bake them at 375°F for 10–15 minutes on greased sheet, uncovered.
5. Spread out on a flat sheet and freeze at once. Place in bag and store in freezer.

STORAGE: In freezer for up to 4 months. Or refrigerate 2–3 days.

YIELD: About 20 servings.

Microwave Meat Loaf

This standard family dish can be puréed for baby, and it also makes an easy-to-handle finger food.

> 2   **pounds ground meat**
> 1½   **cups herb-seasoned stuffing mix, or 1 cup seasoned bread crumbs (If you are making this only for the baby, you can use unseasoned mix or crumbs)**
> ½   **cup finely chopped carrots**
> 1   **teaspoon salt**
> 1   **whole egg or 2 egg yolks**
> 1   **can (8 ounces) tomato sauce**

1. Combine all ingredients thoroughly in large-size bowl.
2. Place in 1½ quart casserole and cover tightly.
3. Cook on medium for 20–25 minutes or until no longer pink.
4. Let stand for 5 minutes.
5. Purée as for Cooked Ground Meat (page 227) or cut into small pieces for finger food.

STORAGE: In refrigerator 3–4 days; or freeze up to 4 months.

YIELD: 6–8 adult servings or about 20 baby servings.

Meatballs

This is a good finger food that you can feed your baby in place of the controversial hot dog. You can use various ground meats or poultry, or try solid cubed meat with the other ingredients in a food processor for one-step mixing.

  2   **pounds ground meat**
  ½   **cup wheat germ**
  ¼   **cup (regular or quick-cooking) rolled oats**
  2   **eggs, beaten**
      oil
      water or vegetable juice

1. Mix all ingredients together in large-size bowl.
2. Shape the mixture into small balls or sticks, each the size of 1 serving (you should have about 20 pieces).
3. Brown lightly in 1 tablespoon oil in large-size frying pan. Add about ½ inch of water or vegetable juice to pan. Cover the pan tightly and simmer over low heat for 30 minutes. Or place covered pan in 350°F oven for 30 minutes. Or steam unbrowned meatballs over boiling water for 20 minutes (30 minutes for pork).
4. Drain and cool.

STORAGE: Refrigerate 3–4 days or freeze for up to 4 months.

YIELD: 20 meatballs or 20 servings.

VARIATION

Substitute bread crumbs, mashed potatoes, cooked rice, or cereal for the rolled oats and wheat germ.

Spareribs

This is a good teething and finger food. As soon as your baby has even a few teeth, he will be able to gnaw the bone clean. You can use either pork spareribs or breast of lamb, which is very inexpensive. You can cook them by either roasting or braising. Pork must be *thoroughly* cooked. If ribs are very meaty and the meat comes off in too-large pieces, trim before serving to your baby.

Roasted Spareribs

spareribs
molasses or catsup (optional)

1. Preheat oven to 325°F.
2. Place spareribs in shallow pan, cover with aluminum foil, and roast for ½ hour. Pour off the fat. You can also precook the ribs by simmering them in water to cover for ½ hour. The object is to remove most of the fat.
3. Increase the oven temperature to 400°F, and roast the ribs, uncovered, for 1 hour or until fork tender. You can baste them with a little catsup or molasses if desired.

STORAGE: In the refrigerator for up to 3 days. Or freeze in individual servings for up to 2 months.

Braised Spareribs

spareribs
butter, margarine, or oil
water, tomato juice, or apple juice

1. Cut into single ribs.
2. Brown the ribs in small amount of butter in a medium-size frying pan over medium-high heat.
3. Add enough water to almost cover the ribs. Cover the pan and simmer over low heat about 1½ hours. Add more liquid as necessary.

STORAGE: Same as for Roasted Spareribs.

Steamed Drumsticks

Your baby may be able to eat steamed chicken legs or drumsticks as soon as he has teeth. You can begin by cutting most of the flesh away and letting him chew on the meat next to the bone.

Chicken drumsticks

1. Preheat oven to 350°F.
2. Wrap each drumstick in aluminum foil or place in baking dish with a little water and cover tightly.
3. Bake in oven for 30 minutes. Or steam over boiling water for 30 minutes or until tender. Remove skin.

STORAGE: In the refrigerator for up to 3 days. Or freeze separately for up to 4 months. You can then reheat in the foil.

• **MICROWAVE VARIATION**
Place drumsticks in a single layer, thicker ends on the outside, on dish. Cover tightly and cook on high for 8 minutes per pound of drumsticks. Let stand 5–10 minutes. Continue as directed.

Liver

Liver is one highly nutritious meat that most babies can chew as finger food. You can use either beef, calf, or chicken liver. It is very easy to prepare. Place whole pieces of liver in a pot with a small amount of boiling water or use your steamer. Cover and simmer over low heat for 5 to 10 minutes. Do not overcook the liver, because it will become tough. You can even serve it slightly pink. Cut out any veins or outside membrane and slice into very thin small pieces before serving.

Do not freeze cooked liver because it will become tough when reheated. If you are buying liver only for your baby, you can cut the raw liver into single servings and freeze it up to three months.

Other Meats Bacon may be served as a finger food. However, you must remember that it is mostly fat with very little meat, so you should not count it as a serving of a protein food. It is also a highly salted food and should not be served too often.

Delicatessen meats, such as boiled or baked ham and roast beef, can be served as instant finger foods, if they are sliced very thin. They are expensive, but very convenient, and your baby really eats very little. Do not use luncheon meats, salami, or bologna, except as a last resort. They usually contain preservatives and artificial flavorings and color. Besides, they are an even more expensive source of protein then plain ham or roast beef.

Hamburgers, medium broiled, can be cut in small pieces. Be careful how you buy ground meat (see Chapter 10).

Frankfurters also can be used as finger foods, but, please, only as a last resort. The controversy over this old stand-by food concerns the many chemical additives, the artificial flavorings and colors that are used, and the low percentage of meat or protein. "All-meat" frankfurters do not contain any poultry products, and the "all-beef" contain only beef as their meat ingredient. However, both of these higher-priced types of frankfurters can contain nonfat dry milk, cereals, and starch. You are paying a high price for these ingredients and, actually, the lower-priced frankfurters can be just as nutritious. If you do serve them to your baby, read the list of ingredients and buy the brand with the smallest amount of additives and fillers. *Always cut frankfurters into small pieces to prevent choking.*

Fish

Fish is a good protein finger food that is soft enough for your baby to chew and swallow. Read the fish section in Chapter 10 for details on the types of fish and methods of preparation. You can serve your baby small flakes of the cooked fish or use the following recipe for fish sticks. If your family eats fish, separate a few flakes for your baby. Do not freeze the cooked fish flakes because they will become tough. When your baby is one year old, you can try serving him canned tuna and salmon flakes.

Steamed Fish Sticks

This is a good protein food that your baby can feed himself. (Adults can enjoy them as a delicious hors d'oeuvre served with horseradish.) This is most easily prepared in a food processor—you can then combine steps 1 and 2. When serving, remember to *cut into small pieces to prevent choking.*

> 3 **pounds whitefish, pike, etc. (frozen fillets, thawed, are easy to use)**
> 2 **small onions, chopped**
> 2 **eggs, beaten**
> 3 **tablespoons cracker meal or wheat germ**
> ½ **cup water or vegetable liquid (approximately)**
>   **Sliced carrot, onion, and celery (optional)**

1. Finely chop or grind the raw fish fillets.
2. Mix the fish, onions, eggs, and cracker meal in a medium-size bowl until well blended, adding a small amount of water.
3. Form the chopped fish mixture into sticks about the size of a short frankfurter. You may also shape into balls. You should have about 30 pieces.
4. In the bottom of your steamer basket, or any pot you use for steaming, place a few slices of carrot, onion, and celery. This is to raise the fish above the water and add a mild flavor, but the vegetables are not really necessary if you have a steamer.
5. Place the fish sticks on top of the vegetables, cover tightly, and steam over a low heat for 2 hours. Add water as necessary.
6. Cool, arrange the sticks on a flat sheet, and freeze in meal-size portions.

STORAGE: In refrigerator for up to 4 days. Or in freezer for up to 2 months.

YIELD: About 30 pieces.

Cheese

Cheese is a protein food that contains the same nutrients as milk. It is not a source of iron, as are the other protein foods. However it is a convenient finger food that is readily available. Your baby will enjoy chewing the sliced semifirm cheeses such as American, Swiss, Muenster, and Cheddar.

When buying cheese, read the labels carefully to avoid those types that contain additives, artificial flavor and color, or fillers, or that have a high salt or fat content. Remember that the words *imitation*, *flavored*, *cheese food* indicate that the product is not pure cheese.

Appendix A

RDA Supplemental Table:
Estimated Sodium, Chloride, and Potassium
Minimum Requirements of Healthy Persons[a]

AGE	WEIGHT (KG)[a]	SODIUM (MG)[a,b]	CHLORIDE (MG)[a,b]	POTASSIUM (MG)[c]
Months				
0–5	4.5	120	180	500
6–11	8.9	200	300	700
Years				
1	11.0	225	350	1,000
2–5	16.0	300	500	1,400
6–9	25.0	400	600	1,600
10–18	50.0	500	750	2,000
>18[d]	70.0	500	750	2,000

[a] No allowance has been included for large, prolonged losses from the skin through sweat.
[b] There is no evidence that higher intakes confer any health benefit.
[c] Desirable intakes of potassium may considerably exceed these values (about 3,500 mg for adults).
[d] No allowance included for growth. Values for those below eighteen years assume a growth rate at the fiftieth percentile reported by the National Center for Health Statistics and averaged for males and females.

Food and Nutrition Board, National Academy of Sciences—National Research Council: Recommended Dietary Allowances[a] (Revised 1989; Designed for the Maintenance of Good Nutrition of Practically All Healthy People in the United States)

Category	Age (years) or Condition	Weight[b] (kg)	Weight[b] (lb)	Height[b] (cm)	Height[b] (in)	Pro-tein (g)	FAT-SOLUBLE VITAMINS Vitamin A (µg RE)[c]	Vitamin D (µg)[d]	Vitamin E (mg α-TE)[e]	Vitamin K (µg)
Infants	0.0–0.5	6	13	60	24	13	375	7.5	3	5
	0.5–1.0	9	20	71	28	14	375	10	4	10
Children	1–3	13	29	90	35	16	400	10	6	15
	4–6	20	44	112	44	24	500	10	7	20
	7–10	28	62	132	52	28	700	10	7	30
Males	11–14	45	99	157	62	45	1,000	10	10	45
	15–18	66	145	176	69	59	1,000	10	10	65
	19–24	72	160	177	70	58	1,000	10	10	70
	25–50	79	174	176	70	63	1,000	5	10	80
	51+	77	170	173	68	63	1,000	5	10	80
Females	11–14	46	101	157	62	46	800	10	8	45
	15–18	55	120	163	64	44	800	10	8	55
	19–24	58	128	164	65	46	800	10	8	60
	25–50	63	138	163	64	50	800	5	8	65
	51+	65	143	160	63	50	800	5	8	65
Pregnant						60	800	10	10	65
Lactating	1st 6 months					65	1,300	10	12	65
	2nd 6 months					62	1,200	10	11	65

[a] The allowances, expressed as average daily intakes over time, are intended to provide for individual variations among most normal persons as they live in the United States under usual environmental stresses. Diets should be based on a variety of common foods in order to provide other nutrients for which human requirements have been less well defined.

[b] Weights and heights of reference adults are actual medians for the U.S. population of the designated age. The use of these figures does not imply that the height-to-weight ratios are ideal.

Vita-min C (mg)	Thi-amin (mg)	Ribo-fla-vin (mg)	Nia-cin (mg NE)[f]	Vita-min B6 (mg)	Fo-late (µg)	Vita-min B12 (µg)	Cal-cium (mg)	Phos-pho-rus (mg)	Mag-ne-sium (mg)	Iron (mg)	Zinc (mg)	Io-dine (µg)	Sele-nium (µg)
30	0.3	0.4	5	0.3	25	0.3	400	300	40	6	5	40	10
35	0.4	0.5	6	0.6	35	0.5	600	500	60	10	5	50	15
40	0.7	0.8	9	1.0	50	0.7	800	800	80	10	10	70	20
45	0.9	1.1	12	1.1	75	1.0	800	800	120	10	10	90	20
45	1.0	1.2	13	1.4	100	1.4	800	800	170	10	10	120	30
50	1.3	1.5	17	1.7	150	2.0	1,200	1,200	270	12	15	150	40
60	1.5	1.8	20	2.0	200	2.0	1,200	1,200	400	12	15	150	50
60	1.5	1.7	19	2.0	200	2.0	1,200	1,200	350	10	15	150	70
60	1.5	1.7	19	2.0	200	2.0	800	800	350	10	15	150	70
60	1.2	1.4	15	2.0	200	2.0	800	800	350	10	15	150	70
50	1.1	1.3	15	1.4	150	2.0	1,200	1,200	280	15	12	150	45
60	1.1	1.3	15	1.5	180	2.0	1,200	1,200	300	15	12	150	50
60	1.1	1.3	15	1.6	180	2.0	1,200	1,200	280	15	12	150	55
60	1.1	1.3	15	1.6	180	2.0	800	800	280	15	12	150	55
60	1.0	1.2	13	1.6	180	2.0	800	800	280	10	12	150	55
70	1.5	1.6	17	2.2	400	2.2	1,200	1,200	320	30	15	175	65
95	1.6	1.8	20	2.1	280	2.6	1,200	1,200	355	15	19	200	75
90	1.6	1.7	20	2.1	260	2.6	1,200	1,200	340	15	16	200	75

[c] Retinol equivalents. 1 retinol equivalent = 1 µg retinol or 6 µg β-carotene.
[d] As cholecalciferol. 10 µg cholecalciferol = 400 IU of vitamin D.
[e] α-Tocopherol equivalents. 1 mg d-α tocopherol = 1 α-TE.
[f] 1 NE (niacin equivalent) is equal to 1 mg of niacin or 60 mg of dietary tryptophan.

Summary Table: Estimated Safe and Adequate Daily Dietary Intakes of Selected Vitamins and Minerals[a]

CATEGORY	AGE (YEARS)	VITAMINS		TRACE ELEMENTS[b]				
		BIOTIN (µG)	PANTO-THENIC ACID (MG)	COPPER (MG)	MANGA-NESE (MG)	FLUO-RIDE (MG)	CHRO-MIUM (µG)	MOLYB-DENUM (µG)
Infants	0–0.5	10	2	0.4–0.6	0.3–0.6	0.1–0.5	10–40	15–30
	0.5–1	15	3	0.6–0.7	0.6–1.0	0.2–1.0	20–60	20–40
Children and	1–3	20	3	0.7–1.0	1.0–1.5	0.5–1.5	20–80	25–50
adolescents	4–6	25	3–4	1.0–1.5	1.5–2.0	1.0–2.5	30–120	30–75
	7–10	30	4–5	1.0–2.0	2.0–3.0	1.5–2.5	50–200	50–150
	11+	30–100	4–7	1.5–2.5	2.0–5.0	1.5–2.5	50–200	75–250
Adults		30–100	4–7	1.5–3.0	2.0–5.0	1.5–4.0	50–200	75–250

[a] Because there is less information on which to base allowances, these figures are not given in the main table of RDA and are provided here in the form of ranges of recommended intakes.

[b] Since the toxic levels for many trace elements may be only several times usual intakes, the upper levels for the trace elements given in this table should not be habitually exceeded.

Appendix B: Nutritive Values of Foods

The following table is compiled from:
United States Department of Agriculture
Home and Garden Bulletin No. 72, *The Nutritive Values of Foods*
Agriculture Handbook No. 8, *Composition of Foods*.

I have found that knowing the nutritional composition of foods is very useful for understanding their nutritional cost. These values are a basis for comparing the kinds and amounts of nutrients in different foods or different forms of the same food. For example, lamb liver is as high, if not higher, in the important nutrients as steak; however, it is considerably less expensive. Just look through and check the foods that you usually serve, then pick out the ones that are economical.

You do not need to use these values in planning your baby's daily diet, although you might want to compare the nutrients he consumes in a typical day with the advisable daily intakes that are described in chapter 1.

The values for calories and nutrients are the amounts present in the edible part of the items, unless noted otherwise. For many of the prepared items, values have been calculated from the ingredients in typical recipes. If a food is fortified with one or more nutrients, the information is on the label. The values shown in this table are based on products from several manufacturers and may differ slightly from those in a specific product.

NUTRITIVE VALUE OF FOODS

(A dash in the columns for nutrients shows that no suitable value could be found although there is reason to believe that a measurable amount of the nutrient may be present)

Food, approximate measure, and weight (in grams)	Water	Food energy	Protein	Fat	Fatty acids Saturated (total)	Fatty acids Unsaturated linoleic	Carbohydrate	Calcium	Iron	Vitamin A value	Thiamin	Riboflavin	Niacin	Ascorbic acid
	Grams	Per- cent	Calo- ries	Grams	Grams	Grams	Grams	Grams	Milli- grams	Milli- grams	Inter- national units	Milli- grams	Milli- grams	Milli- grams	Milli- grams

MILK, CHEESE, CREAM, IMITATION CREAM; RELATED PRODUCTS

Food, approximate measure, and weight (in grams)	Grams	Water	Food energy	Protein	Fat	Saturated (total)	Unsaturated linoleic	Carbohydrate	Calcium	Iron	Vitamin A value	Thiamin	Riboflavin	Niacin	Ascorbic acid
Milk:															
Fluid:															
Whole, 3.5% fat .... 1 cup	244	87	160	9	9	5	Trace	12	288	.1	350	.07	.41	.2	2
Nonfat (skim) .... 1 cup	245	90	90	9	Trace	—	—	12	296	.1	10	.09	.44	.2	2
Partly skimmed, 2% nonfat milk solids added .... 1 cup	246	87	145	10	5	3	Trace	15	352	.1	200	.10	.52	.2	2
Canned, concentrated, undiluted:															
Evaporated, unsweetened .... 1 cup	252	74	345	18	20	11	1	24	635	.3	810	.10	.86	.5	3
Condensed, sweetened .... 1 cup	306	27	980	25	27	15	1	166	802	.3	1,100	.24	1.16	.6	3
Dry, nonfat instant:															
Low-density (1⅓ cups needed for reconstitution to 1 quart)	68	4	245	24	Trace	—	—	35	879	.4	[2]20	.24	1.21	.6	5
High-density (⅞ cup needed for reconstitution to 1 quart) .... 1 cup	104	4	375	37	1	—	—	54	1,345	.6	[2]30	.36	1.85	.9	7
Buttermilk:															
Fluid, cultured, made from skim milk ...... 1 cup	245	90	90	9	Trace	—	—	12	296	.1	10	.10	.44	.2	2

Cheese and related products (continued). The nutrient columns (grams, water %, food energy, protein, fat, saturated fatty acids, oleic, linoleic, carbohydrate, calcium, iron, vitamin A, thiamin, riboflavin, niacin, ascorbic acid) are carried over from the preceding page.

Food																
Cheese:																
Cheddar ... 1 ounce	28	37	115	7	9	5	3	Trace	1	213	.3	370	.01	.13	Trace	0
Cottage, large or small curd: Creamed ... 1 cup	245	78	260	33	10	6	3	Trace	7	230	.7	420	.07	.61	.2	0
Uncreamed ... 1 cup	200	79	170	34	1	Trace	Trace	Trace	5	180	.8	20	.06	.56	.2	0
Cream ... 1 ounce	28	51	107	2	11	6	3	Trace	1	18	Trace	440	Trace	.07	Trace	0
Parmesan, grated ... 1 tablespoon	5	17	25	2	2	1	1	Trace	Trace	68	Trace	60	Trace	.04	Trace	0
Parmesan ... 1 ounce	28	17	130	12	9	5	3	Trace	1	383	.1	360	.01	.25	.1	0
Swiss ... 1 ounce	28	39	105	8	8	4	3	Trace	1	262	.3	320	Trace	.11	Trace	0
Pasteurized processed cheese:																
American ... 1 ounce	28	40	105	7	9	5	3	Trace	1	198	.3	350	.01	.12	Trace	0
Swiss ... 1 ounce	28	40	100	8	8	4	3	Trace	1	251	.3	310	Trace	.11	Trace	0
Pasteurized process cheese food, American:																
1 tablespoon	14	43	45	3	3	2	1	Trace	1	80	.1	140	Trace	.08	Trace	0
1 ounce	28	49	80	5	6	3	2	Trace	2	160	.2	250	Trace	.15	Trace	0
Cream:																
Half-and-half (cream and milk) ... 1 tablespoon	15	80	20	1	2	1	1	Trace	1	16	Trace	70	Trace	.02	Trace	Trace
Light, coffee or table ... 1 tablespoon	15	72	30	1	3	2	1	Trace	1	15	Trace	130	Trace	.02	Trace	Trace
Sour ... 1 tablespoon	12	72	25	Trace	2	1	1	Trace	1	12	Trace	100	Trace	.02	Trace	Trace
Imitation cream products (made with vegetable fat): Creamers:																
Powdered ... 1 teaspoon	2	2	10	Trace	1	Trace	Trace	0	1	1	Trace	[a]Trace	0	0	—	—
Liquid (frozen) ... 1 tablespoon	15	77	20	Trace	2	1	Trace	0	2	2	—	[a]10	0	0	—	—
Malted milk: Dry powder, approx. 3 heaping teaspoons per ounce ... 1 ounce	28	3	115	4	2	—	—	—	20	82	.6	290	.09	.15	.1	0
Milk desserts: Custard, baked ... 1 cup	265	77	305	14	15	7	5	1	29	297	1.1	930	.11	.50	.3	1
Ice cream: Regular (approx. 10% fat) ... 1 cup	133	63	255	6	14	8	5	Trace	28	194	.1	590	.05	.28	.1	1
Rich (approx. 16% fat) ... 1 cup	148	63	330	4	24	13	7	1	27	115	Trace	980	.03	.16	.1	1
Ice milk ... 1 cup	131	67	200	6	7	4	2	Trace	29	204	.1	280	.07	.29	.1	1

Food, approximate measure, and weight (in grams)	Water (Per cent)	Food energy (Calories)	Protein (Grams)	Fat (Grams)	Fatty acids Saturated (total) (Grams)	Fatty acids Unsaturated linoleic (Grams)	Carbohydrate (Grams)	Calcium (Milligrams)	Iron (Milligrams)	Vitamin A value (International units)	Thiamin (Milligrams)	Riboflavin (Milligrams)	Niacin (Milligrams)	Ascorbic acid (Milligrams)
Yoghurt:														
Made from partially skimmed milk ....1 cup.......... 245	89	125	8	4	2	Trace	13	294	.1	170	.10	.44	.2	2
Made from whole milk ....1 cup.......... 245	88	150	7	8	5	Trace	12	272	.1	340	.07	.39	.2	2
EGGS														
Eggs, large, 24 ounces per dozen:														
Raw or cooked in shell or with nothing added:														
Whole, without shell..........1 egg.......... 50	74	80	6	6	2	Trace	Trace	27	1.1	590	.05	.15	Trace	0
White of egg..........1 white.......... 33	88	15	4	Trace	—	—	Trace	3	Trace	0	Trace	.09	Trace	0
Yolk of egg..........1 yolk.......... 17	51	60	3	5	2	Trace	Trace	24	.9	580	.04	.07	Trace	0
Scrambled with milk and fat..........1 egg.......... 64	72	110	7	8	3	Trace	1	51	1.1	690	.05	.18	Trace	0
MEAT, POULTRY; RELATED PRODUCTS														
Bacon (20 slices per lb. raw), broiled or fried, crisp..........2 slices.......... 15	8	90	5	8	3	1	1	2	.5	0	.08	.05	.8	—
Beef,[2] cooked:														
Cuts braised, simmered, or pot-roasted..........3 ounces.......... 85	53	245	23	16	8	Trace	0	10	2.9	30	.04	.18	3.5	—
Hamburger (ground beef), broiled:														
Lean..........3 ounces.......... 85	60	185	23	10	5	Trace	0	10	3.0	20	.08	.20	5.1	—
Regular..........3 ounces.......... 85	54	245	21	17	8	Trace	0	9	2.7	30	.07	.18	4.6	—
Roast, oven-cooked, no liquid added:														
Relatively fat, such as rib..........3 ounces.......... 85	40	375	17	34	16	1	0	8	2.2	70	.05	.13	3.1	—

Food	Amount	Grams	Water (%)	Food energy (Calories)	Protein (g)	Fat (g)	Saturated fat (g)	Unsaturated (g)	Carbohydrate (g)	Calcium (mg)	Iron (mg)	Vitamin A (I.U.)	Thiamine (mg)	Riboflavin (mg)	Niacin (mg)	Ascorbic acid (mg)
Relatively lean, such as heel or round	3 ounces	85	62	165	25	7	3	Trace	0	11	3.2	10	.06	.19	4.5	—
Steak, broiled:																
Relatively fat, such as sirloin	3 ounces	85	44	330	20	27	13	1	0	9	2.5	50	.05	.16	4.0	—
Relatively lean, such as round	3 ounces	85	55	220	24	13	6	Trace	0	10	3.0	20	.07	.19	4.8	—
Beef, canned:																
Corned beef	3 ounces	85	59	185	22	10	5	Trace	0	17	3.7	20	.01	.20	2.9	—
Corned beef hash	3 ounces	85	67	155	7	10	5	Trace	9	11	1.7	—	.01	.08	1.8	—
Beef, dried or chipped	2 ounces	57	48	115	19	4	2	Trace	0	11	2.9	—	.04	.18	2.2	—
Beef potpie, baked, 4¼-inch diam., weight before baking about 8 ounces	1 pie	227	55	560	23	33	9	2	43	32	4.1	1,860	.25	.27	4.5	7
Chicken, cooked:																
Flesh only, broiled	3 ounces	85	71	115	20	3	1	1	0	8	1.4	80	.05	.16	7.4	—
Chicken, canned, boneless	3 ounces	85	65	170	18	10	3	2	0	18	1.3	200	.03	.11	3.7	3
Chicken potpie, baked 4¼-inch diam., weight before baking about 8 ounces	1 pie	227	57	535	23	31	10	3	42	68	3.0	3,020	.25	.26	4.1	5
Heart, beef, lean, braised	3 ounces	85	61	160	27	5	—	—	1	5	5.0	20	.21	1.04	6.5	1
Kidney, braised beef	3.5 ounces	100	53	252	33	12	—	—	8	18	13.1	1,150	.51	4.82	10.7	—
Lamb, cooked:																
Chop, broiled	4 ounces	112	47	400	25	33	18	1	0	10	1.5	—	.14	.25	5.6	—
Leg, roasted	3 ounces	85	54	235	22	16	9	Trace	0	9	1.4	—	.13	.23	4.7	—
Shoulder, roasted	3 ounces	85	50	285	18	23	13	1	0	9	1.0	—	.11	.20	4.0	—
Liver:																
Beef, sauteed	3.5 ounces	100	56	229	26	11	—	—	5.3	11	8.8	53,400	.26	4.19	16.5	27
Calf, sauteed	3.5 ounces	100	51	261	29	13	—	—	2.4	13	14.2	32,700	.24	4.17	16.5	37
Lamb, broiled	3.5 ounces	100	50	261	32	12	—	—	2.8	11	17.9	74,500	.40	5.11	24.9	36
Chicken, simmered	3.5 ounces	100	65	165	20	4	—	—	3.1	16	8.5	12,300	.17	2.69	11.7	16
Pork, cured, cooked:																
Ham, light cure, lean and fat, roasted	3 ounces	85	54	245	18	19	7	2	0	8	2.2	0	.40	.16	3.1	—

Food, approximate measure, and weight (in grams)	Grams	Water Per cent	Food energy Calories	Protein Grams	Fat Grams	Fatty acids Saturated (total) Grams	Fatty acids Unsaturated linoleic Grams	Carbohydrate Grams	Calcium Milligrams	Iron Milligrams	Vitamin A value International units	Thiamin Milligrams	Riboflavin Milligrams	Niacin Milligrams	Ascorbic acid Milligrams
Luncheon meat:															
Boiled ham, sliced ....2 ounces	57	59	135	11	10	4	1	0	6	1.6	0	.25	.09	1.5	—
Pork, fresh,[3] cooked:															
Chop, thick, with bone ....1 chop, 3.5 ounces	98	42	260	16	21	8	2	0	8	2.2	0	.63	.18	3.8	—
Roast, oven-cooked, no liquid added ....3 ounces	85	46	310	21	24	9	2	0	9	2.7	0	.78	.22	4.7	—
Cuts simmered ....3 ounces	85	46	320	20	26	9	2	0	8	2.5	0	.46	.21	4.1	—
Sausage:															
Bologna, slice, 3-in. diam. x⅛-inch ....2 slices	26	56	80	3	7	—	—	Trace	2	.5	—	.04	.06	.7	—
Braunschweiger, slice 2-in. diam. x¼ in. ....2 slices	20	53	65	3	5	—	—	Trace	2	1.2	1,310	.03	.29	1.6	—
Deviled ham, canned ....1 tablespoon	13	51	45	2	4	2	Trace	0	1	.3	—	.02	.01	.2	—
Frankfurter, heated (8 per lb. purchased pkg.) ....1 frank	56	57	170	7	15	—	—	1	3	.8	—	.08	.11	1.4	—
Salami, dry type ....1 ounce	28	30	130	7	11	—	—	Trace	4	1.0	—	.10	.07	1.5	—
Salami, cooked ....1 ounce	28	51	90	5	7	—	—	Trace	3	.7	—	.07	.07	1.2	—
Turkey, roasted flesh only ....3.5 ounces	100	62	190	32	6	—	—	0	8	1.8	—	.05	.18	7.7	—
Veal, medium fat, cooked, bone removed:															
Cutlet ....3 ounces	85	60	185	23	9	5	Trace	0	9	2.7	—	.06	.21	4.6	—
Roast ....3 ounces	85	55	230	23	14	7	Trace	0	10	2.9	—	.11	.26	6.6	—
FISH AND SHELLFISH:															
Bluefish, baked with table fat ....3 ounces	85	68	135	22	4	—	—	0	25	.6	40	.09	.08	1.6	—

							Fatty acids									
							Saturated (total)	Oleic	Linoleic								
Cod, broiled	3.5 ounces	100	65	170	29	5	—	—	—	0	31	1.0	180	.08	.11	3.0	—
Crabmeat, canned	3 ounces	85	77	85	15	2	—	—	—	1	38	.7	—	.07	.07	1.6	—
Fish sticks, breaded, cooked	10 sticks or 8 ounce pkg.	227	66	400	38	20	5	4	10	15	25	0.9	—	.09	.16	3.6	—
Flounder, baked	3.5 ounces	100	58	202	30	8	—	5	—	0	23	1.4	—	.07	.08	2.5	0
Haddock, breaded, fried	3 ounces	85	66	140	17	5	1	—	Trace	5	34	1.0	—	.03	.06	2.7	2
Halibut, broiled	3.5 ounces	100	67	171	25	7	—	1	—	0	16	.8	680	.05	.07	8.3	—
Ocean perch, breaded, fried	3 ounces	85	59	195	16	11	—	—	—	6	28	1.1	—	.08	.09	1.5	—
Salmon, pink, canned	3 ounces	85	71	120	17	5	1	1	Trace	0	[4]167	.7	60	.03	.16	6.8	—
Sardines, Atlantic, canned in oil, drained solids	3 ounces	85	62	175	20	9	—	—	—	0	372	2.5	190	.02	.17	4.6	—
Shad, baked with table fat and bacon	3 ounces	85	64	170	20	10	—	—	—	0	20	.5	20	.11	.22	7.3	—
Shrimp, canned, meat	3 ounces	85	70	100	21	1	—	—	—	1	98	2.6	50	.01	.03	1.5	—
Swordfish, broiled with butter or margarine	3 ounces	85	65	150	24	5	—	—	—	0	23	1.1	1,750	.03	.04	9.3	—
Tuna, canned in oil, drained solids	3 ounces	85	61	170	24	7	2	1	1	0	7	1.6	70	.04	.10	10.1	—
MATURE DRY BEANS AND PEAS, NUTS, PEANUTS; RELATED PRODUCTS																	
Almonds, shelled, whole kernels	1 cup	142	5	850	26	77	6	52	15	28	332	6.7	0	.34	1.31	5.0	Trace
Beans, dry: Common varieties as Great Northern, navy, and others: Cooked, drained: Great Northern	1 cup	180	69	210	14	1	—	—	—	38	90	4.9	0	.25	.13	1.3	0
Navy (pea)	1 cup	190	69	225	15	1	—	—	—	40	95	5.1	0	.27	.13	1.3	0
Canned, solids and liquid: White with— Frankfurters (sliced)	1 cup	255	71	365	19	18	—	—	1	32	94	4.8	330	.18	.15	3.3	Trace

Food, approximate measure, and weight (in grams)	Water	Food energy	Protein	Fat	Fatty acids		Carbohydrate	Calcium	Iron	Vitamin A value	Thiamin	Riboflavin	Niacin	Ascorbic acid
					Saturated (total)	Unsaturated linoleic								
	Percent	Calories	Grams	Grams	Grams	Grams	Grams	Milligrams	Milligrams	International units	Milligrams	Milligrams	Milligrams	Milligrams
Pork and tomato sauce............1 cup	71	310	16	7	2	1	49	138	4.6	330	.20	.08	1.5	5
Pork and sweet sauce............1 cup	66	385	16	12	4	1	54	161	5.9	—	.15	.10	1.3	—
Red kidney............1 cup	76	230	15	1	—	—	42	74	4.6	10	.13	.10	1.5	—
Lima, cooked, drained............1 cup	64	260	16	1	—	—	49	55	5.9	—	.25	.11	1.3	—
Cashew nuts, roasted............1 cup	5	785	24	64	11	4	41	53	5.3	140	.60	.35	2.5	—
Coconut, fresh meat only: Shredded or grated, firmly packed............1 cup	51	450	5	46	39	Trace	12	17	2.2	0	.07	.03	.7	4
Cowpeas or blackeye peas, dry, cooked............1 cup	80	190	13	1	—	—	34	42	3.2	20	.41	.11	1.1	Trace
Lentils, cooked............1 cup	72	212	16	Trace	—	—	38	50	4.2	40	.14	.12	1.2	0
Peanuts, roasted, salted, halves............1 cup	2	840	37	72	16	21	27	107	3.0	—	.46	.19	24.7	0
Peanut butter............1 tablespoon	2	95	4	8	2	2	3	9	.3	—	.02	.02	2.4	0
Peas, split, dry, cooked............1 cup	70	290	20	1	—	1	52	28	4.2	100	.37	.22	2.2	—
Pecans, halves............1 cup	3	740	10	77	5	15	16	79	2.6	140	.93	.14	1.0	2
Soybeans, cooked............1 cup	71	260	22	11.4	—	7	22	146	5.4	60	.42	.18	1.2	0
Walnuts, black or native, chopped............1 cup	3	790	26	75	4	36	19	Trace	7.6	380	.28	.14	.9	—
VEGETABLES AND VEGETABLE PRODUCTS														
Asparagus, green: Cooked, drained: Spears, ½-in. diam. at base............4 spears	94	10	1	Trace	—	—	2	13	.4	540	.10	.11	.8	16
Pieces, 1½ to 2-in. lengths............1 cup	94	30	3	Trace	—	—	5	30	.9	1,310	.23	.26	2.0	38

Canned, solids and liquid	1 cup	244	94	45	5	1	—	—	7	44	4.1	1,240	.15	.22	2.0	37
Beans:																
Lima, cooked, drained	1 cup	170	71	190	13	1	—	—	34	80	4.3	480	.31	.17	2.2	29
Snap:																
Green:																
Cooked, drained	1 cup	125	92	30	2	Trace	—	—	7	63	.8	680	.09	.11	.6	15
Canned, solids and liquid	1 cup	239	94	45	2	Trace	—	—	10	81	2.9	690	.07	.10	.7	10
Yellow or wax:																
Cooked, drained	1 cup	125	93	30	2	Trace	—	—	6	63	0.8	290	.09	.11	.6	16
Canned, solids and liquid	1 cup	239	94	45	2	1	—	—	10	81	2.9	140	.07	.10	.7	12
Sprouted mung beans, cooked, drained	1 cup	125	91	35	4	Trace	—	—	7	21	1.1	30	.11	.13	.9	8
Beets:																
Cooked, drained, peeled:																
Diced or sliced	1 cup	170	91	55	2	Trace	—	—	12	24	.9	30	.05	.07	.5	10
Canned, solids and liquid	1 cup	246	90	85	2	Trace	—	—	19	34	1.5	20	.02	.05	.2	7
Beet greens, leaves and stems, cooked, drained	1 cup	145	94	25	3	Trace	—	—	5	144	2.8	7,400	.10	.22	.4	22
Blackeye peas. See Cowpeas.																
Broccoli, cooked, drained:																
Stalks cut into ½-in. pieces	1 cup	155	91	40	5	1	—	—	7	136	1.2	3,880	.14	.31	1.2	140
Chopped, yield from 10-oz. frozen pkg.	1¾ cups	250	92	65	7	1	—	—	12	135	1.8	6,500	.15	.30	1.3	143
Brussels sprouts	1 cup	155	88	55	7	1	—	—	10	50	1.7	810	.12	.22	1.2	135
Cabbage, common:																
Raw, finely shredded or chopped	1 cup	90	92	20	1	Trace	—	—	5	44	.4	120	.05	.05	.3	42
Cooked	1 cup	145	94	30	2	Trace	—	—	6	64	.4	190	.06	.06	.4	48
Cabbage, celery or Chinese, raw, cut in 1-in. pieces	1 cup	75	95	10	1	Trace	—	—	2	32	.5	110	.04	.03	.5	19

Food, approximate measure, and weight (in grams)	Grams	Water	Food energy	Protein	Fat	Fatty acids Saturated (total)	Fatty acids Unsaturated linoleic	Carbohydrate	Calcium	Iron	Vitamin A value	Thiamin	Riboflavin	Niacin	Ascorbic acid
	Grams	Percent	Calories	Grams	Grams	Grams	Grams	Grams	Milligrams	Milligrams	International units	Milligrams	Milligrams	Milligrams	Milligrams
Carrots:															
Raw:															
Whole, 5½×1 inch......1 carrot	50	88	20	1	Trace	—	—	5	18	.4	5,500	.03	.03	.3	4
Grated......1 cup	110	88	45	1	Trace	—	—	11	41	.8	12,100	.06	.06	.7	9
Cooked, diced......1 cup	145	91	45	1	Trace	—	—	10	48	.9	15,220	.08	.07	.7	9
Cauliflower, cooked, flowerbuds......1 cup	120	93	25	3	Trace	—	—	5	25	.8	70	.11	.10	.7	66
Celery, raw:															
Stalk, large outer......1 stalk	40	94	5	Trace	Trace	—	—	2	16	.1	100	.01	.01	.1	4
Pieces, diced......1 cup	100	94	15	1	Trace	—	—	4	39	.3	240	.03	.03	.3	9
Collards, cooked......1 cup	190	91	55	5	1	—	—	9	289	1.1	10,260	.27	.37	2.4	87
Corn, sweet:															
Cooked......1 ear	140	74	70	3	1	—	—	16	2	.5	[a]310	.09	.08	1.0	7
Canned, solids and liquid......1 cup	256	81	170	5	2	—	—	40	10	1.0	[a]690	.07	.12	2.3	13
Cowpeas, cooked, immature seeds......1 cup	160	72	175	13	1	—	—	29	38	3.4	560	.49	.18	2.3	28
Cucumbers, 10-ounce:															
Raw, pared......1 cucumber	207	96	30	1	Trace	—	—	7	35	.6	Trace	.07	.09	.4	23
Dandelion greens, cooked......1 cup	180	90	60	4	1	—	—	12	252	3.2	21,060	.24	.29	—	32
Endive, curly (including escarole)......2 ounces	57	93	10	1	Trace	—	—	2	46	1.0	1,870	.04	.08	.3	6
Kale, leaves including stems, cooked......1 cup	110	91	30	4	1	—	—	4	147	1.3	8,140	—	—	—	68
Lettuce, raw:															
Butterhead, as Boston types; head, 4-inch diameter......1 head	220	95	30	3	Trace	—	—	6	77	4.4	2,130	.14	.13	.6	18
Crisphead, as iceberg; head......1 head	454	96	60	4	Trace	—	—	13	91	2.3	1,500	.29	.27	1.3	29

Looseleaf, or bunching varieties, leaves ....2 large	50	94	10	1	Trace	—	—	—	2	34	.7	950	.03	.04	.2	9
Mushrooms, canned, solids and liquid ....1 cup	244	93	40	5	Trace	—	—	—	6	15	1.2	Trace	.04	.60	4.8	4
Mustard greens, cooked ....1 cup	140	93	35	3	1	—	—	—	6	193	2.5	8,120	.11	.19	.9	68
Okra, cooked ....8 pods	85	91	25	2	Trace	—	—	—	5	78	.4	420	.11	.15	.8	17
Onions:																
Cooked ....1 cup	210	92	60	3	Trace	—	—	—	14	50	.8	80	.06	.06	.4	14
Young green, small, without tops ....6 onions	50	88	20	1	Trace	—	—	—	5	20	.3	Trace	.02	.02	.2	12
Parsley, raw, chopped ....1 tablespoon	4	85	Trace	Trace	Trace	—	—	—	Trace	8	.2	340	Trace	.01	Trace	7
Parsnips, cooked ....1 cup	155	82	100	2	1	—	—	—	23	70	.9	50	.11	.12	.2	16
Peas, green:																
Cooked ....1 cup	160	82	115	9	1	—	—	—	19	37	2.9	860	.44	.17	3.7	33
Canned, solids and liquid ....1 cup	249	83	165	9	1	—	—	—	31	50	4.2	1,120	.23	.13	2.2	22
Peppers, sweet: Raw, about 5 per pound: Green pod without stem and seeds ....1 pod	74	93	15	1	Trace	—	—	—	4	7	.5	310	.06	.06	.4	94
Cooked, boiled, drained ....1 pod	73	95	15	1	Trace	—	—	—	3	7	.4	310	.05	.05	.4	70
Potatoes, medium (about 3 per pound raw): Baked, peeled after baking ....1 potato	99	75	90	3	Trace	—	—	—	21	9	.7	Trace	.10	.04	1.7	20
Boiled, peeled after boiling ....1 potato	136	80	105	3	Trace	—	—	—	23	10	.8	Trace	.13	.05	2.0	22
French-fried, piece 2×½×½ inch: Cooked in deep fat ....10 pieces	57	45	155	2	7	2	2	4	20	9	.7	Trace	.07	.04	1.8	12
Frozen, heated ....10 pieces	57	53	125	2	5	1	1	2	19	5	1.0	Trace	.08	.01	1.5	12
Mashed: Milk added ....1 cup	195	83	125	4	1	—	—	—	25	47	.8	50	.16	.10	2.0	19
Pumpkin, canned ....1 cup	228	90	75	2	1	—	—	—	18	57	.9	14,590	.07	.12	1.3	12
Spinach: Cooked ....1 cup	180	92	40	5	1	—	—	—	6	167	4.0	14,580	.13	.25	1.0	50
Canned, drained solids ....1 cup	180	91	45	5	1	—	—	—	6	212	4.7	14,400	.03	.21	.6	24

Food, approximate measure, and weight (in grams)		Water	Food energy	Protein	Fat	Fatty acids		Carbohydrate	Calcium	Iron	Vitamin A value	Thiamin	Riboflavin	Niacin	Ascorbic acid
						Saturated (total)	Unsaturated linoleic								
	Grams	Percent	Calories	Grams	Grams	Grams	Grams	Grams	Milligrams	Milligrams	International units	Milligrams	Milligrams	Milligrams	Milligrams
Squash:															
Cooked:															
Summer, diced.....1 cup..... 210		96	30	2	Trace	—	—	7	52	.8	820	.10	.16	1.6	21
Winter, baked, mashed.....1 cup..... 205		81	130	4	1	—	—	32	57	1.6	8,610	.10	.27	1.4	27
Sweet potatoes:															
Cooked, medium, 5×2 inches:															
Baked, peeled after baking.....1 sweet potato... 110		64	155	2	1	—	—	36	44	1.0	8,910	.10	.07	.7	24
Boiled, peeled after boiling.....1 sweet potato... 147		71	170	2	1	—	—	39	47	1.0	11,610	.13	.09	.9	25
Candied, 3½×2¼ inches.....1 sweet potato... 175		60	295	2	6	2	1	60	65	1.6	11,030	.10	.08	.8	17
Canned, vacuum or solid pack.....1 cup..... 218		72	235	4	Trace	—	—	54	54	1.7	17,000	.10	.10	1.4	30
Tomatoes:															
Raw, approx. 3-in. diam., 2⅛ in. high.....1 tomato..... 200		94	40	2	Trace	—	—	9	24	.9	1,640	.11	.07	1.3	[7]42
Canned, solids and liquid.....1 cup..... 241		94	50	2	1	—	—	10	14	1.2	2,170	.12	.07	1.7	41
Tomato catsup:															
Tablespoon.....1 tablespoon..... 15		69	15	Trace	Trace	—	—	4	3	.1	210	.01	.01	.2	2
Tomato juice, canned:															
Cup.....1 cup..... 243		94	45	2	Trace			10	17	2.2	1,940	.12	.07	1.9	39
Turnips, cooked, diced.....1 cup..... 155		94	35	1	Trace			8	54	.6	Trace	.06	.08	.5	34
Turnip greens, cooked.....1 cup..... 145		94	30	3	Trace			5	252	1.5	8,270	.15	.33	.7	68

FRUITS AND FRUIT PRODUCTS

Apples, raw (about

Food, approximate measure	Grams	Water (%)	Food energy (cal.)	Protein (g)	Fat (g)	Saturated	Oleic	Linoleic	Carbohydrate (g)	Calcium (mg)	Iron (mg)	Vitamin A (I.U.)	Thiamine (mg)	Riboflavin (mg)	Niacin (mg)	Ascorbic acid (mg)
Apple juice, bottled or canned .... 1 cup	248	88	120	Trace	Trace	—	—	—	30	15	1.5	—	.02	.05	.2	2
Applesauce, canned: Sweetened .... 1 cup	255	76	230	1	Trace	—	—	—	61	10	1.3	100	.05	.03	.1	3[3]
Unsweetened or artificially sweetened .... 1 cup	244	88	100	1	Trace	—	—	—	26	10	1.2	100	.05	.02	.1	2[2]
Apricots: Raw (about 12 per lb.)[3] .... 3 apricots	114	85	55	1	Trace	—	—	—	14	18	.5	2,890	.03	.04	.7	10
Canned in heavy syrup .... 1 cup	259	77	220	2	Trace	—	—	—	57	28	.8	4,510	.05	.06	.9	10
Dried, uncooked (40 halves per cup) .... 1 cup	150	25	390	8	1	—	—	—	100	100	8.2	16,350	.02	.23	4.9	19
Cooked, unsweetened, fruit and liquid .... 1 cup	285	76	240	5	1	—	—	—	62	63	5.1	8,550	.01	.13	2.8	8
Apricot nectar, canned .... 1 cup	251	85	140	1	Trace	—	—	—	37	23	.5	2,380	.03	.03	.5	8[4]
Avocados, whole fruit, raw[5]: California (mid- and late-winter) .... 1 avocado	284	74	370	5	37	7	17	5	13	22	1.3	630	.24	.43	3.5	30
Florida (late summer, fall) .... 1 avocado	454	78	390	4	33	7	15	4	27	30	1.8	880	.33	.61	4.9	43
Bananas, raw, medium size[2] .... 1 banana	175	76	100	1	Trace	—	—	—	26	10	.8	230	.06	.07	.8	12
Banana flakes .... 1 cup	100	3	340	4	1	—	—	—	89	32	2.8	760	.18	.24	2.8	7
Blackberries, raw .... 1 cup	144	84	85	2	1	—	—	—	19	46	1.3	290	.05	.06	.5	30
Blueberries, raw .... 1 cup	140	83	85	1	1	—	—	—	21	21	1.4	140	.04	.08	.6	20
Cantaloup, raw, medium, 5-inch diameter[5] .... ½ melon	385	91	60	1	Trace	—	—	—	14	27	.8	6,540[6]	.08	.06	1.2	63
Cherries, canned, red, sour, pitted, water pack .... 1 cup	244	88	105	2	Trace	—	—	—	26	37	.7	1,660	.07	.05	.5	12
Cranberry-juice cocktail, canned .... 1 cup	250	83	165	Trace	Trace	—	—	—	42	13	.8	Trace	.03	.03	.1	40[10]
Cranberry sauce, sweetened, canned, strained .... 1 cup	277	62	405	Trace	Trace	—	—	—	104	17	.6	60	.03	.03	.1	6
Dates, pitted, cut .... 1 cup	178	22	490	4	1	—	—	—	130	105	5.3	90	.16	.17	3.9	0
Figs, dried, large .... 1 fig	21	23	60	1	Trace	—	—	—	15	26	.6	20	.02	.02	.1	0

Food, approximate measure, and weight (in grams)	Grams	Water	Food energy	Protein	Fat	Fatty acids Saturated (total)	Fatty acids Unsaturated linoleic	Carbohydrate	Calcium	Iron	Vitamin A value	Thiamin	Riboflavin	Niacin	Ascorbic acid
	Grams	Percent	Calories	Grams	Grams	Grams	Grams	Grams	Milligrams	Milligrams	International units	Milligrams	Milligrams	Milligrams	Milligrams
Fruit cocktail, canned, in heavy syrup ...1 cup	256	80	195	1	Trace	—	—	50	23	1.0	360	.05	.03	1.3	5
Grapefruit:															
Raw, medium, 3¾-in. diam.[5]															
White ...½ grapefruit	241	89	45	1	Trace	—	—	12	19	.5	10	.05	.02	.2	44
Pink or red ...½ grapefruit	241	89	50	1	Trace	—	—	13	20	.5	540	.05	.02	.2	44
Canned, syrup pack ...1 cup	254	81	180	2	Trace	—	—	45	33	.8	30	.08	.05	.5	76
Grapefruit juice:															
Fresh ...1 cup	246	90	95	1	Trace	—	—	23	22	.5	(11)	.09	.04	.4	92
Canned, white:															
Unsweetened ...1 cup	247	89	100	1	Trace	—	—	24	20	1.0	20	.07	.04	.4	84
Sweetened ...1 cup	250	86	130	1	Trace	—	—	32	20	1.0	20	.07	.04	.4	78
Frozen, concentrate, unsweetened:															
Diluted with 3 parts water, by volume ...1 cup	247	89	100	1	Trace	—	—	24	25	.2	20	.10	.04	.5	96
Dehydrated crystals prepared with water ...1 cup	247	90	100	1	Trace	—	—	24	22	.2	20	.10	.05	.5	91
Grapes, raw[6] ...1 cup	153	82	65	1	1	—	—	15	15	.4	100	.05	.03	.2	3
Grape juice:															
Canned or bottled ...1 cup	253	83	165	1	Trace	—	—	42	28	.8	—	.10	.05	.5	Trace
Frozen concentrate, sweetened:															
Diluted with 3 parts water, by volume ...1 cup	250	86	135	1	Trace	—	—	33	8	.3	10	.05	.08	.5	(11)
Grape juice drink, canned ...1 cup	250	86	135	Trace	Trace	—	—	35	8	.3	—	.03	.03	.3	(12)
Lemon juice, raw ...1 cup	244	91	60	1	Trace	—	—	20	17	.5	50	.07	.02	.2	112
Lemonade concentrate:															
Diluted with 4⅓ parts water, by volume ...1 cup	248	88	110	Trace	Trace	—	—	28	2	Trace	Trace	Trace	.02	.2	17
Lime juice:															

Food	Measure	Grams	Water (%)	Food energy	Protein	Fat	Fatty acids: Saturated	Unsaturated: Oleic	Unsaturated: Linoleic	Carbohydrate	Calcium	Iron	Vitamin A	Thiamin	Riboflavin	Niacin	Ascorbic acid
Fresh	1 cup	246	90	65	1	Trace	—	—	—	22	22	.5	20	.05	.02	.2	79
Canned, unsweetened	1 cup	246	90	65	1	Trace	—	—	—	22	22	.5	20	.05	.02	.2	52
Limeade concentrate, frozen: Diluted with 4⅓ parts water, by volume	1 cup	247	90	100	Trace	Trace	—	—	—	27	2	Trace	Trace	Trace	Trace	Trace	5
Oranges, raw, 2⅝-in. diam., all commercial varieties[3]	1 orange	180	86	65	1	Trace	—	—	—	16	54	.5	260	.13	.05	.5	66
Orange juice, fresh, all varieties	1 cup	248	88	110	2	1	—	—	—	26	27	.5	500	.22	.07	1.0	124
Canned, unsweetened	1 cup	249	87	120	2	Trace	—	—	—	28	25	1.0	500	.17	.05	.7	100
Frozen concentrate: Diluted with 3 parts water, by volume	1 cup	249	87	120	2	Trace	—	—	—	29	25	.2	550	.22	.02	1.0	120
Dehydrated crystals, prepared with water	1 cup	248	88	115	2	1	—	—	—	27	25	.5	500	.20	.07	1.0	109
Orange-apricot juice drink	1 cup	249	87	125	1	Trace	—	—	—	32	12	.2	1,440	.05	.02	.5	[10]40
Orange and grapefruit juice: Frozen concentrate: Diluted with 3 parts water, by volume	1 cup	248	88	110	1	Trace	—	—	—	26	20	.2	270	.16	.02	.8	102
Papayas, raw, ½-inch cubes	1 cup	182	89	70	1	Trace	—	—	—	18	36	.5	3,190	.07	.08	.5	102
Peaches: Raw: Whole, medium, 2-inch diameter	1 peach	114	89	35	1	Trace	—	—	—	10	9	.5	[13]1,320	.02	.05	1.0	7
Sliced	1 cup	168	89	65	1	Trace	—	—	—	16	15	.8	[13]2,230	.03	.08	1.6	12
Canned, yellow-fleshed, solids and liquids: Syrup pack, heavy: Halves or slices	1 cup	257	79	200	1	Trace	—	—	—	52	10	.8	1,100	.02	.06	1.4	7
Water pack	1 cup	245	91	75	1	Trace	—	—	—	20	10	.7	1,100	.02	.06	1.4	7
Dried, uncooked	1 cup	160	25	420	5	1	—	—	—	109	77	9.6	6,240	.02	.31	8.5	28
Cooked, unsweetened, 10-12 halves and juice	1 cup	270	77	220	3	1	—	—	—	58	41	5.1	3,290	.01	.15	4.2	6

Food, approximate measure, and weight (in grams)	Water	Food energy	Protein	Fat	Fatty acids — Saturated (total)	Fatty acids — Unsaturated linoleic	Carbohydrate	Calcium	Iron	Vitamin A value	Thiamin	Riboflavin	Niacin	Ascorbic acid
	Percent	Calories	Grams	Grams	Grams	Grams	Grams	Milligrams	Milligrams	International units	Milligrams	Milligrams	Milligrams	Milligrams
Frozen:														
Carton, 12 ounces, not thawed........1 carton........340	76	300	1	Trace	—	—	77	14	1.7	2,210	.03	.14	2.4	[14]135
Pears:														
Raw, 3x2½-inch diameter[2]........1 pear........182	83	100	1	1	—	—	25	13	.5	30	.04	.07	.2	7
Canned, solids and liquid: Syrup pack, heavy; Halves or slices........1 cup........255	80	195	1	1	—	—	50	13	.5	Trace	.03	.05	.3	4
Pineapple:														
Raw, diced........1 cup........140	85	75	1	Trace	—	—	19	24	.7	100	.12	.04	.3	24
Canned, heavy syrup pack, solids and liquid: Crushed........1 cup........260	80	195	1	Trace	—	—	50	29	.8	120	.20	.06	.5	17
Sliced, slices and juice........2 small or 1 large........122	80	90	Trace	Trace	—	—	24	13	.4	50	.09	.03	.2	8
Pineapple juice, canned........1 cup........249	86	135	1	Trace	—	—	34	37	.7	120	.12	.04	.5	[8]22
Plums, all except prunes: Raw, 2-inch diameter, about 2 ounces[3]........1 plum........60	87	25	Trace	Trace	—	—	7	7	.3	140	.02	.02	.3	3
Canned, syrup pack (Italian prunes): Plums (with pits) and juice[4]........1 cup........256	77	205	1	Trace	—	—	53	22	2.2	2,970	.05	.05	.9	4
Prunes, dried, "softenized," medium: Uncooked[5]........4 prunes........32	28	70	1	Trace	—	—	18	14	1.1	440	.02	.04	.4	1
Cooked, unsweetened........1 cup........270	66	295	2	1	—	—	78	60	4.5	1,860	.08	.18	1.7	2
Prune juice, canned or bottled........1 cup........256	80	200	1	Trace	—	—	49	36	10.5	—	.03	.03	1.0	[5]5
Raisins, seedless, 1 cup........165	18	480	4	Trace	—	—	128	102	5.8	30	.18	.13	.8	2

Food	Amount	Grams	Water (%)	Food energy (cal.)	Protein (g)	Fat (g)	Saturated	Oleic	Linoleic	Carbohydrate (g)	Calcium (mg)	Iron (mg)	Vitamin A (I.U.)	Thiamin (mg)	Riboflavin (mg)	Niacin (mg)	Ascorbic acid (mg)
Raspberries, red:																	
Raw	1 cup	123	84	70	1	1	—	—	—	17	27	1.1	160	.04	.11	1.1	31
Frozen, 10-ounce carton, not thawed	1 carton	284	74	275	2	1	—	—	—	70	37	1.7	200	.06	.17	1.7	59
Rhubarb, cooked, sugar added	1 cup	272	63	385	1	Trace	—	—	—	98	212	1.6	220	.06	.15	.7	17
Strawberries																	
Raw	1 cup	149	90	55	1	1	—	—	—	13	31	1.5	90	.04	.10	1.0	88
Frozen, 10-ounce carton, not thawed	1 carton	284	71	310	1	1	—	—	—	79	40	2.0	90	.06	.17	1.5	150
Tangerines, raw, medium	1 tangerine	116	87	40	1	Trace	—	—	—	10	34	.3	360	.05	.02	.1	27
Tangerine juice, canned, sweetened	1 cup	249	87	125	1	1	—	—	—	30	45	.5	1,050	.15	.05	.2	55
Watermelon, raw	1 wedge	925	93	115	2	1	—	—	—	27	30	2.1	2,510	.13	.13	.7	30
GRAIN PRODUCTS																	
Bagel, 3-in. diam.	1 bagel	55	29	165	6	2	—	—	—	30	8	1.2	0	.15	.11	1.4	0
Barley, pearled, light, uncooked	1 cup	200	11	700	16	2	Trace	1	1	158	32	4.0	0	.24	.10	6.2	0
Biscuits, baking powder, from home recipe with enriched flour, 2-in. diam.	1 biscuit	28	27	105	2	5	1	2	1	13	34	.4	Trace	.06	.06	.1	Trace
Biscuits, baking powder, from mix, 2-in. diam.	1 biscuit	28	28	90	2	3	1	1	1	15	19	.6	Trace	.08	.07	.6	Trace
Bran flakes (40% bran), added thiamin and iron	1 cup	35	3	105	4	1	—	—	—	28	25	12.3	0	.14	.06	2.2	0
Bran flakes with raisins, added thiamin and iron	1 cup	50	7	145	4	1	—	—	—	40	28	13.5	Trace	.16	.07	2.7	0
Breads:																	
Boston brown bread, slice 3x3¾ in.	1 slice	48	45	100	3	1	—	—	—	22	43	.9	0	.05	.03	.6	0
Cracked-wheat bread: Slice	1 slice	25	35	65	2	1	—	—	—	13	22	.3	Trace	.03	.02	.3	Trace
French or Vienna bread: Enriched, 1 lb. loaf	1 loaf	454	31	1,315	41	14	3	—	2	251	195	10.0	Trace	1.27	1.00	11.3	Trace

Food, approximate measure, and weight (in grams)		Water	Food energy	Protein	Fat	Fatty acids		Carbohydrate	Calcium	Iron	Vitamin A value	Thiamin	Riboflavin	Niacin	Ascorbic acid
						Saturated (total)	Unsaturated linoleic								
	Grams	Percent	Calories	Grams	Grams	Grams	Grams	Grams	Milligrams	Milligrams	International units	Milligrams	Milligrams	Milligrams	Milligrams
Italian bread:															
Enriched, 1 lb. loaf ....1 loaf	454	32	1,250	41	4	Trace	2	256	77	10.0	0	1.32	.91	11.8	0
Raisin bread:															
Slice ....1 slice	25	35	65	2	1	—	—	13	18	.3	Trace	.01	.02	.2	Trace
Rye bread:															
American, light (⅓ rye, ⅔ wheat):															
Slice ....1 slice	25	36	60	2	Trace	—	—	13	19	.4	0	.05	.02	.4	0
Pumpernickel, loaf, 1 lb. ....1 loaf	454	34	1,115	41	5	—	—	241	381	10.9	0	1.04	.64	5.4	0
White bread, enriched:															
Slice ....1 slice	25	36	70	2	1	—	—	13	21	.6	Trace	.06	.05	.6	Trace
Slice, toasted ....1 slice	22	25	70	2	1	—	—	13	21	.6	Trace	.06	.05	.6	Trace
Whole-wheat bread:															
Slice ....1 slice	28	36	65	3	1	—	—	14	24	.8	Trace	.09	.03	.8	Trace
Slice, toasted ....1 slice	24	24	65	3	1	—	—	14	24	.8	Trace	.09	.03	.8	Trace
Breadcrumbs, dry, grated.......1 cup	100	6	390	13	5	1	1	73	122	3.6	Trace	.22	.30	3.5	Trace
Buckwheat flour, light, sifted ....1 cup	98	12	340	6	1	—	—	78	11	1.0	0	.08	.04	.4	0
Bulgur, canned, seasoned.......1 cup	135	56	245	8	4	—	—	44	27	1.9	0	.08	.05	4.1	0
Cookies:															
Brownies with nuts:															
Made from home recipe with enriched flour ....1 brownie	20	10	95	1	6	1	1	10	8	.4	40	.04	.02	.1	Trace
Made from mix ....1 brownie	20	11	85	1	4	1	1	13	9	.4	20	.03	.02	.1	Trace
Chocolate chip:															
Made from home recipe with enriched flour ....1 cookie	10	3	50	1	3	1	1	6	4	.2	10	.01	.01	.1	Trace

Food, approximate measure	Weight (g)	Water (%)	Food energy (cal.)	Protein (g)	Fat (g)	Saturated (g)	Oleic (g)	Linoleic (g)	Carbohydrate (g)	Calcium (mg)	Iron (mg)	Vitamin A (I.U.)	Thiamine (mg)	Riboflavin (mg)	Niacin (mg)	Ascorbic acid (mg)
Commercial............1 cookie	10	3	50	1	2	1	1	Trace	7	4	.2	10	Trace	Trace	Trace	Trace
Fig bars, commercial............1 cookie	14	14	50	1	1	—	—	—	11	11	.2	20	Trace	.1	.1	Trace
Corn flakes, added nutrients:																
Plain............1 cup	25	4	100	2	Trace	—	—	—	21	4	.4	0	.11	.02	.5	0
Corn (hominy) grits, degermed, cooked:																
Enriched............1 cup	245	87	125	3	Trace	—	—	—	27	2	.7	[15]150	.10	.07	1.0	0
Cornmeal:																
Whole ground, unbolted, dry............1 cup	122	12	435	11	5	1	2	2	90	24	2.9	[15]620	.46	.13	2.4	0
Degermed, enriched: Dry form............1 cup	138	12	500	11	2	—	—	—	108	8	4.0	[15]610	.61	.36	4.8	0
Cooked............1 cup	240	88	120	3	1	—	—	—	26	2	1.0	[15]140	.14	.10	1.2	0
Corn muffins, made with enriched degermed cornmeal and enriched flour; muffin 2⅜-in. diam.............1 muffin	40	33	125	3	4	2	2	Trace	19	42	.7	[15]120	.08	.09	.6	Trace
Crackers:																
Graham, 2½-in. square............4 crackers	28	6	110	2	3	1	1	1	21	11	.4	0	.01	.06	.4	0
Saltines............4 crackers	11	4	50	1	1	—	—	—	8	2	.1	0	Trace	Trace	.1	0
Doughnuts, cake type............1 doughnut	32	24	125	1	6	1	4	1	16	13	[16].4	30	[16].05	[16].05	[16].4	Trace
Farina, quick-cooking, enriched, cooked............1 cup	245	89	105	3	Trace	—	—	—	22	147	[17].7	0	[17].12	[17].07	[17]1.0	0
Macaroni, cooked: Enriched: Cooked, until tender............1 cup	140	72	155	5	1	—	—	—	32	8	[17]1.3	0	[17].20	[17].11	[17]1.5	0
Unenriched: Cooked, until tender............1 cup	140	72	155	5	1	—	—	—	32	11	.6	0	.01	.01	.4	0
Macaroni (enriched) and cheese, baked............1 cup	200	58	430	17	22	10	9	2	40	362	1.8	860	.20	.40	1.8	Trace
Canned............1 cup	240	80	230	9	10	4	4	1	26	199	1.0	260	.12	.24	1.0	Trace
Muffins, with enriched white flour; muffin, 3-inch diam.............1 muffin	40	38	120	3	4	1	2	Trace	17	42	.6	40	.07	.09	.6	Trace
Noodles (egg noodles), cooked: Enriched............1 cup	160	70	200	7	2	—	—	—	37	16	[17]1.4	110	[17].22	[17].13	[17]1.9	0
Unenriched............1 cup	160	70	200	7	2	—	—	—	37	16	1.0	110	.05	.03	.6	0

Food approximate measure, and weight (in grams)	Grams	Water Per-cent	Food energy Calories	Protein Grams	Fat Grams	Fatty acids Saturated (total) Grams	Fatty acids Unsaturated linoleic Grams	Carbohydrate Grams	Calcium Milligrams	Iron Milligrams	Vitamin A value International units	Thiamin Milligrams	Riboflavin Milligrams	Niacin Milligrams	Ascorbic acid Milligrams
Oatmeal or rolled oats, cooked ... 1 cup	240	87	130	5	2	—	1	23	22	1.4	0	.19	.05	.2	0
Pancakes, 4-inch diam.:															
Wheat, enriched flour (home recipe) ... 1 cake	27	50	60	2	2	Trace	Trace	9	27	.4	30	.05	.06	.4	Trace
Buckwheat (made from mix with egg and milk) ... 1 cake	27	58	55	2	2	Trace	Trace	6	59	.4	60	.03	.04	.2	Trace
Plain or buttermilk (made from mix with egg and milk) ... 1 cake	27	51	60	2	2	1	Trace	9	58	.3	70	.04	.06	.2	Trace
Pizza (cheese) 5½-in. sector; ⅛ of 14-in. diam. pie ... 1 sector	75	45	185	7	6	2	Trace	27	107	.7	290	.04	.12	.7	4
Popcorn, popped, plain ... 1 cup	6	4	25	1	Trace	—	—	5	1	.2	—	—	.01	.1	0
Pretzels:															
Dutch, twisted ... 1 pretzel	16	5	60	2	1	—	—	12	4	.2	0	Trace	Trace	.1	0
Thin, twisted ... 1 pretzel	6	5	25	1	Trace	—	—	5	1	.1	0	Trace	Trace	Trace	0
Stick, regular, 3⅛ inches ... 5 sticks	3	5	10	Trace	Trace	—	—	2	1	Trace	0	Trace	Trace	Trace	0
Rice, brown ... 1 cup	205	70	238	5	1	—	—	51	24	1.0	0	.18	.04	2.8	0
Rice, white:															
Enriched:															
Raw ... 1 cup	185	12	670	12	1	—	—	149	44	[18]5.4	0	[18].81	[18].06	[18]6.5	0
Cooked ... 1 cup	205	73	225	4	Trace	—	—	50	21	[18]1.8	0	[18].23	[18].02	[18]2.1	0
Instant, ready-to-serve ... 1 cup	165	73	180	4	Trace	—	—	40	5	[18]1.3	0	[18].21	[18]—	[18]1.7	0
Unenriched, cooked ... 1 cup	205	73	225	4	Trace	—	—	50	21	.4	0	.04	.02	.8	0
Parboiled, cooked ... 1 cup	175	73	185	4	Trace	—	—	41	33	[18]1.4	0	[18].19	[18]—	[18]2.1	0

Food	Amount	Grams	Water (%)	Food energy (cal)	Protein (g)	Fat (g)	Saturated (g)	Oleic (g)	Linoleic (g)	Carbohydrate (g)	Calcium (mg)	Iron (mg)	Vitamin A (IU)	Thiamin (mg)	Riboflavin (mg)	Niacin (mg)	Ascorbic acid (mg)
Rice, puffed, added nutrients	1 cup	15	4	60	1	Trace	—	—	—	13	3	.3	0	.07	.01	.7	0
Rolls, enriched:																	
Cloverleaf or pan:																	
Home recipe	1 roll	35	26	120	3	3	1	1	Trace	20	16	.7	30	.09	.09	.8	Trace
Commercial	1 roll	28	31	85	2	2	Trace	1	Trace	15	21	.5	Trace	.08	.05	.6	Trace
Frankfurter or hamburger	1 roll	40	31	120	3	2	1	1	Trace	21	30	.8	Trace	.11	.07	.9	Trace
Rye wafers, whole-grain, 1⅞x3½ inches	2 wafers	13	6	45	2	Trace	—	—	—	10	7	.5	0	.04	.03	.2	0
Spaghetti, cooked, tender stage, enriched	1 cup	140	72	155	5	1	—	—	—	32	11	1.3[17]	0	.20[17]	.11[17]	1.5[17]	0
Spaghetti with meat balls and tomato sauce:																	
Home recipe	1 cup	248	70	330	19	12	4	6	1	39	124	3.7	1,590	.25	.30	4.0	22
Canned	1 cup	250	78	260	12	10	2	5	1	28	53	3.3	1,000	.15	.18	2.3	5
Waffles, with enriched flour, 7-in. diam.	1 waffle	75	41	210	7	7	2	4	1	28	85	1.3	250	.13	.19	1.0	Trace
Waffles, made from mix, enriched, egg and milk added, 7-in. diam.	1 waffle	75	42	205	7	8	3	3	1	27	179	1.0	170	.11	.17	.7	Trace
Wheat, puffed, added nutrients	1 cup	15	3	55	2	Trace	—	—	—	12	4	.6	0	.08	.03	1.2	0
Wheat, shredded, plain	1 biscuit	25	7	90	2	1	—	—	—	20	11	.9	0	.06	.03	1.1	0
Wheat flakes, added nutrients	1 cup	30	4	105	3	Trace	—	—	—	24	12	1.3	0	.19	.04	1.5	0
Wheat flours:																	
Whole wheat, from hard wheats, stirred	1 cup	120	12	400	16	2	Trace	1	1	85	49	4.0	0	.66	.14	5.2	0
All-purpose or family flour, enriched:																	
Sifted	1 cup	115	12	420	12	1	—	—	—	88	18	3.3[17]	0	.51[17]	.30[17]	4.0[17]	0
Unsifted	1 cup	125	12	455	13	1	—	—	—	95	20	3.6[17]	0	.55[17]	.33[17]	4.4[17]	0
Self-rising, enriched	1 cup	125	12	440	12	1	—	—	—	93	331	3.6[17]	0	.55[17]	.33[17]	4.4[17]	0
Cake or pastry flour, sifted	1 cup	96	12	350	7	1	—	—	—	76	16	.5	0	.03	.03	.7	0
Wheat germ, toasted	1 cup	65	3	260	20	8	—	—	3	33	31	6	0	1.1	.66	3.5	6.6

FATS, OILS

Food, approximate measure, and weight (in grams)	Grams	Water (Per-cent)	Food energy (Calories)	Pro-tein (Grams)	Fat (Grams)	Fatty acids Satu-rated (total) (Grams)	Fatty acids Unsat-urated linoleic (Grams)	Carbo-hydrate (Grams)	Cal-cium (Milli-grams)	Iron (Milli-grams)	Vita-min A value (International units)	Thi-amin (Milli-grams)	Ribo-flavin (Milli-grams)	Niacin (Milli-grams)	Ascor-bic acid (Milli-grams)
Butter:															
Regular ... 1 tablespoon	14	16	100	Trace	12	6	Trace	Trace	3	0	[10]470	—	—	—	0
Whipped, 6 sticks or 2, 8-oz. containers per pound ... 1 tablespoon	9	16	65	Trace	8	4	Trace	Trace	2	0	[10]310	—	—	—	0
Fats, cooking:															
Lard ... 1 cup	205	0	1,850	0	205	78	20	0	0	0	0	0	0	0	0
1 tablespoon	13	0	115	0	13	5	1	0	0	0	0	0	0	0	0
Vegetable fats ... 1 cup	200	0	1,770	0	200	50	44	0	0	0	—	0	0	0	0
1 tablespoon	13	0	110	0	13	3	3	0	0	0	—	0	0	0	0
Margarine:															
Regular ... 1 tablespoon	14	16	100	Trace	12	2	3	Trace	3	0	[20]470	—	—	—	0
Soft, 2, 8-oz. tubs per pound ... 1 tablespoon	14	16	100	Trace	11	2	4	Trace	3	0	[20]470	—	—	—	0
Mayonnaise ... 1 tablespoon	14	15	100	Trace	11	2	6	Trace	3	.1	40	Trace	.01	Trace	—
Oils, salad or cooking:															
Corn ... 1 tablespoon	14	0	125	0	14	1	7	0	0	0	—	0	0	0	0
Cottonseed ... 1 tablespoon	14	0	125	0	14	4	7	0	0	0	—	0	0	0	0
Olive ... 1 tablespoon	14	0	125	0	14	2	1	0	0	0	—	0	0	0	0
Peanut ... 1 tablespoon	14	0	125	0	14	3	4	0	0	0	—	0	0	0	0
Safflower ... 1 tablespoon	14	0	125	0	14	1	10	0	0	0	—	0	0	0	0
Soybean ... 1 tablespoon	14	0	125	0	14	2	7	0	0	0	—	0	0	0	0
SUGARS, SWEETS															
Honey, strained or extracted ... 1 tablespoon	21	17	65	Trace	0	—	—	17	1	.1	0	Trace	.01	.1	Trace
Jams and preserves ... 1 tablespoon	20	29	55	Trace	Trace	—	—	14	4	.2	Trace	Trace	.01	Trace	Trace
Jellies ... 1 tablespoon	18	29	50	Trace	Trace	—	—	13	4	.3	Trace	Trace	.01	Trace	1

Molasses, cane:															
Light (first extraction) ... 1 tablespoon	20	24	50	—	—	—	—	13	33	.9	—	.01	.01	—	—
Blackstrap (third extraction) ... 1 tablespoon	20	24	45	—	—	—	—	11	137	3.2	—	.02	.04	.4	Trace
Syrups:															
Sorghum ... 1 tablespoon	21	23	55	—	—	—	—	14	35	2.6	—	—	.02	.4	—
Table blends, chiefly corn, light and dark ... 1 tablespoon	21	24	60	0	0	0	0	15	9	.8	0	0	0	0	0
Sugars:															
Brown, firm packed ... 1 cup	220	2	820	0	0	0	0	212	187	7.5	0	.02	.07	.4	0
White:															
Granulated ... 1 cup	200	Trace	770	0	0	0	0	199	0	.2	0	0	0	0	0
... 1 tablespoon	11	Trace	40	0	0	0	0	11	0	Trace	0	0	0	0	0
Powdered, stirred before measuring ... 1 cup	120	Trace	460	0	0	0	0	119	0	.1	0	0	0	0	0
MISCELLANEOUS ITEMS															
Bouillon cubes, approx. ½ in. ... 1 cube	4	4	5	1	Trace	—	—	Trace	—	—	—	—	—	—	—
Gelatin:															
Plain, dry powder in envelope ... 1 envelope	7	13	25	6	Trace	—	—	0	—	—	—	—	—	—	—
Dessert powder, 3-oz. package ... 1 package	85	2	315	8	0	—	—	75	—	—	—	—	—	—	—
Gelatin dessert, prepared with water ... 1 cup	240	84	140	4	0	—	—	34	—	—	—	—	—	—	—
Olives, pickled:															
Green ... 4 medium or 3 extra large or 2 giant	16	78	15	Trace	2	Trace	Trace	Trace	8	.2	40	Trace	—	—	—
Ripe: Mission ... 3 small or 2 large	10	73	15	Trace	2	Trace	Trace	Trace	9	.1	10	Trace	Trace	—	—
Pickles, cucumber:															
Dill, medium, whole, 3¾ in. long, 1¼ in. diam. ... 1 pickle	65	93	10	Trace	Trace	—	—	1	17	.7	70	Trace	.01	Trace	4

Food, approximate measure, and weight (in grams)	Water	Food energy	Protein	Fat	Fatty acids Saturated (total)	Fatty acids Unsaturated linoleic	Carbohydrate	Calcium	Iron	Vitamin A value	Thiamin	Riboflavin	Niacin	Ascorbic acid
	Percent	Calories	Grams	Grams	Grams	Grams	Grams	Milligrams	Milligrams	International units	Milligrams	Milligrams	Milligrams	Milligrams
Fresh, sliced, 1½ in. diam., ¼ in. thick....2 slices....15	79	10	Trace	Trace	—	—	3	5	.3	20	Trace	Trace	Trace	1
Sweet, gherkin, small, whole, approx. 2½ in. long, ¾ in. diam....1 pickle....15	61	20	Trace	Trace	—	—	6	2	.2	10	Trace	Trace	Trace	1
Popcorn. See Grain Products.														
Pudding, home recipe with starch base:														
Vanilla (blanc mange)....1 cup....255	76	285	9	10	5	Trace	41	298	Trace	410	.08	.41	.3	2
Pudding mix, dry form,														
4-oz. package....1 package....113	2	410	3	2	1	Trace	103	23	1.8	Trace	.02	.08	.5	0
Sherbet....1 cup....193	67	260	2	2	—	—	59	31	Trace	120	.02	.06	Trace	4
Soups:														
Canned, condensed, ready-to-serve:														
Prepared with an equal volume of milk:														
Cream of chicken....1 cup....245	85	180	7	10	3	3	15	172	.5	610	.05	.27	.7	2
Cream of mush- room....1 cup....245	83	215	7	14	4	5	16	191	.5	250	.05	.34	.7	1
Tomato....1 cup....250	84	175	7	7	3	1	23	168	.8	1,200	.10	.25	1.3	15
Prepared with an equal volume of water:														
Bean with pork....1 cup....250	84	170	8	6	1	2	22	63	2.3	650	.13	.08	1.0	3
Beef broth, bouil- lon consommé....1 cup....240	96	30	5	0	0	—	3	Trace	.5	Trace	Trace	.02	1.2	—
Beef noodle....1 cup....240	93	70	4	3	1	1	7	7	1.0	50	.05	.07	1.0	Trace
Cream of chicken....1 cup....240	92	95	3	6	3	3	8	24	.5	410	.02	.05	.5	Trace
Cream of mush- room....1 cup....240	90	135	2	10	1	5	10	41	.5	70	.02	.12	.7	Trace
Minestrone....1 cup....245	90	105	5	3	1	—	14	37	1.0	2,350	.07	.05	1.0	—
Split pea....1 cup....245	85	145	9	3	1	Trace	21	29	1.5	440	.25	.15	1.5	1
Tomato....1 cup....245	90	90	2	3	Trace	1	16	15	.7	1,000	.05	.05	1.2	12

Food, approximate measure		Grams	Water	Food energy	Protein	Fat	Saturated (total)	Unsaturated, Oleic	Unsaturated, Linoleic	Carbohydrate	Calcium	Iron	Vitamin A	Thiamin	Riboflavin	Niacin	Ascorbic acid
Vegetable beef	1 cup	245	92	80	5	2	—	—	—	10	12	.7	2,700	.05	.05	1.0	—
Vegetarian	1 cup	245	92	80	2	2	—	—	—	13	20	1.0	2,940	.05	.05	1.0	—
Dehydrated, dry form:																	
Chicken noodle (2-oz. package)	1 package	57	6	220	8	6	2	2	1	33	34	1.4	190	.30	.15	2.4	3
Onion mix (1½-oz. package)	1 package	43	3	150	6	5	1	2	1	23	42	.6	30	.05	.03	.3	6
Tomato-vegetable with noodles (2½-oz. package)	1 package	71	4	245	6	6	2	2	1	45	33	1.4	1,700	.21	.13	1.8	18
Frozen, condensed:																	
Cream of potato:																	
Prepared with equal volume of milk	1 cup	245	83	185	8	10	5	3	Trace	18	208	1.0	590	.10	.27	.5	Trace
Prepared with equal volume of water	1 cup	240	90	105	3	5	3	2	Trace	12	58	1.0	410	.05	.05	.5	—
Cream of shrimp:																	
Prepared with equal volume of milk	1 cup	245	82	245	9	16	—	—	—	15	189	.5	290	.07	.27	.5	Trace
Prepared with equal volume of water	1 cup	240	88	160	5	12	—	—	—	8	38	.5	120	.05	.05	.5	—
Tapioca, dry, quick-cooking	1 cup	152	13	535	1	Trace	—	—	—	131	15	.6	0	0	0	0	0
Tapioca cream pudding	1 cup	165	72	220	8	8	4	2	Trace	28	173	.7	480	.07	.30	.2	2
White sauce, medium	1 cup	250	73	405	10	31	16	10	1	22	288	.5	1,150	.10	.43	.5	2
Yeast:																	
Brewer's, dry	1 tablespoon	8	5	25	3	Trace	—	—	—	3	17	1.4	Trace	1.25	.34	3.0	Trace
Yogurt. See Milk, Cheese, Cream, Imitation Cream.																	

[1]Value applies to unfortified product; value for fortified low-density product would be 1,500 I.U., and the fortified high-density product would be 2,290 I.U.

[2]Contributed largely from beta-carotene used for coloring.

[3]Outer layer of fat on the cut was removed to within approximately ½-inch of the lean. Deposits of fat within the cut were not removed.

[4]If bones are discarded, value will be greatly reduced.

[5]Measure and weight apply to entire vegetable or fruit including parts not usually eaten.

[6]Based on yellow varieties; white varieties contain only a trace of cryptoxanthin and carotenes, the pigments in corn that have biological activity.

[7]Year-round average. Samples marketed from November through May, average 29 milligrams per 200-gram tomato; from June through October, around 52 milligrams. This is the amount from the fruit. Additional ascorbic acid may be added by the manufacturer. Refer to the label for this information.

[8]Value for varieties with orange-colored flesh; value for varieties with green flesh would be about 540 I.U.

[9]Value listed is based on products with label stating 30 milligrams per 6 fl. oz. serving.

[10]For white-fleshed varieties; for red-fleshed varieties, 1,080 I.U. per cup.

[11]Present only if added by the manufacturer. Refer to the label for this information.

[12]Based on yellow-fleshed varieties; for white-fleshed varieties value is about 50 I.U. per 114-gram peach and 80 I.U. per cup of sliced peaches.

[13]This value includes ascorbic acid added by manufacturer.

[14]This value is based on product made from yellow varieties of corn; white varieties contain only a trace.

[15]Based on product made with enriched flour. With unenriched flour, approximate values per doughnut are: Iron, 0.2 milligram; thiamin, 0.01 milligram; riboflavin, 0.03 milligram; niacin, 0.2 milligram.

[16]Iron, thiamin, riboflavin, and niacin are based on the minimum levels of enrichment specified in standards of identity promulgated under the Federal Food, Drug, and Cosmetic Act.

[17]Iron, thiamin, riboflavin, and niacin are based on the minimum levels of enrichment specified in standards of identity promulgated under the Federal Food, Drug, and Cosmetic Act. Riboflavin is based on unenriched rice. When the minimum level of enrichment for riboflavin specified in the standards of identity becomes effective the value will be 0.12 milligram per cup of parboiled rice and white rice.

[18]Year-round average.

[19]Based on the average vitamin A content of fortified margarine. Federal specifications for fortified margarine require a minimum of 15,000 I.U. of vitamin A per pound.

Appendix C: Personal Feeding Chart

Please use the following pages to note the foods you introduce and your baby's reaction to them. In case of allergic reactions, this record will be very useful to your doctor, to baby sitters, and for your own quick reference in selecting foods.

PERSONAL FEEDING CHART

DATE	AGE GIVEN	BEVERAGES	CEREAL	FRUIT	VEGETABLE	DAIRY	PROTEIN	LIKE	DISLIKE	ALLERGY	COMMENTS

REACTION

PERSONAL FEEDING CHART

DATE	AGE GIVEN	BEVERAGES	CEREAL	FRUIT	VEGETABLE	DAIRY	PROTEIN	LIKE	DISLIKE	ALLERGY	COMMENTS

REACTION

Bibliography

Government Publications

The U.S. government publishes many informative booklets on nutrition and health as well as food purchase, preparation, and storage. Many are free; others are very inexpensive. The following list is from the *Consumer Information Catalogue* (Winter 1991–92). You can also write for a free copy of the current *Consumer Information Catalogue*. There is no service fee for the catalog. All orders for free booklets require a $1.00 service fee. To order, make your check or money order payable to "Superintendent of Documents." Do not send stamps as payment. If you order both free and sales booklets, you may combine the $1.00 service fee and the sales price in one check or money order.

If you order *only* free booklets, mail your order to:

> S. James
> Consumer Information Center-2A
> P. O. Box 100
> Pueblo, CO 81002

If you order *only* sales booklets or *both* sales and free booklets, mail your order to:

> R. Woods
> Consumer Information Center-2A
> P. O. Box 100
> Pueblo, CO 81002

Remember to include the $1.00 fee if you order any free booklets.

Nutrition

Diet, Nutrition and Cancer Prevention: The Good News. This booklet will help you select, prepare, and serve healthier foods. Includes a list of high-fiber and low-fat foods. 15 pp. (1986. NIH) 526Y. Free.

Dietary Guidelines for Americans. Seven dietary guidelines to help you stay healthy based on recent nutrition research. Charts suggested body weights, calories used in various exercises, and a guide for selecting healthy food every day. 28 pp. (1990. USDA / HHS) 527Y. Free.

Eating for Life. Explains how making the right food choices can reduce your risk of developing cancer and heart diseases. Offers tips on buying and preparing food as well as on menu selection when eating out. 23 pp. (1988. NIH) 113Y. $1.00.

Eating To Lower Your High Blood Cholesterol. Menus, guidelines, cooking tips, and comparison charts of fat and cholesterol to help teach you how to eat properly and lower your blood cholesterol. 53 pp. (1987. NIH) 114Y. $2.00.

Feeding Baby: Nature and Nurture. Explains why breast milk is best for babies and answers your questions about vitamins. Compares milk based and soy based formulas, and explores the dangers of confusing soy beverages with soy based formulas. 4 pp. (1990. FDA) 507Y. Free.

Food News for Consumers. Up-to-date articles on food safety, health and nutrition, and recent findings on a variety of food concerns. Annual subscription-4 issues. (USDA) 251. $5.00.

The Grazing of America: A Guide to Healthy Snacking. "Grazing" is becoming the American way of eating. Learn how to choose the best snacks for your age and lifestyle. 6 pp. (1989. FDA) 530Y. Free.

A Simple Guide to Complex Carbohydrates. What they are and why they are vital to a healthy diet. Dispels the popular myth that starch equals calories and lists healthy sources of starch and fiber. 5 pp. (1989. FDA) 536Y. Free.

A Word About Low Sodium Diets. Tips on how to reduce your sodium intake. Gives recipes with salt substitutes. 5 pp. (1986. FDA) 538Y. Free.

Purchase, Preparation, and Storage

Fish and Seafood Made Easy. Tips on how to select, store, and prepare fish and shellfish. Includes recipes, suggested spices and sauces, and a chart comparing the taste and texture of most seafood. 29 pp. (1989. DOC) 421Y. 50¢.

Food Irradiation—Toxic to Bacteria, Safe for Humans. Irradiation kills harmful organisms so they cannot survive or multiply in your food. Learn how this safe and effective process works and why it is especially useful in certain foods. 4 pp. (1991. FDA) 529Y. Free.

Is that Newfangled Cookware Safe? Discusses advantages and safety concerns of seven popular types of cookware from aluminum to nonstick coatings to cast iron. 4 pp. (1991. FDA) 531Y. Free.

Keeping Up with the Microwave Revolution. Examines FDA research on food packaging designed for use in microwave ovens. Also explains how microwaves work and gives cooking tips. 5 pp. (1990. FDA) 593X. Free.

Preventing Food-Borne Illness. Discusses symptoms, prevention tips, and safe storage. Also charts common disease-causing organisms and where they come from. 7 pp. (1991. FDA) 534Y. Free.

Quick Consumer Guide to Safe Food Handling. How to reduce the risk of food poisoning when shopping for, preparing, serving, and reheating food. Charts how long some foods can be safely frozen or refrigerated. 8 pp. (1990. USDA) 535Y. Free.

Weighing Food Safety Risks. How to judge the risks of consuming chemicals like aflatoxins and pesticides such as alar in apples. 4 pp. (1989. FDA) 537Y. Free.

OTHER PUBLICATIONS AND RESOURCES

Here are some other useful publications and organizations:

Books

Jane Brody. *Jane Brody's Good Food Book*. New York: Bantam Books, 1987.

Jane Brody. *Jane Brody's Nutrition Book*. New York: Bantam Books, 1982.

Ellen Buchman Ewald. *Recipes for a Small Planet*. New York: Ballantine, 1973.

Janet Dailey. *Keeping Food Fresh*. Garden City, NY: The Dial Press, 1985.

Michael F. Jacobson, Ph.D., Lisa Y. Lefferts, Anne Witte Garland. *Safe Food*. Los Angeles: Living Planet Press, 1991.

Barbara Kafka. *Microwave Gourmet Healthstyle Cookbook*. New York: William Morrow & Co., 1989.

Frances Moore Lappé. *Diet for a Small Planet*. New York: Ballantine, 1982.

Fredrick J. Stare, Robert E. Olson, and Elizabeth M. Whelan. *Balanced Nutrition; Beyond the Cholesterol Scare*. Holbrook, MA: Bob Adams, Inc., 1989.

U.S. Department of Agriculture. *Nutrition and Your Health: Dietary Guidelines for Americans*, 3rd ed. 1990. Order from: USDA, Room 325-A, 6505 Belcrest Road, Hyattsville, MD 20782.

Organizations

American Academy of Pediatrics
P.O. Box 927
141 Northwest Point Boulevard
Elk Grove Village, IL 60009–0927

Center for Science in the Public Interest
1875 Connecticut Ave. N.W.
Suite 300, Washington, D.C. 20009-5728

La Leche League International
9616 Minneapolis Avenue
P. O. Box 1209
Franklin Park, IL 60131
Hotline: 1-800-LA LECHE

U.S. Department of Agriculture
Meat and Poultry Hotline: 1-800-535-4555
Staffed by home economists, the hotline
operates weekdays from 10:00 A.M. to 4:00
P.M. Eastern Time.

CHOKING PREVENTION AND FIRST AID FOR INFANTS AND CHILDREN

When children begin eating table foods, parents must be very careful. Older infants and children under age four are at greatest risk for choking on food and small objects. Choking occurs when food or objects enter the airway (trachea). Blocking the airway prevents oxygen from getting to the lungs and to the brain. If the brain goes without oxygen for more than four minutes, brain damage or death may occur. Each year over 3,000 men, women, and children in the United States die from accidental choking. About one in ten of these deaths is in children under the age of five. Many of these deaths can be avoided.

The American Academy of Pediatrics (AAP) and the American Trauma Society (ATS) believe that parents often can prevent choking. The AAP and the ATS offer the following choking prevention and first aid information for children and infants.

Dangerous Foods Do not feed children under four years old any round, firm foods unless they're chopped completely. These types of foods are common choking dangers. Infants and young children sometimes don't grind or chew their food well, so they sometimes attempt to swallow it whole. Common choking dangers for infants and children include:

FOODS	HOUSEHOLD ITEMS
hot dogs	balloons
chunks of meat	marbles
grapes	small toy parts
hard candy	pen caps
popcorn	
chunks of peanut butter	
raisins	
raw carrots	

Prevention

- Keep dangerous foods from children until four years of age.
- Insist that children eat while sitting at the table, never while running or playing.
- Prepare and cut food appropriately for young children and teach them to chew their foods well.
- Supervise mealtime for young children. Many choking cases occur when older brothers or sisters offer unsafe foods to a younger child.
- Avoid toys with small parts and keep other small household items out of reach of young children.

First Aid

1. Find out if the child can breathe, cry or speak. See if the child has a strong cough. (A strong cough means there is little or no blockage. It may also dislodge the item if there is blockage.)

2. If the child is breathing, coughing, or speaking, carefully watch him. Do not start first aid if there is a strong cough or if there is little or no blockage. This can turn partial blockage into complete blockage.

3. Begin the following first aid if:
   - the child cannot breathe at all
   - the child's airway is so blocked that there's only a weak cough and loss of color.

FOR INFANTS UNDER ONE YEAR OLD

1. Make sure you or someone else has called for emergency medical services.

2. Place the infant face and head down on your forearm at a 60-degree angle. (See figure A.) Support the head and neck. Rest your forearm firmly against your body for extra support. *Note:* If the infant is large, you may want to lay the child face down over your lap. Firmly support the head, holding it lower than the trunk.

3. Give four rapid back blows with the heel of your hand, striking high between the shoulder blades.

4. If the blockage is not relieved, turn the infant over. Lay the child down, face up, on a firm surface. Give four rapid chest thrusts over the breastbone using two fingers.

5. If breathing does not start, open the mouth with thumb held over tongue and fingers wrapped around lower jaw. This is called the tongue-jaw lift. It draws the tongue away from the back of the throat and may help clear the airway. If you can see the foreign body, it may be removed with a sideways sweep of a finger. Never poke the finger straight into the throat. But be very careful of finger sweeps because they may cause further blockage.

6. If the infant does not begin to breathe right away, place your mouth over the mouth and nose of the infant. Attempt two quick, shallow breaths. Because of the infant's size, use quick and short breaths.

7. Repeat steps one through six.

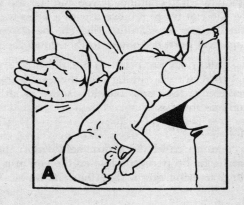

FOR CHILDREN OVER ONE YEAR OLD

1. Make sure you or someone you know has called for emergency medical services.

2. Place the child on his back. (See figure B.) Kneel at his feet. Put the heel of one hand in the midline between the navel and ribcage. Place the second hand on top of the first. Then press firmly, but gently, into the abdomen with a rapid inward and upward thrust. Repeat this six to ten times. These abdominal thrusts are called the Heimlich maneuver.

3. If breathing does not start, open the airway using the tongue-jaw lift technique. If you can see the foreign body, you can try to remove it with a sideways sweep of the finger. Be careful, though, because finger sweeps may push the object further down the airway.

4. If the child does not begin to breathe right away, attempt to restore breathing with the mouth-to-mouth technique. If this fails, repeat a series of six to ten abdominal thrusts.

5. Repeat steps one through four.

Note: In a larger child, the abdominal thrusts (Heimlich maneuver) may be performed when the victim is standing, sitting, or lying down. (See figure C.)

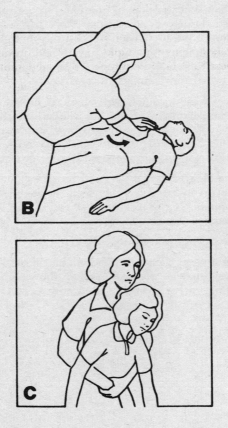

The Growth Charts

Parents have a valid concern that their children receive optimal nutrition, especially during the first year when growth is most rapid. Deficiencies can develop through malabsorption or undetected infections, as well as poor nutrition. The Committee on Nutrition of the American Academy of Pediatrics states that *"the growth chart is the single most useful clinical tool for the assessment of nutritional status."* Growth charts should be maintained and preserved, either by parents, pediatrician, or both, as part of a child's health record.

The following charts to record the growth of the individual child from birth to three years of age were constructed by the National Center for Health Statistics in collaboration with the Center for Disease Control. The charts are based on data from the Fels Research Institute, Yellow Springs, Ohio. These data are appropriate for young boys and girls in the general U.S. population. The charts provide reference percentiles and a place to record:

- Length for age
- Weight for age
- Head circumference for age
- Weight for length

A percentile is a measure of how many children out of a group of 100 fall below a specific point. When a child is on the 95th percentile line of weight for age it means that 95 children out of 100 of the corresponding age and sex have the same weight or less, and only 5 children weigh more. For example, the 50th percentile on a girl's weight chart means that one-half the girls surveyed weighed 18 pounds or less at eight months of age.

Your pediatrician will interpret your child's measurements the first few months and will determine the percentile and whether he or she is showing optimal growth. If you are concerned about your infant's growth, comparison with peers on the growth charts usually indicates that your child may be small, but is still normal and thriving. As the visits become less frequent, you will be taking your own measurements, and plotting the growth lines.

As you can see on the NCHS Growth Charts, growth during the first two years follows a steady increase. The most important thing to watch out for is a slowing of growth that causes the line to flatten out or decline. For example, if your child is in the 40th percentile until eight months of age, then starts dropping to lower percentiles, you should bring this to the attention of your doctor—though rapid changes are less likely to be significant when they occur within the range from the 25th to the 75th percentile. If your child is above the 95th percentile or below the 5th percentile, you should also consult your doctor.

The most frequent causes of a slowing or failure to thrive are caloric or emotional deprivation; however, poor absorption of nutrients and chronic disease may also be causes.

WHEN YOUR CHILD IS OVERWEIGHT

More common is too rapid an increase in growth, especially on the weight charts. According to the Committee on Nutrition, *obesity, or some degree of overweight, is the most important nutritional disorder in the United States today*. An estimated *10 to 30 percent of children* fall into this category. As you have seen, overweight contributes to heart disease, respiratory infections, and diabetes. Cute chubby babies tend to become overweight children (often teased), and overweight adults (prone to illnesses).

You should be able to tell by sight if your infant is gaining too much weight for his or her length (or height). You can also use the Weight for Length Growth Chart—if your child is in a high percentile, it is a good clue that he or she is overweight. Bring this to the attention of your pediatrician to determine whether feeding habits are causing this high weight gain and how to control it. Infants and young children should not have to "lose weight." Since there is such rapid growth, it is usually enough to slow down the amount of weight gain. Do not arbitrarily put your child "on a diet."

Some preventive measures include: breast-feeding (where an infant consumes only the amount he desires); delay in introducing solid foods until four to six months; not insisting that your child finish the last bite or drop in a bottle; elimination or reduction of sugar in foods; following the recommended allowances for calories; prompting physical exercise. In general, food should be given only in response to hunger, not as a pacifier or reward. Just keep in mind that *optimal growth does not mean the fastest or greatest rate of growth*.

HOW TO KEEP THE GROWTH CHARTS

The first few months after birth, you will probably take your child to the pediatrician for monthly checkups. At this time, the doctor will take these measurements, which you can record on the appropriate chart. You might ask to be shown how to take the measurements yourself. You should also check these measurements on your own scale and with a specific measuring ruler and unstretchable tape to ensure that they are calibrated or measure the same as the doctor's. Then, when you are no longer making monthly visits, you can still maintain accurate charts.

Remember to measure at about the same day of each month, at the same time of day, and with the same degree of undress, preferably nude or with minimal clothing and without shoes. Measure length with the child lying on his or her back, fully extended. Use a beam balance scale, if possible, or use the same scale each time.

First, record all measurements on the following list according to date. To record each measurement on the appropriate chart, simply find the child's age on the horizontal scale; then follow a vertical line from that point to the horizontal level of the child's measurement. Where the two lines intersect make a cross mark with a contrasting pen. In graphing weight for length, place the cross mark directly above the child's length at the horizontal level of his weight. The next time your child is measured, join the new set of cross marks to the previous set by straight lines. You will have a continuing growth line that should follow a curve similar to that of the percentile lines, and you will be able to determine which percentile your child is in.

HOW TO INTERPRET
THE GROWTH TABLES

Where your child starts out on the growth chart percentiles depends upon several factors. Heredity, the stature of parents and grandparents, plays a large role in determining whether your child is short (in the 10th percentile) or tall (in the 90th percentile). Studies have shown, though, that environment (the amount and type of food consumed) more strongly affects the weight of a child than does heredity. Overweight parents tend to have overweight children because they follow the same eating habits.

Another important factor is whether your child was premature, in which case his or her weight may be low in terms of actual age. However, premature or low-birth-weight infants (less than 5.5 pounds) usually grow more rapidly in early infancy than normal infants. Nutritional deprivation during pregnancy may also result in low birth weight of infants, who tend to remain in the lower growth percentiles if nutritional deprivation continues.

The average American baby weighs about eight pounds at birth, loses several ounces, then regains birth weight by the tenth to fourteenth day. Weight gain continues at a little over one pound per month. *In general, birth weight should be doubled by six months and tripled by one year of age.*

NAME _____ RECORD # _____

DATE OF BIRTH _____

DATE OF MEASUREMENT	AGE IN MONTHS	RECUMBENT LENGTH	WEIGHT	HEAD CIRCUMFERENCE	

NAME _____ RECORD # _____

DATE OF BIRTH _____

DATE OF MEASUREMENT	AGE IN MONTHS	RECUMBENT LENGTH	WEIGHT	HEAD CIRCUMFERENCE	

NAME _____ RECORD # _____

DATE OF BIRTH _____

DATE OF MEASUREMENT	AGE IN MONTHS	RECUMBENT LENGTH	WEIGHT	HEAD CIRCUMFERENCE	

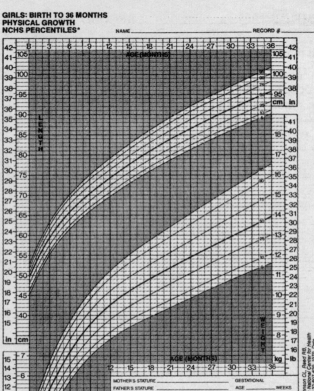

GIRLS: BIRTH TO 36 MONTHS
PHYSICAL GROWTH
NCHS PERCENTILES*

NAME _____ RECORD # _____

AGE (MONTHS)

HEIGHT

AGE (MONTHS)

WEIGHT

MOTHER'S STATURE _____ GESTATIONAL
FATHER'S STATURE _____ AGE _____ WEEKS

DATE	AGE	LENGTH	WEIGHT	HEAD CIRC.	COMMENT
	BIRTH				

* Adapted from: Hamill PVV, Drizd TA, Johnson CL, Reed RB, Roche AF, Moore WM. Physical growth: National Center for Health Statistics percentiles. AM J CLIN NUTR 32:607-629, 1979. Data from the Fels Longitudinal Study, Wright State University School of Medicine, Yellow Springs, Ohio.

© 1982 Ross Laboratories.

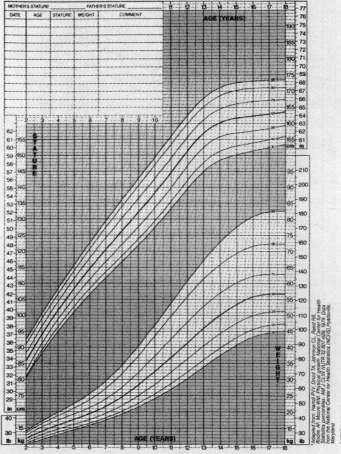

GIRLS: 2 TO 18 YEARS
PHYSICAL GROWTH
NCHS PERCENTILES*

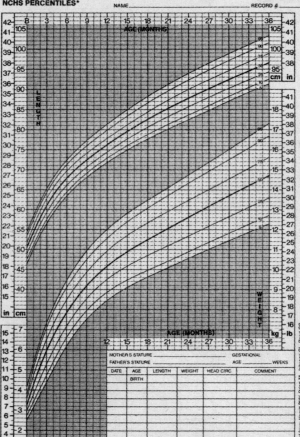

BOYS: BIRTH TO 36 MONTHS
PHYSICAL GROWTH
NCHS PERCENTILES*

NAME_____ RECORD #_____

AGE (MONTHS)
LENGTH
AGE (MONTHS)
WEIGHT

MOTHER'S STATURE _____ GESTATIONAL
FATHER'S STATURE _____ AGE _____ WEEKS

DATE	AGE	LENGTH	WEIGHT	HEAD CIRC	COMMENT
	BIRTH				

*Adapted from: Hamill PVV, Drizd TA, Johnson CL, Reed RB, Roche AF, Moore WM: Physical growth: National Center for Health Statistics percentiles. AM J CLIN NUTR 32:607-629, 1979. Data from the Fels Longitudinal Study, Wright State University School of Medicine, Yellow Springs, Ohio.

© 1982 Ross Laboratories

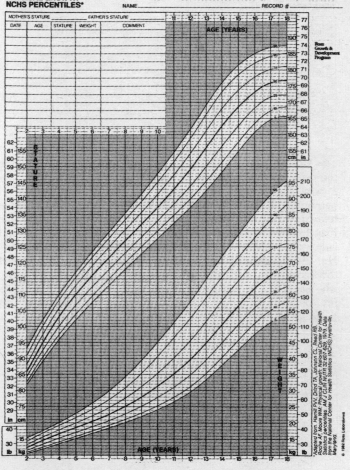

BOYS: 2 TO 18 YEARS
PHYSICAL GROWTH
NCHS PERCENTILES*

NAME_____ RECORD #_____

Ross
Growth &
Development
Program

*Adapted from: Hamill PVV, Drizd TA, Johnson CL, Reed RB,
Roche AF, Moore WM. Physical growth: National Center for Health
Statistics percentiles. AM J CLIN NUTR 32:607-629, 1979. Data
from the National Center for Health Statistics (NCHS), Hyattsville,
Maryland.

© 1982 Ross Laboratories

Sue Castle is the author of several parenting books (including the original version of *The Complete Guide to Preparing Baby Foods*) and writes and produces television programming on parenting, childcare and nutrition for major networks and cable television. She has worked with popular parenting experts like Joan Lunden and she wrote and produced the highly-acclaimed video, "Your Newborn Baby: Everything You Need to Know." Her two daughters, now grown, were babies when she created the recipes for the original edition of this book. Sue Castle, who has a B.A. in psychology from Smith College and an M.A. in Social Psychology from Columbia University, lives in Briarcliff, New York.

Index

Recipe Index

Sound advice in these comprehensive maternity and childcare books from Bantam

☐ 24233-4 **THE FIRST TWELVE MONTHS OF LIFE: YOUR BABY'S GROWTH MONTH BY MONTH**
Frank Caplan $6.50/$7.99

☐ 26438-9 **THE SECOND TWELVE MONTHS OF LIFE**
Frank Caplan $6.50/$8.50

☐ 26967-4 **EARLY CHILDHOOD YEARS**
Theresa Caplan $6.99/$8.50

☐ 26232-7 **THE COMPLETE BOOK OF BREASTFEEDING**—Marvin S. Eiger, M.D.,and Sally Wendkos Olds $5.99/$6.99

☐ 29183-1 **THE COMPLETE NEW GUIDE TO PREPARING BABY FOODS**—(Rev.)--Sue Castle $4.99/$5.99

☐ 27251-9 **FEED ME! I'M YOURS**—Vicky Lansky $4.99/$5.99

☐ 34632-6 **INFANT MASSAGE**
Vimala Schneider McClure $10.95/$13.95

☐ 35339-X **YOUR CHILD'S HEALTH: A PEDIATRIC GUIDE FOR PARENTS**
(Rev.)--Barton D. Schmitt, M.D. $16.95/$20.95

☐ 26114-2 **BETTER HOMES AND GARDENS NEW BABY BOOK** $5.99/$6.99

☐ 27145-8 **NAME YOUR BABY**—Lareina Rule $4.50/$5.99

☐ 27579-8 **UNDERSTANDING PREGNANCY AND CHILDBIRTH**
Sheldon Cherry $4.99/$5.99

Ask for these books at your local bookstore or use this page to order.

Please send me the books I have checked above. I am enclosing $_____ (add $2.50 to cover postage and handling). Send check or money order, no cash or C.O.D.'s please.

Name _____

Address _____

City/State/Zip _____

Send order to: Bantam Books, Dept. HN 18, 2451 S. Wolf Rd., Des Plaines, IL 60018
Allow four to six weeks for delivery.

Prices and availability subject to change without notice. HN 18 8/95

BANTAM'S BEST IN DIET, HEALTH, AND NUTRITION